The Co-operative Game Theory
of the Firm

The Co-operative
Game Theory
of the Firm

MASAHIKO AOKI

CLARENDON PRESS
1984

Oxford University Press, Walton Street, Oxford OX2 6DP
London New York Toronto
Delhi Bombay Calcutta Madras Karachi
Kuala Lumpur Singapore Hong Kong Tokyo
Nairobi Dar es Salaam Cape Town
Melbourne Auckland
and associated companies in
Beirut Berlin Ibadan Mexico City Nicosia

Oxford is a trade mark of Oxford University Press

Published in the United States
by Oxford University Press, New York

British Library Cataloguing in Publication Data
Aoki, Masahiko
The co-operative game theory of the firm.
1. Industrial organization (Economic theory) –
Mathematical models
I. Title
338'.7   HD2326
ISBN 0-19-828485-3

Library of Congress Cataloging in Publication Data
Aoki, Masahiko, 1938-
The co-operative game theory of the firm.
Bibliography: p.
Includes index.
1. Industrial organization – Mathematical models.
2. Business enterprises – Mathematical models.
3. Corporations – Mathematical models. 4. Industrial
relations – Mathematical models. 5. Game theory.
I. Title. II Title: Cooperative game theory of the firm.
HD30.25.A63 1984   338.5'0724   84-14915
ISBN 0-19-828485-3

Set by Grestun Graphics, Oxfordshire
Printed in Great Britain by
Biddles Ltd., Guildford

Preface

The neoclassical theory, which dominates academic thinking, lacks a coherent theory of the firm; the material generally subsumed under that heading is little more than a theory of markets in which the important actors are profit-maximizing entrepreneurs. There is also the vast 'managerial' literature in which the autonomous role of corporate managers is emphasized. But managerial economics has not been entirely successful in meeting the challenge of providing a convincing alternative theory of the modern corporate firm; the frequently-made postulate of 'growth maximizing' or 'sales maximizing' by managers has been criticized as being *ad hoc*.

What is missing in these theories is, in my view, an aspect of the firm of growing importance — namely, as a coalitional structure composed of diverse constituents including shareholders, managers, and employees. I have tried to model this aspect of the modern corporate firm within a cooperative-game framework and have analysed its implications in two articles published in the *American Economic Review* (September 1980 and December 1982) and subsequently incorporated it into Part II of the present book. The model was originally intended as a general model of the firm. In fact, the model includes the neoclassical model of the profit-maximizing firm, the managerial model of the growth-maximizing firm, and the model of the worker-controlled firm as special cases. Unfortunately, however, some readers are apt to misinterpret this model as representing the rather narrow, specific models of collective bargaining, managerialism, Japanese management, etc. My desire to convince readers that the cooperative-game model of the firm implies more than just those specific models was what led me to prepare the present book.

This book is organized in the following manner. The construction and analysis of the cooperative-game model of the firm in Part II is preceded by Part I, which is devoted to an immanent critical review of the orthodox theories of the firm. This part, by showing the inadequacy of the established theories will, it is hoped, provide a compelling introduction to Part II. Part II is then followed by a legal-economic discussion of the institutional structures of modern corporate firms in developed corporate economies in Part III. This part hopefully will help demonstrate that the cooperative-game model can serve as a universal prescriptive norm for diagnosing the efficiency characteristics of modern corporate firms under diverse institutional set-ups.

I have benefited from the kindness and assistance of many individuals and institutions in preparing this book, and I am very grateful to them. Specifically, Professors Richard Freeman, Ryutaro Komiya, Harvey Leibenstein, Robin Marris, Hajime Miyazaki, and Oliver Williamson have read either the entire manuscript or portions thereof and given me useful comments and warm encouragement. Professors Ian MacDonald and Robert Solow kindly permitted me to rephrase and discuss extensively the material of their joint paper, published in the *American Economic Review* (December 1982), in chapter 6 of the present book. The American Economic Association also consented to this arrangement as well as to the use of the aforementioned papers of mine that were published in the *American Economic Review*. Dr. R. J. Coleman of the Commission of the European Communities has been kind enough to spare his busy time to inform me about the progress of the discussions surrounding the *Draft Fifth Directive on Harmonization of the Company Laws of the Member States*. Professor Amartya Sen set up a happy liaison between the Press and the author. Patient typing of the manuscript was performed at various stages by Misses Ayako Ogawa, Yoshiko Seiyama, and Tomoko Kashima. Research leading to this book was partially supported by the Fulbright Commission of Japan and the Ministry of Education of Japan under Grant No. 56330003.

Finally, and of course not least, I am thankful to my wife, Reiko, and two daughters, Maki and Kyoko, for their warmest moral support over the last five years during the preparation of this book in such diverse localities as Cambridge, Mass., Kyoto, and Stanford.

Stanford
Summer 1984

Contents

Part I

Re-examination of the Orthodox Theories of the Firm

Chapter 1

Introduction

No matter what individual 'capitalist' nation we choose to consider — and there is a great variety in social type — we cannot fail but notice the preponderance of large business firms in its economic structure. Through their activities, these concerns generate a substantial proportion of national incomes, in such diverse forms as wages, salaries, contributions to social securities and pension funds, dividends, retained profits, and so on. The business firm serves as a nexus for concurrent and fairly steady relationships among various claimants for those incomes. Yet, the orthodox academic view regarding the objective of the business firm, economic as well as legal, remains surprisingly simple. It is postulated that the business firm — in its typical form, the corporation — is managed, or at least should be managed, in the sole interest of the body of shareholders: employed workers and salaried managers are recruited from markets by the corporation solely to serve as instruments in achieving this goal.

I will discuss the orthodox economic model built on the above view in greater detail below, but it seems useful at the outset to distinguish two aspects of the model, 'descriptive' and 'normative'. The descriptive aspect posits that the axiom of shareholders' sovereignty is a reasonable, scientific assumption on the basis of which essential characteristics of the complex operations of the business firm can be explained and predicted. According to this model, the remuneration of employees' services is seen to be determined externally in the market-place, and all residual income accrues to the shareholders. The behaviour of the firm is then understood as reactions to market stimuli in order to maximize the residual gain. The orthodox model viewed as a normative device, on the other hand, admits that actual corporate behaviour may deviate from the norm of shareholders' utility maximization, but asserts that not only corporate performance, but also overall efficiency of the economy, would be improved if the divergence were to be checked. The implication is that the manager ought to (be made to) act as a shareholders' agent and that the workers should refrain from making excessive wage demands beyond the competitive rate through intra-firm bargaining apparatus.

The objective of this book is to propose and analyse a new model of the corporate firm as an alternative to the orthodox view and to work out its implications as regards issues related to the structure of corporate decision-making and industrial relations in the corporate economy. In order to develop the motivation of this study, let me state a few observations and related questions that appear somewhat at odds with the orthodox paradigm.

First, the orthodox model posits that the firm combines and discharges human and material resources flexibly so as to maximize profits (or share values) in response to the market signals of the wage rates and prices. However, we observe that the large firm internalizes its own employment structure, into which workers enter only at certain job classifications that constitute a 'port of entry' (Kerr, 1954, pp. 101–3; see also Dunlop, 1966). The remainder of jobs is, to a significant extent, shielded from the direct influence of competitive force in the external labour market. These jobs are, in many cases, filled by promotion and transfer of the workers who have already gained entry to the firm; and wage increases often result from a promotion from one grade of jobs to the next. Thus, inside the firm, pricing and allocation of labour is governed by a set of administrative rules and procedures.

What is the essence of the workings of such an internal labour market? Some might argue that it is nothing but a miniature copy of the market mechanism. But, as we shall see in Chapter 2, the firm emerges partly because the 'visible hand' (Chandler, 1977) of administrative procedure can guide processes of generating, using, transmitting, and storing certain kinds of labour skills and knowledge more efficiently than the 'invisible hand' of market forces. As a consequence, external market forces do not fully govern, even if they do partly condition, the determination of the employment condition prevailing within the internal employment structure.

The structure and workings of the 'internal labour market' have been fairly well documented in recent efforts by labour economists,[1] but the integration of these studies with the theory of the firm, which purports to explain and predict business behaviour, is yet to be developed. For instance, it may be worth asking questions such as: In order for the firm to be efficient, how is the internal pay structure to be related to the choice of other managerial decision variables? Does the emergence of an internal employment structure have any impact on criteria on which managerial performances are to be judged? If employees are nothing but an exogenous factor of production to the firm, however, questions of these nature are never warranted.

By the same token, the material assets of a business firm are not as malleable as has been hitherto assumed; and it is only shares, which entitle the owners to a bundle of certain rights in the corporation, such as dividends, voting, and appraisal,[2] that one can easily transfer on the market. Thus the business firm is not a mere mechanical 'black box' that transforms atomistic factors of production into marketable outputs. Rather, it is a more rich entity in which the management regulates the allocation of its own resources, human and material. We ought to look inside the black box.

It was the recognition of this imperative that gave rise to the managerial theory of the firm, as an alternative to the orthodox theory, which presupposes a more independent role for the corporate manager who regulates internal allocation. What I would like to propose, however, is to examine the impact of the emergence of the internal organization of the employees in general – not just the managers – on corporate behaviour. The conspicuous recent phenomenon of inter-firm mobilities of managers, engineers, and skilled workers in high-technology industry may appear to downgrade the importance and relevancy of 'internalness' of the employment structure. I would contend, however, that what one can deduce from this phenomenon is the increasing importance of human resources *vis-à-vis* material resources as assets of the firm. Modes of internal uses of human resources, and the welfare of holders of those resources, are becoming factors more explicitly recognized in, and highly relevant to, corporate decision-making in order that firms gain competitive advantages.

Second, as the market-oriented conception of employment is giving way to a conception based upon a notion of a relatively more stable attachment of employees to a particular firm, the business firm is assuming another function in addition to its traditional role as a producing unit; that is the function of an insurance institution. With 'implicit contracts' (Azariadis, 1975) of continuing employment, possibly interrupted by temporary lay-offs, the firm seems to reduce at least some of the variability that otherwise would accompany wage incomes. Also, the firm plays an increasing role in the provision of its own pension benefits to retired employees and of sick pay to indisposed absentees. In reducing work risk and income risk, the firm is offering a joint product: employment plus an incomplete insurance service. In spite of this new function of the firm, should the internal distribution of the firm be still viewed as a zero-sum game between employees and owners of the firm, or can extra gain be generated by shifting risk among constituents of the firm? If so, how is that gain disposed of? Is the Keynesian demand control still effective to stimulate new employments even if the security of jobs for existing employees becomes one of the managerial targets of the firm?

Third, although not a few businessmen still treat labour unions as detrimental to their objectives, open management–union confrontation is increasingly regarded as counterproductive. Rather, it is being often observed that productivities at the shop-floor are enhanced where workers participate in working out methods of improving the quantity and quality of production. Also employees and their organizations in many places have insisted upon increasing recognition being given to the human aspects of the production process. Not only that, employees are increasingly seen to have interests in the overall functioning of firms to which they devote a large part of their lives. When conditions permit, employees and their organizations will no doubt seek to influence the decisions of firms through the exercise of their bargaining power at all levels of the economy. However, searches by industrial nations for a proper solution to accommodate employees' voices in the decision-making structure of the firm, inconclusive as yet, seem to be moving in diverse directions.

In Anglo-American unionized industries, for example, traditional collective bargaining is generally regarded as the most viable channel through which industrial democracy can be enhanced. Collective bargaining agreements aside, however, management seems free to pursue its own objectives, conceivably that of share-value maximization. In continental Europe, notably in Germany and Scandinavian countries, industrial democracy is formalized through legal frameworks of corporate governance. The supervisory council (Aufsichtsrat) of the German corporation, which selects the management, is required to contain a certain number of employee representatives depending upon the size of the enterprise. In the Japanese corporation the interplay of power between the body of shareholders is more tacit. It may be viewed as arbitrated by management, which recruits its important members mostly from the promotional hierarchy of the employees and which claims to be the benevolent guardian of the interests of the concern as a whole (including the interests of the workers as well as the shareholders). In many of the top non-unionized corporations in the United States, as well, personnel departments play an ever-increasing role in their management team, and their personnel policies are widely recognized as being more equitable and less adversarial than in typical unionized corporations.[3]

Obviously, there must be cultural roots and institutional inertia to this national diversity in industrial relations and corporate structures; but the trend towards a recognition of employees' voices in decision-making structures of the firm seems universal. Do the different institutional solutions to accommodate the employees' voices have any implication for the efficiency of corporate behaviour? Is one participation scheme more efficient over other schemes, given a relative bargaining power of the employees *vis-à-vis* the employer? Will the statutory introduction of employee participation necessarily have adverse consequences as regards managerial incentives to be efficient and to invest?

In my assessment, an out-of-proportional attention has been given to the monetary aspect of the recent stagflationary phenomenon. However, it is at the level of enterprises that prices of products, wages of various jobs, amounts of employment, and so on are actually determined. Is there not an internal driving force within the firm to generate such a phenomenon? Is not stagnation caused partly as a consequence of the increasing power of incumbent employees?

In order to address these and related issues, it seems to be necessary to attempt a *new* economic model of the firm, one that treats the employees as an integral part of the firm rather than as an exogenous factor to it. Such a view is overshadowed by Alfred Marshall, although he did not pursue its logical implications for the behaviour of the firm. He states:

The point of view of the employer however does not include the whole gains of the business: for there is another part which attaches to his employees. Indeed, in some cases and for some purposes, nearly the whole income of a business may be regarded as a quasi-rent, that is an income determined for the time by the state of the market for its wares, with but little reference to the cost of preparing for their work the various things and persons engaged in it. In other words it is a *composite quasi-rent* divisible among the different persons in the business by bargaining, supplemented by custom and by notions of fairness — results, which are brought about by causes that bear some analogy to those that, in early forms of civilization, have put the producer's surplus from the land almost permanently into the hands not of single individuals, but of cultivating firms. (Marshall, 1920, p. 626)

A major purpose of this book is to formalize the nature of 'bargaining' (as well as of 'customs' and 'fairness') to which Marshall referred, and to examine its possible consequences on the internal distribution of value-added within the corporate firm and its possible impact on corporate policy towards the external market. The market behaviour of the corporate firm will be understood as a reaction to fluctuating environmental and internal conditions which seeks to maintain 'organizational equilibrium' between the shareholders and the employees, or 'organizational homeostasis'. Let me hasten to add, however, that the word 'bargaining' need not be narrowly interpreted to imply only the collective bargaining institution. Unless otherwise specified, the word will be used in this book in its most general sense, covering *implicit* bargaining arbitrated and adjudicated by the manager, as well as collective bargaining.

Part I of the book deals with a survey of orthodox theories of the firm. It is not intended to be an impartial and encyclopaedic survey, but rather a personal overview of the literature on the subject to motivate the present study.[4] The theories to be treated are the neoclassical theory and the managerial theory, as well as the theory of the worker-controlled firm.

These three theories have one feature in common: they regard the firm as being managed in the sole interests of a particular group of its participants, identified as either shareholders, managers, or workers. They try to capture the essence of the firm by focusing their analytical attentions on the utility maximization of a dominant class of participants, taking the satisfaction levels to be achieved by the other classes of participants as given. For instance, in the neoclassical theory, only the shareholders (entrepreneurs) are explicitly recognized as rational maximizers. The manager appears only implicitly as their agent (or explicitly, in the case of the newly developing principal-agency theory), and the workers' interests appear only in the form of a labour supply function to which the manager adjusts in finding the solution that is optimal to the shareholders. These orthodox theories offer clues to understanding certain facets of the firm, but I would argue that what is missing in them is an explicit treatment of interactions among shareholders, managers, and employees.

There are important, albeit unorthodox, theories of the firm that take into account the interactions of different elements of the firm in one way or another. Among them are the organizational theory of Herbert Simon (1952-3; also Cyert and March, 1963), the X-efficiency theory of Harvey Leibenstein (1966, 1976, 1982), the 'exit-voice' theory of Albert Hirschman (1970), and the transactional cost theory of Oliver Williamson (1975, 1982). I shall have occasion to refer to those theories. It suffices now to say that my model, to be introduced in Part II, is similar in 'spirit' to theirs, but is analytically distinct in its game-theoretic approach. More specifically, I shall view the firm as a coalition with the shareholders' body and the employees' body as its members, and regard market behaviour of the firm and internal distribution therein as a co-operative game solution (the bargaining solution). Under this framework, decisions within the firm are reckoned as outcomes implicitly or explicitly agreed upon by the

members of the firm and characterized by *balancing the powers* of the members
as well as *internal efficiency* from the viewpoint of the members.

The co-operative game theory is a general theory of the firm in the sense that
it includes the orthodox neoclassical theory of the firm and the theory of the
worker-controlled firm as two special cases. That is, the neoclassical model of
the firm corresponds to the case in which the internal bargaining power of
employees, appropriately defined, is nil; and the model of the worker-managed
firm corresponds to the case in which the internal bargaining power of the shareholder body is nil. However, the real firm may be thought of as lying somewhere
between the two extremes. When both parties have strictly positive bargaining
power, my model will behave differently from either of the two, not only
quantitatively but in certain qualitative respects as well.

The model to be constructed in Part II is descriptive, in the sense that it purports to explain and predict the internal distribution within the firm as well as
its behaviour towards external markets, assuming that it maintains an internal
balance of power among its members while pursuing 'internal' efficiency of its
policy. However, actual decisions by firms may not approximate internal efficiency, either because the actual bargaining situation is not transparent to
members of the firm owing to informational blockage, because decisions are
actually made unilaterally by an agent of a particular member of the firm at the
sacrifice of other members, or for some other reason. Under this circumstance,
the model may be viewed as a normative device, built on the principle of
efficiency-cum-fairness.[5]

Part III will describe three legal models of corporate structure and industrial
relations, each differentiated from the other as regards the manner in which the
position of employees in the decision-making structure of the firm is acknow-
ledged. I shall then discuss the efficiency properties of these differing corporate
structures, using my game-theoretic model of the firm as a frame of reference.
Although the three models are highly stylized, they are meant to reflect fundamental features of the Anglo-American unionized firm, the German (European)
co-determination firm, and the American non-union firm as well as the Japanese
firm.

Ten years ago, the recieved Anglo-American legal model of the corporation
(the company) was parallel to the neoclassical model of the firm. Being based on
the contractual principle, it took the view that employees were not members of
the corporation (the company) and that their rights sprang from the employment contract alone, the terms of which were likely to be determined as a result
of collective bargaining. A leading authority on British company law criticized
the state of the legal theory in 1969 as follows:

In so far as there is any true association in the modern public company it is
between management and workers rather than between the shareholders *inter se*
or between them and the management. But the fact that the workers form an
integral part of the company is ignored by the law. In legal theory the relationship between a company and its employees is merely the contractual relationship

of master and servant and the servants no more form part of the company than do its creditors. . . . [This] orthodox legal view is unreal in that it ignores the undoubted fact that the employees are members of the company for which they work to a far greater extent than are the shareholders whom the law persists in regarding as its proprietors. If the relationship between management and share-holders gives rise to problems which company law has still not satisfactorily solved, the relationship between management and labour presents problems which company law has not even recognised as being its concern. (Gower, 1969, pp. 10–11)

Since then, however, the economic, social, and political environment has altered considerably. In the United Kingdom, the legal aspects of worker participation and industrial democracy began to be discussed in earnest in the 1970s, partly because of the possible need to harmonize UK company law with those of other European Communities nations.[6] In the United States, too, the structure of corporate governance became a very active topic of public discussion. Among factors stimulating such discussion are public interests in the shareholder democ-racy and corporate accountability encouraged by the Securities and Exchange Commission under the former chairmanship of Harold Williams; the increased size of institutional shareholdings accompanying the growth of pension funds; the representation of former President Douglas Fraser of the United Auto Workers on the Chrysler Board; widely held concern over the productivity slow-down of the corporate sector; a reflection on the wisdom of myopic share-price maximization as the discipline on management. Meanwhile, the efficiency and equity implications of such apparently exotic features of the Japanese firm as lifetime employment, enterprise unionism, corporative managerial philosophy, and so on attracted world-wide attention. These are not entirely historical residues that are to fade away; on the contrary, they are results of the relatively recent developments within a modern corporate-legal framework.

At this stage we need not dwell on these developments; it suffices to point out that the comparative legal models of the corporation are now much richer than the neoclassical economic model of the firm. Part III will be concerned with an 'economic' aspect, that is the 'efficiency' aspect, of three stylized 'legal' structures of the firm. It is meant to be a primitive attempt to open a dialogue between the legal theory of the corporation and the economic theory of the firm.

Chapter 2

The Neoclassical Theory of the Firm

This chapter is concerned with a critical survey of the neoclassical theory of the firm. Although there exists more than one version of what may be called the 'neoclassical theory of the firm', each can be characterized by two common features.

1   The firm is seen as a technological black box which combines marketed factors of production (with firm-specific resources) to produce marketable outputs. Its technological possibilities are usually represented by the production function, which specifies the amount of output corresponding to each feasible combination of factor inputs.

2   The rates of remuneration for the factors of production explicitly recognized in the model, such as capital and labour, are assumed to be determined on a market that is *external* to the firm.

The sales price of the firm's output is assumed to be determined either by the market or by the firm facing a certain demand condition prevailing in the market. The residual of revenue from sales of outputs after the payments to the marketed factors of production, which is called profit (quasi-rent), is the analytical focal point of the neoclassical analysis. Depending on the way this residual is treated, two notions of the *entrepreneur* may be distinguished.

Leon Walras maintains that the firm reaches a subjective equilibrium when the residue is wiped out through competition among entrepreneurs. In his treatment, the entrepreneur is nothing but a co-ordinator of production, taking technology and resource prices as given.[1] In the other view, the residual is due to the productivities of firm-specific resources that are not transferable through the market. The entrepreneur is identified with the owner of those resources, and the firm is supposed to reach a subjective equilibrium when the residue is maximized. I will argue below that the existence of firm-specific resources cannot be ignored for an understanding of the workings of the firm.

But what kind of animal is the firm-specific resource? What is specific and unique to the firm? If we pose this question in a related, but slightly different, way we may encounter the famous Coase problem, 'to discover why a firm emerges at all in a specialized exchange economy' (Coase, 1937, p. 335). The scrutiny of Coase's own answer to this question, which appears somewhat vague, would lead one almost on to an entrance of the black box. Neoclassicists have increasingly come to regard the firm as a bundle of contractual relationships which are different from the spot market transaction by nature. Yet they hold firmly to the second presumption, that the terms of contracts are basically determined by external market situations and that there is only one type of residual claimants, i.e. entrepreneurs. But a re-examination of the neoclassical argument will lead us beyond what may be thought of as the neoclassical boundary: it is difficult to maintain that firm-specific resources are endowed in a single, monolithic agent such as the entrepreneur (as a proxy for the body of shareholders). The firm must be viewed as a sort of coalition of financial as well as human resource-holders. But, then, can there be such a thing as *the* single, well-defined objective of the firm?

The Walrasian entrepreneur as a co-ordinator

The neoclassical system as formulated by Walras is composed of only one type of maximizers – households – and two types of co-ordinators – entrepreneurs and an auctioneer.

Each household owns either capital, land, personal abilities, or some combination of these resources, and controls the supply of its service to the markets; revenue from the sales constitutes the income that is available for the purchases of consumer goods and/or new capital goods. Households make their decision on the amounts of sales of productive services and formulate demands for goods so as to maximize their utilities. The only maximizers recognized explicitly in the model are households.

Entrepreneurs buy the services of resources and outputs of other entrepreneurs in specific proportions to produce their products. It is assumed that the amount of output changes equiproportionally with the scale of the factor input combination. The prices of goods and services are set by the auctioneer, who adjusts them according to the Law of Supply and Demand. Given a system of prices, the excess of sales price of entrepreneurial output over the cost of production may be either positive, null, or negative. This excess is termed *bénéfice de l'entreprise* by Walras. A positive or negative *bénéfice* is a sign of disequilibrium, and entrepreneurs respond to this signal according to the Law of Cost Price; that is, they increase their scale of production when the *bénéfice* is positive and reduce it when the *bénéfice* is negative. The presumption that firms strive for higher incomes and lower losses through entry and exit seems implicit in the formulation of the Law of Cost Price. However, entrepreneurs in their purely functional roles are only catalytic agents, who become active to accelerate combinations of atomistic factors of production only when the *bénéfice* is positive. 'Thus, in a state of equilibrium, entrepreneurs make neither profit nor loss' (Walras, 1954, p. 225). 'Profit in the sense of *bénéfice de l'entreprise* . . . depends upon exceptional and not upon normal circumstances and . . . theoretically it ought to be ignored' (p. 423).

In general equilibrium, in which state the demand for, and the supply of, each good are equal and the cost of production of each good is just covered by its sales price, 'the greatest possible satisfaction of consumers' wants', i.e. the state that is nowadays referred to as a 'Pareto optimum', obtains. Thus in the Walrasian system, entrepreneurs, together with the auctioneer, act as mere co-ordinators to bring harmony to the competitive pursuit of self-interests by resource-holding households. Entrepreneur and resource-holder may be alternative aspects that are simultaneously present in a single individual. However, his role as a neutral co-ordinating entrepreneur and as a utility-maximizing resource-holder must be distinguished. 'Entrepreneurs make their living not as entrepreneurs but as land-owners, laborers, or capitalists' (p. 225).

The functionalist view of entrepreneur by Walras gave some useful insights into an aspect of the firm that had been ignored in the classical and Marxian frame of thinking, which looks upon the firm as an institution of exploitation. Yet this insightful functionalist view was made possible inevitably with simple abstractions in some other respects. Particularly, it was presumed that the only information needed by the Walrasian entrepreneur to perform his task, apart from the technological information he was endowed with initially, was provided by the auctioneer in the form of market prices. He did not need any direct in-formation concerning the characteristics (tastes, expectations, the amount of resource endowment, and so on) of economic agents who supplied the services of owned resources to the firm.

The Walrasian auctioneer is only a fictitious personification of the Law of Supply and Demand. But whose decision is it actually to set prices according to this law? There is a very suggestive paper by Kenneth Arrow (1959), who proposes to understand that the auctioneer's role is actually performed by the firm. He argues that, in disequilibrium, when demand for, and supply of, goods and/or services are unequal, even in an objectively competitive market each buyer and seller can be regarded as a monopolist or monopsonist respectively, and the main force of changing prices is vested in the more concentrated side of the market, in sellers in case of most commodities and in buyers in case of unorganized labour.

Let us condsider, for instance, a case in which the aggregate demand for homogeneous and unorganized labour exceeds its supply. Assume that labour is not mobile in the *short run* without incurring an additional cost. Then the rep-resentative firm must raise its wage offer to increase its employment of labour, but cannot thereby attract all the supply at one time. This implies that the firm is faced with a subjective supply curve that is upward-sloping. Suppose that the firm sets the wage so as to maximize *bénéfice*. Under the conditions specified, however, it is equally to the benefit of other (average) firms to raise their wage offers. The firm under consideration will thus have to revise the estimation of its subjective supply curve upward at the same time that a profit maximizing point on it is being explored. Hence, as long as demand is higher than supply, wage rates are likely to be raised. If the process is stable, *bénéfice* is supposed to dis-appear eventually, as the monopsonic power of the firm stems only from the transitory cost to be incurred by workers. The line of argument suggests, how-ever, that even the competitive firm is under stricter informational requirements in the process of wage adjustment (in the processes of price adjustment in gen-eral) than the pure Walrasian entrepreneur, since it needs to estimate the whole curvature of its short-run labour supply, and not merely to be informed of a single wage rate.

In the Arrovian view, the firm is thus supposed to perform the dual roles of an entrepreneurial co-ordinator and a price-setter, albeit only out of equilibrium. Specifically, it combines various resources in an appropriate way and at the same time sets the rate of remuneration of their services. It will be seen that these dual roles are, in a way, the essential function of the firm under more general circumstances.

The entrepreneur as a maximizer

In the system of Walras, profit in the sense of *bénéfice* disappears in general equilibrium, because there is supposed to exist no factor of production (at least in the long run) that is immobile between firms without cost, so that all the revenue of the firm is exhausted after payment to factors of production supplied through the markets. But what if there are firm-specific resources that are indispensable to a firm as factors of production, but are not transferable to other firms without cost? The endowment of the firm-specific resources is fixed at any moment of time, so that returns from additional applications to them of other marketed factors in a specified combination would sooner or later be diminishing. A product residue after the deduction of the products of marketed factors (products being the marginal contribution of a single factor unit multiplied by the number of units) could become positive. The residual is considered as accruable to the productivities of the firm-specific resources and is called profit or quasi rent.

If firm-specific resources are of a homogeneous nature as regards quality, and if there is no uncertainty as to the results of their usage, then whether their ownership is concentrated in one individual or dispersed among many individuals is immaterial. The maximization of profit would coincide with the interest(s) of either him or them, as far as share of each in profit is proportional to the quantity supplied. So, non-Walrasian neoclassicists can identify the entrepreneur as the one who combines the marketed resources so as to maximize returns from firm-specific resources, either in his capacity as a sole owner of the resources or as an agent of the body of owners. Classical capitalists who provide for capital and manage production by themselves fit this image of entrepreneur best; however owner–managers are not dominant figures at the present stage of history. Some contemporary authors, therefore, construct models in which households, in their capacity as shareholders, have shares in maximized profits (quasi-rents). The Arrow–Debreu (1954) model of a 'private ownership economy' is a notable example. In this model the manager of the firm is retreated to obscurity. But what are the firm-specific resources jointly owned by the shareholders?

The Coase problem

Instead of answering the question directly, let us twist it slightly and ask our-
selves why the firm emerges at all in a market exchange system. By understanding
the genesis of the firm, its essence may be revealed to us.

As is well known, this question was first posed in a celebrated article by
Ronald Coase (1937). His own answer to the question was that there are 'costs
of using the price mechanism' which may be reduced or eliminated by entrepreneurial co-ordination. Specifically, he points to two kinds of such cost: the
cost of 'discovering what the relevant prices are' (Coase, 1937, p. 390), and the
cost that may be saved by making 'a long-term contract for the supply of some
article or services' (p. 391) instead of successive shorter-term contracts.

Let us consider the latter cost to begin with. Coase regards the emergence of
these long-term contracts, particularly in employment relations, as likely, 'owing
to the risk attitude of the people concerned' (p. 337). More precisely, however,
it ought to be an asymmetry of the risk attitude between employees and employers that motivates them to agree to long-term employment contracts rather
than using the spot market.

Imagine a representative producer, equipped with certain stocks of capital
and facing his own labour pool. He also faces a product market in which demand
price is uncertain. If the supply of, and the demand for, labour services are
equated through the spot market of labour, then the resulting wage rate would
be determined at the level of the marginal value product of unit labour service,
evaluated at prevailing product price. The wage rate would fluctuate contingent
upon the occurrence of new states of nature affecting the product market.

Now, suppose that the employer is risk-neutral, i.e. that he is indifferent
between a prospect of uncertain profits and a certain profit, provided that the
expected average of the prospective fluctuating profits is equal to the certain
profit. On the other hand, suppose that the suppliers of labour services (let us
assume them homogeneous) are risk-averse, i.e. that they prefer the guarantee
of a fixed wage rate to the prospect of fluctuating wages in the spot market,
provided the fixed wage rate is not less than the expected average of the prospective wages by more than some positive value. The difference between an acceptable fixed wage rate and the expected average of prospective wage rates in the
spot market is an insurance premium which the employee is willing to pay for
the guarantee of a fixed wage.

In this circumstance, the employer and the employee both could be better off
by agreeing to an employment contract that guarantees the employee, regardless
of product market conditions, a fixed wage rate less than the expected average
of the spot wage rates. Needless to say, there is a upper bound to the insurance
premium that the employees are willing to pay. Neoclassicists presume that the
employer has the bargaining power to extract the maximum insurance premium
from the employees for the guarantee,[2] because the competition in the labour
market would push up the insurance premium payable so that there is no difference, from the viewpoint of employees, between the utility derivable from the

guarantee of a fixed wage and the expected utility derivable from fluctuating spot wages. In other words, the whole saving of the cost of using the spot market would accrue to the employer.

The above reasoning would suggest that an aspect of the firm can be characterized as a bundle of long-run risk-shifting employment contracts. However, on the relevancy of long-run contracts to the emergence of the firm, Coase has more to say:

> Now, owing to the difficulty of forecasting, the longer the period of the contract is for the supply of commodity or service, the less possible, and indeed, the less desirable it is for the person purchasing to specify what the other contracting party is expected to do. It may well be a matter of indifference to the person supplying the service or commodity which of several courses of action is taken, but not to the purchaser of that service or commodity. But the purchaser will not know which of these several courses he will want the supplier to take. Therefore, the service which is being provided is expressed in general terms. . . . The details of what the supplier is expected to do is . . . decided later by the purchaser. When the direction of resources (within the limits of the contract) becomes dependent on the buyer in this way, that relationship which I term a 'firm' may be obtained. (Coase, 1937, pp. 391–2)

When precise information is not available at present, but useful information is expected in future, one can gain by holding economic resources in a flexible form and postponing the specification of the use of these resources until new information evolves, because that would expand opportunities. This is one of the reasons why economic agents normally hold portions of their assets in a liquid form (money) in spite of the (opportunity) cost of liquidity premium.[3] If the employer can place the employees under his direction within a certain bound, he would gain a similar kind of flexibility. By the same token as a liquidity premium arises in the financial market, 'option value' would arise in the long-term employment contract for the expansion of an employer's future options. Who appropriates this option value, then? If the employees are really 'indifferent' as to how their services are used, it is reasonable to assume that this value is appropriated by the employer as a free good. However, as the employees become more independent, as a result of either higher educational achievements or the influence of egalitarian ideals in the enveloping society, it becomes doubtful that they will submit themselves to managerial discretionary power without any compensation. Does the shift of uncertainty to the employer provide such compensation? Neoclassicists seem to presume, as indicated above, that no net gain is accruable to employees through such risk-shifting.

If the employer acquires exclusively the whole savings of the cost of using the market in the face of uncertainty, i.e. both the option value and the sum of the maximum insurance premium payable, then the formation of the firm is not a product of exchange, but rather the result of unilateral choice by the employer. The employees are at best indifferent between the spot market and the long-term employment contract with the payment of the maximum premium. Rather, they may be even worse off, if they are not indifferent towards the exercise of employer's discretionary power over them. Does the employer's ability to organize production bestow on him such bargaining power as to enable him to reap the whole savings of the cost? Or is it more reasonable to assume that there will be some kind of sharing of the saving between the employer and the employees? An attempt to answer this question constitutes the crux of this chapter. But before taking the problem any further, consider one more important issue related to risk-shifting: why is it reasonable to presuppose that the employer is more inclined to take risks than the employees? Is he endowed with a natural faculty for taking risks? Are entrepreneurs, being inherently 'confident and venturesome', willing to relieve their 'doubtful and timid' (Knight, 1921, pp. 279–80) employees of all risk?

The asymmetry of risk attitudes and the modern corporation

We have seen that risk-bearing by the employer would generate economic value measured by the sum of the maximum insurance premiums payable by all the employees. In this respect, the firm-specific resources may be identified with the risk-taking ability of the employer. How is this ability endowed, particularly in the context of the corporate system? As is well known, it was Frank Knight who discussed the risk-taking ability of shareholders systematically for the first time.

According to Knight (1921), the manager of the business firm faces two elements of uncertainty: he must estimate the future demand that he is to satisfy, and he must estimate the future results of his productive operation in attempting to satisfy that demand. Technological direction based on forecasts as well as production control by the manager reduces uncertainties, but does not eliminate them completely. Yet the marketed factors of production must be placed under organizational control before results of productive and marketing operations of the firm are known. If the owners of marketed factors have neither the ability nor the inclination to take risks, the manager must take the responsibility for forecasting and control by guaranteeing them a fixed remuneration determined on the market regardless of the results of his decision. Thus,

[w]hen . . . the managerial function comes to require the exercise of judgement involving *liability to error*, and when in consequence the assumption of *responsibility* for the correctness of his opinion becomes a condition prerequisite to getting the other members of the group to submit to the manager's direction, the nature of the function is revolutionized: *the manager becomes an entrepreneur*. (Knight, 1921, p. 276; the last italics are added)

A problem remains as to who personifies entrepreneurship, in Knight's sense of the word, in the case of a corporate firm in which the manager who makes decisions receives a salary and seems to take no 'risk', whereas the shareholders who take the risk make no decision. Knight argues that the crucial decision in an organization such as the corporate firm is to select the person who makes decisions, and that any other sort of decision-making or exercise of judgement is automatically reduced to a routine function. Therefore, although ultimate decisions of the corporation may seem to lie in the hands of the manager, this is illusory. The ultimate decision lies with the shareholders, who select the manager. Furthermore, shareholders' resources are placed in an exposed position with respect to losses incurred by the business, and thus guarantee the owners of other marketed factors of production against failure to receive full contractual remuneration. Hence, it is argued, the principle of inseparability of control and responsibility is still valid, and ultimate entrepreneurship is located with the shareholders, particularly in 'the small groups of "insiders" who are the real owners of the business' (Knight, 1921, p. 359).

Knight's opinion, interesting as it may be, has been criticized in view of apparent phenomena of the wide dispersal of shareownership that accelerated in the first half of the century (see for instance Gordon, 1966). More recently, however, Arrow and Lind (1970) developed an interesting argument as to why the body of shareholders may be risk-neutral, even if (actually we ought to say 'because') shareownership is widely dispersed.

Assume an economy wherein wealth-holders diversify their portfolios among sufficiently numerous statistically uncorrelated stocks. In this economy, take a firm in which an investment would yield uncertain returns. There is a cost of risk-bearing that must be subtracted from the expected return in order to compute the value of the investment to each individual, if he is risk-averse. But suppose that the number of shareholders is very large and that the number of shares of the firm held by each is a very small component of each one's total wealth. Then, undoubtedly, individual risk costs involved in the investment in this firm would become negligible. But, rather unexpectedly, Arrow and Lind proved further that their sum over all shareholders tended to become negligible, as well, if the number of shareholders became sufficiently large; for, as the number of shareholders became large, their individual cost diminished in a higher order than the increase in the number of shareholders. It follows then that, if the manager is acting in the interests of the shareholders, he will behave as a risk-neutral agent. The entrepreneur, as the one who has the ability to bear risk, may be identified with the collectivity of many small shareholders. His ability to take risk arises from a combined effect of risk-pooling in one firm and risk-spreading on financial markets.

On the other hand, because of the limitation of human learning capacity and the present institution of a fixed work day in the business firm, it is neither wise nor possible for suppliers of labour services to diversify their investment in human capital and to hold several jobs simultaneously. As a result, individuals in their capacity as suppliers of labour services are likely to be more risk-averse than the collectivity of many small shareholders. The asymmetry of risk attitudes between the employees and the employers is a natural consequence of the ingenious social contrivance of the corporate institution. And through this institution, the market system can cope with the uncertain world in spite of the limitation of individuals' capacities to take risk.

The firm as a risk-sharing contrivance

Although the body of shareholders may be treated as relatively more risk-taking than the employee, however, the Arrow–Lind conditions mentioned above for the shareholders to be completely neutral towards risk may be considered too ideal. Actually, there are important reasons why large corporations may not behave in a risk-neutral fashion. First, in order to control a firm, a shareholder must hold a large proportion of the total shares of the firm, which may not be a negligible component of his wealth. Then, even if the number of shareholders is large, the risk attitude of this dominant shareholder would be heavily reflected in the policy-making of the firm, and the shareholder may not be neutral towards risk. Second, even if risk should be neglected from the shareholders' point of view, the manager's career and income may be intimately related to the firm's performance, and he may show a tendency to 'play safe' in formulating corporate policy. Third, to the extent that performances of firms are mutually correlated, i.e. that the state of nature relevant to the income formation of firms is identifiable with a market factor common to all firms (the state of the business cycle), the possibility of shareholders' risk-spreading will be reduced.

If the body of shareholders cannot be treated as risk-neutral in aggregation, then some kind of risk-sharing between the employer and the employees may become optimal under certain conditions other than fixed wage contracts. Below, the nature of such a risk-sharing contract is illustrated. At the outset, the material may appear to the readers somewhat technical and only elaborative, but actually it contains an important logical step towards further development of the discussion.

If the employer as well as the employees is risk-averse, any fixed wage contract may not be Pareto-superior, over the spot market, in an *ex ante* sense (before the actual sales revenue of the firm is known), even if the employer is relatively more risk-taking than the employees. In other words, it can happen that both the employer and the employees are at least equally well off in terms of expected utilities, and that at least one of them is strictly better off, if they remain under the spot market instead of entering any kind of fixed wage contract. The risk-averse employer may not wish to absorb the risk alone within the bound of the insurance premium that the employees are willing to pay. On the other hand, if the employees' incomes are adjusted to their realized marginal product in the spot market *ex post* (after the actual sales revenue of the firm is known), the employer shifts some of the risk involved in value production to the employees. But the spot market does not appear as the predominant institution in allocating labour, even if it does play a peripheral role, in spite of the possibility that some corporations behave as risk-averters.

When both an employer and employees are risk-averters, some kind of well-designed risk-sharing device within the firm would be a better arrangement for both the parties than either the spot market or fixed wage contracts. Risk-sharing may take the form of a bonus, a profit-sharing plan, or a flexible wage adjustment, in which workers' incomes are at least partly contingent on the business performance of the employing firm. In general, an *ex ante* optimal risk-sharing rule cannot be formulated simply:[4] a risk-sharing rule is Pareto-optimal in an *ex ante* sense if any departure from it would necessarily lower the expected utility of at least one of the parties involved. But under a special condition specified below, Pareto-optimal risk-sharing always exists between a fixed number of the employees and the employer in a simple class of *linear* risk-sharing rule:

$$\omega = \alpha + \beta x$$

where ω is employee's earnings, α and β are non-negative parameters, and x is the sales revenue of the firm per employee, which is an uncertain variable. Under rules of this kind, the employees are partly guaranteed certain incomes and partly engaged in a proportional sharing of the as-yet-unknown revenue with the employer. In order for a risk-sharing rule in this class to be optimal, it must hold that the maximum insurance premiums per small risk that the employer and the employees are willing to pay are both constant and independent of the levels of their expected incomes; more technically, it corresponds to the case in which the measure of absolute risk aversion of both the employees and the employer are constant.[5]

Suppose now that this condition holds. The following diagrammatical exposition illustrates the Pareto optimality of linear risk-sharing rules. For simplicity's sake, assume that the amount of physical output of the firm is a function $f(\cdot)$ of the number of employed workers n, and that there is uncertainty only in sales price p of the product; i.e., $x = pf(n)/n$, where the expected average of uncertain price $E[p]$ is assumed to equal one. In Fig. 2.1 any arbitrary linear risk-sharing can be represented as a point in terms of the employees' relative share β in the firm's revenue and their expected income,

$$E\omega = \alpha + \beta \frac{f(n)}{n}.$$

Draw a straight line $G(\alpha, \beta)$ through a point $(\beta, E\omega)$ with slope f/n. The intercept of the line with the ordinate represents the value of α that, together with the value of β, gives rise to the expected income $E\omega$. The spot market distribution is represented by the point M whose abscissa corresponds to the employees' share $S_\omega = nf'(n)/f(n)$, which is constant regardless of the state of the market and whose ordinate corresponds to the expected marginal value product of labour $f'(n)$.

The curve $F(\beta)$ represents the set of those linear risk-sharings under which each employee is equally well off, in terms of his expected utility, as under the spot market (we assume of course that the employees are homogeneous). Since the employees are risk-averters, they are willing to trade off a higher expected income for a lower but less variable income. Now consider curve $H(\beta)$. It represents the set of linear risk-sharing under which the employer is equally well off in terms of his expected utility as under the spot market. If the employer is risk-averse, then the curve is downward-sloping from M to the left, since he requires a higher risk premium in the form of a reduction in employees' incomes if he is to absorb more risk. If the employer is risk-neutral, on the other hand, the curve would stretch out of the point M horizontally, for obvious reasons.

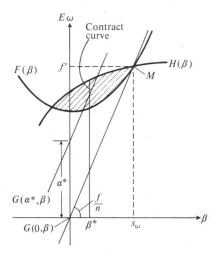

Fig. 2.1

If and only if the employer is relatively more risk-taking than the employees, there is a lens-shaped area enclosed by the graphs of F and H as depicted. This shaded area represents the set of linear risk-sharings whose outcomes are expected to be Pareto-superior to the outcomes of the spot market. The vertical distance of the lens-shaped area for each value of β represents the cost saving from not using the spot market when the employees' proportional share is equal to that value of β. This saving is measured in terms of expected income per employee. It is maximized at $\beta = \beta^*$, where the slope of F and H are equal. The intersection of the line $\beta = \beta^*$ with the lens-shaped area corresponds to the Edgeworth contract curve. That is, if α^* is chosen so that the corresponding graph of G cuts through the lens-shaped area at $\beta = \beta^*$, then the choice of α^*, together with β^*, constitutes a Pareto-optimal linear risk-sharing. We cannot change either α^* or β^*, nor can we change both, without lowering the expected utility of at least one party.

A choice of α^* specifies the distribution of the cost saving from not using the spot market between the employer and the employees. However, neoclassicists seem to assume that the saving can be appropriated exclusively by the employer. For instance, Paul Samuelson argues:

It is *not* clear that higher total worker income will result from such profit-sharing schemes. What the worker gives up in assured wage may be just matched by what he receives on the average over the years in variable bonuses. *Only if the overall productivity of the firm is enhanced by the feeling of participation will there be any net gain of society's income* (and any such gain will be divided up among both workers and property owners). One must emphasize these trite banalities because enthusiasts for profit-sharing are always making unsubstantiated claims that somehow something-for-nothing is achieved by such schemes. (Samuelson, 1977, p. 16; italics in original)

Samuelson's contention that no benefit can be created by mere departures from a fixed wage contract, represented by a point for which $\beta = 0$, to risk-sharing schemes (profit-sharing schemes) is not correct, as illustrated above, unless the employer is risk-neutral (this is the case in which the curve H is horizontal), so that the maximum cost saving is attainable at $\beta^* = 0$. Samuelson also asserts that a switch from the fixed wage contract to a risk-sharing scheme is possible only as a move from the intercept of the curve F north-eastward along the curve. However, the employees are indifferent between entering the spot market (the point M) and being bound by a risk-sharing arrangement represented by a point on the curve F. If the employees withdraw from this risk-sharing arrangement, only the employer would be hurt. Therefore, the employees' threat that they will collectively withdraw from the arrangement unless a benefit-sharing agreement satisfactory to them is reached may be exercised effectively, and the employer may rather yield some of the maximum cost-saving at $\beta = \beta^*$ to the employees, inducing them to participate in risk-sharing. This argument holds even if $\beta^* = 0$, i.e. if the employer is risk-neutral.

But how can the employees exercise such an effective threat? Are they not exposed to competition from outsiders who would be satisfied with an infinitesimal increase in the wage rate from the spot rate? We must now introduce the idiosyncratic nature of the body of incumbent employees to complete the argument.

The invisible hand *v*. the visible hand

We turn now to discuss the market-using cost of the first type, i.e. the cost of 'discovering what relevant prices are'. On this cost, Coase did not elaborate. But I would like to argue that the market-using cost relevant to the emergence of the firm is of a fundamental and essential nature. I propose to interpret the market-using cost of the first type as the relative inefficiency of the price mechanism (the 'invisible hand') *vis-à-vis* an alternative mechanism of administrative type (the 'visible hand', in Chandler's (1977) phrase). This section maintains, with the aid of achievements of the theory of decentralized resource allocation, that under certain conditions the visible hand in fact works better in allocating certain kinds of resources from the *informational efficiency* point of view. The next section tries to identify those resources in the context of firm organization. The discussion has special bearing on the nature of employees' skills and knowledge, and will lead us to a conclusion that human resources are essential components of firm-specific resources, and thereby are able to exercise an effective threat over the disposition of the saving of market-using cost.

The theory of decentralized resource allocation, a well developed branch of mathematical economics, regards as its objective the comparison of the performances of various resource allocation mechanisms, the two most notable being the price mechanism and the quantity mechanism.[6] It is well known that, under certain conditions, the price mechanism fails to find prices, or fails to elicit those responses from economic agents that would maintain an optimal allocation of resources. Among these conditions, the presence of economies of scale and the collective goods property in the use of resources are the most relevant for our discussion. But is there any mechanism at all that would perform better than the price mechanism under these conditions? The quantity mechanism is that candidate.[7] In order to treat this issue somewhat precisely, let us employ for a moment the analytical gadget used in the theory of decentralized resource allocation.

Suppose that a well-defined economic objective is given that may be attained through the co-ordination of a very large number of activities using scarce resources. Let us imagine an economic agent who formulates the objective in terms of a utility function, the value of which depends upon the final outputs of the activities. Call him a *helmsman*.[8] Suppose that, the purposive knowledge aside, the helmsman lacks the exact technological knowledge needed to perform those activities necessary for the fulfilment of the objective. Suppose further that such technological knowledge is dispersed among many activity units. The endowment of scarce resources is supposed known only to the helmsman.[9] Thus, knowledge needed for co-ordination to fulfil the objective is decentralized. How, then, can an optimal plan of resource allocation and choices of activities be found? Following Frederik Hayek (1945, pp. 78-9), we might put this question as: 'What is the best way of utilizing knowledge initially dispersed among all the people [?]'.

One possibility is simply to centralize all the useful information at one centre (say, with the helmsman) and let that central agent solve an optimal plan. This may correspond to the conventional notion of the organization, but the large organization is never run in this way. The centralization of knowledge and solution of an optimal plan would be too costly in terms of time and resources. Some important knowledge may not be conveyed to the centre in its original form because of possible noise disturbances in the process of communication; or it may be incomprehensible to the centre because of the limitation of its individual capacity. Also, centralized command of solutions to activity units may run contrary to the individual motives of those managers. A desirable alternative is to limit the exchange of information as little as possible and to decentralize decision-making to where the relevant knowledges are — that is, to let each activity unit choose its productive plan only by communicating to it by means of the simplest signals that summarize such further information as it needs.

One possible candidate for such an ideal set of signals is the price system. Imagine that the helmsman announces prices of goods and resources to activity units and solicits individual responses of demands for, and supplies of, goods and resources. The helmsman aggregates those responses to calculate the final output of each good or resource, and readjusts its price so as to approximate the marginal utility of the corresponding good or resource. A conceivable rule of response for each activity unit is that of profit maximization.

Suppose now that there is the possibility of economies of scale in resource use. Then, if individual activity units are required to follow the profit-maximizing rule, this process of successive revision of prices would never converge to an equilibrium under which the outputs of the activity units maximize the utility function of the helmsman. The invisible hand fails.[10]

An alternative mechanism, the quantity mechanism, runs as follows.[11] The helmsman specifies a tentative allocation of a resource with respect to which economies of scale may be expected. As regards other goods, it may send out ordinary price signals. Each activity unit responds to this system of quantity-price signals by a choice of profit-maximizing activity within the quantity constraint of the centrally controlled resource. It sends back the usual demand–supply signal regarding uncontrolled goods. The helmsman, while making the prices of uncontrolled goods approximate the marginal utilities derivable from them, monitors marginal products of the controlled resources, and revises their tentative allocation. He shifts a portion of the resources from units with comparatively lower marginal productivities to units with comparatively higher marginal productivities. If the resources are allocated initially in a balanced way, then such a revision of allocation will always be implementable, even out of equilibrium, and will be improving as well, in the sense that the utility value will be ever-increasing during the process until an equilibrium is reached. Under a suitable regularity condition, an equilibrium is almost always locally optimal.

The informational requirements for the quantity mechanism defined above may be higher than those for the price mechanism. In the latter, information made available to activity units regarding the resources that exhibit increasing returns to scale takes the form of a *uniform* price, whereas in the quantity mechanism it takes the form of quantities *specific* to each unit. However, the quantity mechanism is more practical and useful for finding an optimal plan.

Next, let us proceed to a comparison of performances of the two mechanisms in the presence of collective goods.[12] Suppose that some produced goods can be used collectively, that is by more than one activity unit, simultaneously and non-exclusively. In this circumstance, if the price mechanism is to be used to find an optimal plan, a separate, independent market of the single collective goods must be operated for each of the units involved in either its production or its use. Different prices of a single collective good must be announced to each user unit by a custodian of that good and must be revised separately according to the Law of Supply and Demand as applied to a pair of producer's supply (I will assume a single producing unit) and each individual unit's demand. The aggregate of individual prices is transmitted to a producing unit which chooses the supply that will maximize profit. In other words, the single collective good must be treated as if there are as many kinds of goods as there are number of units using that good collectively. Therefore, as the number of user units increases, the number of price messages must increase.

In the quantity mechanism applied to collective goods, on the other hand, the helmsman may announce a single message of quantity, i.e. a production target that is at the same time an amount of availability to user units. The helmsman then monitors marginal value products and the marginal production cost of the collective good at units involved in either its use or its production. He aggregates the marginal value products and compares the sum with the marginal cost at the producing unit. If the difference is positive, the helmsman revises the quantity message upward, i.e. directs an increase in production of the collective goods, and vice versa. As regards private goods, the ordinary price mechanism may be supplemented.

In the presence of collective goods, an advantage of the quantity mechanism lies in its remarkable informational efficiency. The helmsman may announce only one quantity message per collective goods, whereas in the price mechanism the custodian must announce a separate price message to each of the activity units involved for a single collective good. It is a quite natural consequence of the fact that what is common in the use of a collective good is its quantity and what is private is its individual economic value.

We have thus seen that, under the presence of economies of scale in resource use and collective goods, the quantity mechanism involves less cost than the price mechanism by either the saving of disequilibrium costs or the economizing on the informational requirement. The formulation of the quantity mechanism in the above is extremely stylized, but it may be reasonable to say that it reflects the essence of the administrative process of resource allocation and co-ordination of activities within the organization of the firm, as contrasted with the workings of the price mechanism. In order to give a more solid base to this claim, I shall next argue that one of the most important resources, of which allocation is largely regulated by administrative procedures within the firm, in fact, exhibits increasing returns to scale and the collective goods property.

Collective nature of the human assets

Capital funds may be cited as important resources which may exhibit increasing returns to scale, and the administrative allocation of investible funds is certainly a unique feature of the multi-divisional corporation. For this, well-known contributions by Alfred Chandler (1977), Oliver Williamson (1975), and others may be referred to. I would therefore like to stress that the skills and knowledge of employees are at least as important resources for the firm as financial assets, and that for them administrative allocation is more efficient than the market mechanism.

In the theory of human capital developed for the last a quarter-century or so, it has been recognized ever more clearly that an un-negligible proportion of employees' skills are formed on the job, and that on-the-job training increases productivity more in those firms providing it. Such training is called *specific training* (see Becker, 1964, p. 19). Specific training involves costs in terms of the value placed on the time and effort of trainees, the 'teaching' provided by others, and the resources used. These costs may be interpreted as a sort of 'set-up cost', which is a clear indication of the presence of economies of scale. Hence, the longer the trainees work for the firm that provided the specific training, the higher the rate of return will be on the investment in training. Such resources exhibiting increasing returns to scale cannot be either generated or utilized in an efficient fashion through allocation and pricing on the spot market. The marginal cost of using a specific skill, once formed, would be smaller relative to the training cost of generating it. If individuals are paid only for the marginal user-costs of specific skills, it is not worth their bearing the costs of specific training. In order to derive the maximum returns from specific training they would instead try to control the supplies of specific skills through the spot market in monopolistic fashion. On the other hand, the employer will not bear the cost of specific training, either, unless there is a guarantee that trainees will not quit the firm after training and that they will yield enough returns to his investment. But through the spot market mechanism there is no assurance that trainees will stay with the firm, and the trainees may make self-disbelieved promises to stay in the expectation that individual advantage will thereby be realized. This strategic misrepresentation of intentions, coined as 'opportunism' by Oliver Williamson (1975), together with the possible monopolistic (monopsonistic) conducts of agents, can lead to the result that, under the spot market mechanism, the generation and use of specific skills will be at less than an efficient level. As was argued in the last section, some type of administrative allocation and pricing needs to be substituted from the efficiency point of view. An aspect of such an administrative rule as the seniority wage and promotion may be understood as a contrivance in which costs and returns to specific training are shared between employer and trainees. Under this rule, employees bear part of the training costs in their earlier years but are guaranteed of its returns in later years. They are thus provided with incentives to stay with the training firm and thereby to yield returns to employer's investment.

This much is recognized in the theory of human capital. However, the approach of the human capital theory is excessively individualistic. Human capital is assumed to be embodied in an individual, and costs of, and returns to, training are assumed to be calculable with respect to the individual, even though it is recognized that the costs and returns may be shared between the trainee and the employer (see Becker, 1964, p. 22). But there seems to be an important class of skills and knowledge that can be formed only in an organizational context and embodied only in a team of employees. The theory of internal labour market emphasizes just that. Peter Doeringer and Michael Piore state:

[P]erformance in some production and most managerial jobs involves a team element, and a critical skill is the ability to operate effectively within the given members of the team. This ability is dependent upon the interaction of the personalities of the members, and the individual's work 'skills' are specific in the sense that skills necessary to work on one team are never quite the same as those required on another. (Doeringer and Piore, 1971, pp. 15–16)

Such special skills are essentially collective goods, as they are not individually appropriable.

A team element is widely recognized to be a feature of managerial jobs (see Marris, 1964, p. 16; Penrose, 1959). But there is ample evidence that performance in production jobs also involves a substantial amount of that element, ranging from a passive conformation to informal work customs to a more conscious workers' involvement in shop-floor production problems. Regarding the former, Doeringer and Piore observe:

[T]he process through which custom is generated at the workplace is closely related to the development of job skills. On-the-job training, for example, depends heavily upon individual habits formed by a set of reinforcements generated by the productive process on the one hand, and through imitation by inexperienced workmen of neighboring employees on the other. . . . Some skills and in fact group customs, and the development of these skills is facilitated by the social cohesion and group pressure which enforce customary law. (Doeringer and Piore, 1971, p. 27)

Work practices at the work-place cannot be established independently from general custom in the enveloping society, and any work custom has aspects that are imported by the work group from the larger community in which it resides. But with this reservation, we may say that each custom has unique, idiosyncratic characteristics, as it develops from repeated interactions among particular personalities. What is more, practices that are repeated, to a great extent, were selected initially on efficiency grounds. Therefore, the acquisition of work customs by workers has a non-transferable value to the firm. Of course, as a result of subsequent development of technology in the society at large, conflicts between work customs and efficiency may arise, and once-efficient customs may be turned into 'collective bads' from the viewpoint of the firm. In the face of such conflict, the firm must adapt work customs to emergent efficiency needs in order to survive. This adaptation will add idiosyncratic characteristics to new customs, as the mode and speed of adaptation will differ depending upon unionization of the firm, managerial character, and so on.

Work customs generated and owned collectively are transferable to new workers through 'social cohesion and group pressures' rather than the market. This implies that work by experienced workers, practising customs at the workplace, and the like also function as a non-excludable input to the skill formation of new workers. In other words, the experienced workers exert an external effect on the new workers, which is another way of saying that the work customs are essentially collective goods.

A more sophisticated form of team co-operation may be found in successful workers' participation in production control, in which groups of workers from the same workshops, or formal (union) representatives of workers at enterprise or plant level, co-operate with management to discuss in-plant production problems and to work out methods of improving production quantity and quality. There is a sign that the idea of workers' participation in production control as a means of improving labour productivities is being accepted by an ever-increasing number of enterprises everywhere.[13] A key element in such idea is the use of work teams at the shop-floor level.

Good communication between management and labour and an involvement of workers in production control would serve as a means of ensuring a high degree of motivation. However, many times the workers' participation results in real improvements in the organization of teamwork which realize the avoidance of quality defects, the more efficient handling of materials and scrap, energy conservation, and so on. In order for such semi-autonomous, collective control of production by workers to be more effective than rigid hierarchical control by technical experts, the sharing of work experience among the workers and their collective learnings-by-doing on the shop-floor seem to be absolutely vital.

From these and other possible observations, it may be said that employees' skills, managerial as well as productive, are, to a non-negligible extent, the products of team efforts and can be neither appropriable nor portable individually. Is it possible, then, to generate and use those collective skills efficiently through the price mechanism? Since collective skills are never appropriable individually, the spot market of labour is not likely to provide a suitable setting in which their use is appropriately rewarded. For instance, *individual* withdrawal of skill supply from the market may not readily affect the maintenance of group customs. Therefore the experienced workers would not be able to derive full value corresponding to their contributions to intergenerational skill transmission if they were to act individually through the spot market. As a result, the willingness and efforts of the experienced workers to transmit their skills may be lower.[14] It is not theoretically impossible to fancy a more complete system of markets including the ones for pricing collective skills. As the analytical construction in the previous section indicates, however, a different future market must be set up to evaluate the use values of collective skills in each of future periods. Bounded rationality of economic agents (Simon, 1972; Williamson, 1975, pp. 21–6) would make it difficult for such an informationally complicated system to be implemented. Clearly, it is more practical to control administratively investments in, and uses of, human resources. Informational efficiency is one of the primary reasons why the firm emerges to regulate the allocation of human resources through non-market, administrative procedures.

To shirk or to be monitored

The role of team property in work processes as a driving force behind the formation of the firm is also stressed by Armer Alchian and Harold Demsetz (1972). According to them, there are two necessary conditions for the emergence of the firm. First, it must be possible to increase productivity through team-oriented production. But since it is costly to meter individual productivities (the marginal products) of individual members of the team, there is an incentive for each member to shirk. It is difficult to restrict shirking through simple market exchange between co-operating inputs. Thus, as the second condition for the emergence of the firm, it must be economical to estimate marginal productivity by observing, specifying, and controlling input behaviour in a non-market fashion. In their opinion, if monitoring of individual performances of co-operating inputs owned by several individuals becomes a specialized, centralized function of an agent who receives the residual product above the marginal products of the other inputs, and if these rights to monitoring and residual claim become transferable, the essential elements of the 'classical' firm obtains.[15]

What is recognized immediately from the above argument is that Alchian and Demsetz's usage of the term 'team' is different from that in the preceding discussion. In their framework, team production is nothing but production in which 'the product is not a mere sum of separable outputs of each cooperating resource' (Alchian and Demsetz, 1972, p. 779). However, the marginal productivity of each member is *not* unmeasurable in principle, even if it is costly to measure. Notice in contrast that I used the term 'team' when skills are not individually appropriable. For them, a team production process is one in which members are replaceable by outsiders having equal intrinsic characteristics. What is essential to their argument is not the collective nature of co-operators' skills, but rather an individual's incentive to shirk when he works as part of a group.

I would not deny the possibility that people will be induced to take more 'leisure' in team production if not monitored and that a reduction in shirking, or a saving of the monitoring cost, can be brought about through the centralized organization of inputs. But, eclectic as it may sound, it appears to go a little too far to say that the metering problem is the only, or even the most important, cause of the existence of the firm.

Further, there are some ambiguities in Alchian and Demsetz's argument as to the nature of the monitor's income. The authors argue that the monitor himself will be effectively monitored not to shirk as a monitor by an incentive given to him: 'give him title to the net earnings of the team, net of payments to other inputs.' But what do the payments to other inputs equal? '[H]opefully, the marginal value products' (1972, p. 782). If the monitor does not contribute to team productivity proper except for reducing the shirking of others, however, the marginal products of the monitored team should exhaust the whole product of team production and nothing would be left for the monitor. Otherwise one must assume that there exists some firm-specific resource besides co-operative inputs explicitly recognized in the model; but accepting its existence amounts to denying that the efficient metering through centralized contracts is the sole *raison d'être* of the firm. In another place, however, the authors argue that 'the monitor earns his residual through reduction in shirking that he brings about' (Alchian and Demsetz, 1972, p. 782). In other words, the whole gain from the organization of 'honest' activities accrues to the monitor.

Why do the team players accept the monitor's control, then? Since the possibility of shirking indicates that team members derive some utilities from a saving of effort expenditure, they are unlikely to accept the latter's control voluntarily for no compensation. It amounts to their abiding the additional displeasure of less leisure, while giving the benefits from their additional efforts entirely to the monitor. This dilemma may be resolved only by departing from the principle of payment according to marginal productivity. The next section will argue that such departure is in fact considered as a likelihood in the modern corporate firm for some other important reasons as well.

The importance and relevancy of monitoring cost to the emergence of the firm is also stressed by a recent work by Williamson (1982). Williamson has been developing a unique analytical framework for the theory of economic organization in general, and the theory of the firm in particular, in which the transaction between agents rather than the choice of an agent is taken as the basic unit of analysis, and in which economizing on various transaction costs is considered a driving force for organizational innovations (the formation of the firm in particular). I have already hinted that his and my orientations are broadly similar (see p. 27).

In one of his recent articles, focused on internal labour organization, Williamson classifies labour transactions of a continuing kind in terms of two dimensions: (1) the degree to which human assets are transaction-specific and (2) the ease with which the productivity of individual workers can be evaluated. The first dimension has been discussed in this book. With respect to the second dimension, Williamson refers to Alchian and Demsetz (1972). However, while the latter contend that the difficulty of evaluating individual productivity in teamwork may be solved by observing the intensity with which an individual works, Williamson is critical of this contention, arguing that the assessment of inputs is much more subtle than mere effort-accounting. For the employees may have to 'co-operate' in helping to devise and implement complex responses to uncertain circumstances, and it may not be efficient from the teamwork point of view that 'the employee attends to own or local goals at the expense of others' (Williamson, 1982, p. 6). What is rightly pointed out here is the co-operative and collective nature of efficient labour organization, as stressed in the last section.

Williamson suggests that, given a high amount of firm-specific learning on the first dimension, an increase in metering difficulty in the second dimension would make the following transition more efficient; i.e. from mere continuing employer relations mutually committed by the employer and the employee to the 'relational team' form of firm organization, in which employees are 'socially conditioned to dedicate themselves to the purpose of the firm', while being given 'considerable job security' as well as 'assurance against exploitation' (Williamson, 1982, p. 7). I interpret this as meaning that metering difficulty is closely associated with the collective goods nature of human assets and that the sharing of benefits arising from the use of them is likely to be a more natural and implied consequence. It is to this claim that I shall now turn.

Organizational rent and intra-firm bargaining

Relying primarily upon neoclassical logic, we have seen that various costs of using the market can be reduced or eliminated by the formation of the firm. In summary, the possibilities of such cost-saving may be listed as follows:

1 the saving of risk cost through risk-sharing employment contract;
2 the generation of option value and a reduction of shirking by administrative allocation and monitoring of labour inputs;
3 the reduction of disequilibrium cost, as well as the control of opportunistic behaviour of agents, by administrative allocation of resources which exhibits increasing returns to scale;
4 the informational efficiency in regulating the formation and utilization of the team element of human resources.

Having explored the Coase problem, we have indirectly answered the original question as well: what constitutes firm-specific resources? Corresponding to each of the above items of cost-saving by the formation of the the firm, we can identify the following firm-specific resources:

1 the relatively higher risk-taking ability of the body of shareholders made possible through the corporate institution;
2 the willingness of the employees to co-operate and the ability of the employer to adapt and monitor production effectively under uncertainty;
3 the skills and knowledge formed on the job and embodied in the employees as well as the ability of the employer to generate and utilize them efficiently; the large-scale funds pooled by shareholders and the manager's ability to allocate them internally in an efficient way;
4 the collective skills formed on the shop-floor and embodied in the team of employees, as well as the ability of the employer to generate and utilize them efficiently.

In sum, the firm-specific resources are not embodied in a single, monolithic agent, but are dispersed among the body of shareholders and the body of employees. Those resources are firm-specific in the sense that they are value-less in isolation and productive only in their steady association with the corporate firm as a nexus for mutual association. At first sight, it may appear that an individual shareholder's association with the firm is casual. However, as noted already, the shareholders' ability to take more risk is the result of collective risk-'pooling' combined with individual risk-spreading. Further, individual shareholders cannot withdraw their funds from the corporation without an appropriate corporate resolution: it is only shares that entitle them to a bundle of certain rights in the corporation that can be transferred on the market (p. 4 above). The body of shareholders is as permanent as the corporation. Also, I have argued in a previous section that an important part of employees' skills and knowledge is utilized more efficiently in a team context and is not individually appropriable. Thus, it may be the body of employees built up over a period of time, rather than particular individual employees, that is firm-specific.

Each item of the cost-saving may actually represent different aspects of a lump surplus generated by the firm and may not be distinguishable neatly one from another. Let us therefore refer to an aggregate of such surplus as the *organizational rent*, indicating that it is generated by the formation of the organization, particularly in the form of a corporation. The next logical step is to ask who appropriates this rent? The answer now seems to be obvious: the holders of the firm-specific resources. However, they are not homogeneous: how is the lump sum distributed among them?

The orthodox view is to regard the organizational rent accruing exclusively to the entrepreneur (the body of shareholders) in the form of profit. Subject to the labour supply function, the entrepreneur maximizes his profits. Perfect divisibility of labour supply is assumed, and searching for the profit-maximizing point on the supply curve entails bargaining between the entrepreneur and the small marginal unit of labour. However, not only may bargaining between employees and employer take place in marginal units, but the employees may also be able to make an all-or-nothing choice of participation or non-participation in the firm as a collectivity. Doing so will enable them to exercise more active bargaining power over the distribution of the organizational rent. This possibility can be readily seen for the case of cost saving of type 3 and 4 above (p. 30). Suppose that workers in the team possess collective skills and/or firm-specific skills formed by on-the-job training, efficient use of which would generate economic gains that are not possible through mere casual combination of marketed labour services. Under this circumstance, if the workers withhold their co-operation collectively, then the shareholder's opportunity will be spoiled. Using this possibility as an effective threat, the workers as a collectivity may acquire a certain bargaining power over the distribution of the organizational rent arising from investment in firm-specific and collective skills.

Regarding the risk cost-saving (point 1 above), a similar reasoning may be applied. If the employees are not allowed to participate in its apportion, they will not be motivated to bind themselves to the long-run risk-sharing contracts and may become indifferent as between staying with the contracting partner and being mobile among more than one employer through the labour market. Therefore they can make a credible threat of withdrawing from the long-term contracts. Since the risk cost-saving can be generated only when the risk-sharing contract is observed in the long run by both parties, the execution of such a threat would annihilate the generation of economic gains to be appropriated by the employer. Therefore the employer would rather agree to the sharing of risk cost-saving in order to motivate the employee to observe the contract. To the extent to which the employees can control their labour supply collectively and shield themselves from the competitive pressure of the external labour market, they will be able to elicit advantageous terms of sharing.

As regards bargaining over other cost savings generated by the hierarchical control of production, the situation has changed considerably since the heyday of classical economics. 'The direction of resources' (Coase, 1937), 'monitoring by centralized contractual agent' (Alchian and Demsetz, 1972), and the operation of the quantity mechanism − all these require some people to specialize in giving orders and some to execute them, but this authority relationship can be logically separated from the division of the fruits of co-operation under authoritative direction. Because of higher employment opportunity, higher social security benefits, and greater personal savings, the fear of hunger is no longer a potent weapon of the employer to force the employees to be blindly obedient.

Also, partly as a result of the continuing influence of the democratic imperative in society at large and partly as a result of a higher level of general education, employees have become more independent and more ready to assert that they are entitled to receive a fair treatment, both materially and otherwise. They are thus willing to exercise their bargaining power, and their ability to do so effectively rests on the strength of their organizations and/or on their latent control of production processes on the shop-floor. Faced with the (collective) assertiveness of the employees, the employer must calculate the cost of a productivity slow-down that could result from his failure to reach an implicit or explicit agreement with the employees regarding sharing of the organizational rent.

Alchian and Demsetz consider that such sharing is viable for a saving of type 2 above only in small teams in which reciprocal monitoring among co-operators is more effective. They argue:

[g]eneral sharing in the residual results in losses from enhanced shirking by the monitor that exceeds the gains from reducing shirking by residual-sharing employees. If this were not so, profit-sharing with employees should have occurred more frequently in Western societies where such organizations are neither banned nor preferred politically. (Alchian and Demsetz, 1972, p. 787)

Sharing of the market-using cost saving need not take the legal form of profit-sharing, however. *De facto* sharing may take a form of wage premium and be practised even under the usual collective bargaining institution or in the form of implicit wage contracts. So the Alchian−Demsetz argument to the effect that the monitor would shirk unless he is guaranteed the whole reduction in shirking is not firmly tenable.

Conclusions

The neoclassical school has developed a systematic theory of markets. Yet, it lacks a coherent theory of the firm; the material generally subsumed under that heading is actually a theory of markets in which firms are important actors. The

Walrasian model of a general equilibrium with production hardly gives us greater insight into the workings of the capitalist economy than is available from the pure exchange model. Recently, neoclassical efforts directed towards the exploration of the internal workings of the firm have been gathering force, as I have mentioned in this chapter, but the firm still remains a bundle of exchange relationships — albeit of special kinds, such as the contractual exchange between the acceptance of authority and the guarantee of a fixed wage — and the entrepreneur is still visualized as the sole beneficiary of the residual income.

However, as I have tried to make clear in this chapter, the logical scrutiny of some of the neoclassical constructs, such as risk-sharing, the quantity mechanism, monitoring, and so on, seems to be that employees and employer can achieve certain gains of their own by co-operation. Only if it is additionally assumed that the employees can effectively threaten to withhold their co-operation in the absence of a satisfactory agreement is sharing of firm-specific gains the logical conclusion. Thus, it seems reasonable to characterize the firm as a field of bargaining among the firm-specific resource-holders including the body of employees, rather than simply as a bundle of individual exchange relationships supplemented by the existence of marketable residual claims (equity). There does not seem to exist, therefore, a single objective of the firm such as the maximization of residual (profits); rather, the firm internalizes a bargaining process in which the conflicting objectives of the firm-specific resource-holders are brought into equilibrium within a framework of the co-operative relations.

Chapter 3

The Managerial Theory of the Firm

Corresponding to the two types of saving of the market-using costs that we discussed in the last chapter, two functions are usually attributed to the entreprencur: risk-bearing and control. However, a conspicuous feature of modern capitalism is the fade-out of the owner-managed firm from the mainstream of the economy, and the rise to a position of dominance of the large corporate enterprise. Needless to say, the management (control) of activities of the large corporation is becoming increasingly complicated, and is therefore entrusted to professional managers. On the other hand, since the optimal portfolio for any investor is likely to be diversified across the shares of many corporations, an individual investor generally has no special interest in personally overseeing the detailed activities of any firm. Because of the wide dispersal of shareownership, the managers of large corporations appear to have captured the power to form corporate policy decisions, freeing themselves from shareholder' direct surveillance. Thus, the two functions that were united in the neoclassical entrepreneur now appear to reside in the two separate types of participants in the firm.

The growing dominance of the corporate firm, the increasing decision-making power of corporate management, and the increasing passive position of the shareholder were documented, and the ethical and economic justifications given by (neo)classical economics to the modern corporation was questioned, by one of the most influential writings on the legal–economic theory, *The Modern Corporation and Private Property*, by Adolf Berle and Gardiner Means (1932). But how does the economic system constituted of large manager-dominated firms behave? Is the system justifiable on moral as well as political and economic grounds? Berle· in his earlier writing (1931) had maintained that corporate powers were held in trust not only for the corporation but also for individual members of it.[1] By so arguing, he tried to resurrect the classical unification of risk-bearing and control by the force of the law. This view came to be criticized by E. Merrick Dodd of Harvard Law School, who argued that the directors of a corporation must (if they had not already) become trustees, not merely for shareholders but also for other constituents of corporation, such as employees, customers, and particularly the entire community (Dodd, 1932). Later, Berle conceded to Dodd, and admitted that modern directors act *de facto* and *de jure* as administrators of a community system, although he remained rather cautious about admitting this as the 'right disposition'.[2]

The managerialist view that the control of large corporations does, or should, develop into a purely neutral technocracy, balancing a variety of claims by various groups in the community on the basis of public policy, albeit established as an influential line of thought in the legal science, has never been accepted by

mainstream economics. Twenty-five years after the publication of the book by
Berle and Means, Edward Mason (1958) raised a legitimate question in a provoca-
tive essay as to why managerial economics had failed, *vis-à-vis* the neoclassical
theory-cum-ideology, to provide an adequate economic theory explaining the
workings of a managerial economic system and an ideology justifying the system.
He enumerated the following possible reasons:

1   The economy might not be as managerial as the literature supposed.
2   The description might be correct, but the managerial economists might not
    as yet have penetrated deeply enough into the system to provide an adequate
    theory-cum-ideology.
3   Corporate managements may not always have behaved in a manner as bene-
    ficial to various participants of the firm as managerialists believed.

Mason thought that there was some truth in all these explanations. A later
development of 'economic' managerialism by Marris (1964), Williamson (1964),
and others may be thought of as an attempt to respond to the challenge posed
by Mason under the second of these reasons, that is, as an attempt to construct
a formalized theory explaining the behaviour of the 'managerial' firm. But in so
doing, they only replaced the neoclassical hypothesis of entrepreneurial utility
maximization with the hypothesis of managerial utility maximization. As a result
they departed from the original premise of managerialism, that the management
acts as intermediary to various participants of the firm, and came to believe that
the manager subjects corporate policy decisions to his own objective. In effect,
they surrender to the charge expressed in reason 3 above by Mason.

In this chapter I shall first discuss the nature of the managerial utility function
as posited by managerial economic theorists. It is usually assumed that managerial utility is related to the size of the firm (in the static case) or to its growth
rate (in the dynamic case), and that the manager maximizes his utility subject
to a constraint imposed by shareholders.[3] This maximizing behaviour of the
manager is often interpreted as being rooted in his egoistic pursuit of prestige,
power, status, higher income, and other personal benefits associated with the
size of the firm. In this vulgarized interpretation, the corporate firm is little
more than a vehicle for satisfying the manager's personal needs. There are likely
to be such personal motives operating behind managerial activities, but such a
super-individualistic interpretation of managerial objectives seems to lose sight of
an important aspect of the manager's role in the modern corporate firm.

A book by Robin Marris (1964), which I find an eloquent presentation of the
managerial theory, contains a more interesting interpretation, however. Marris
attributes the manager's preference for corporate growth to his role as an organ-
izer who integrates the individual pecuniary motives of hierarchically organized
salaried managers. Indeed, he characterizes his theory as 'an attempt to recon-
struct the "internal" theory of the firm' (Marris, 1964, p. i). In the first part of
this chapter I shall focus on this aspect of the managerial theory, an aspect that

economists' preoccupation with analytical manipulation of the growth maximization hypothesis tends to overlook.

The second part of the chapter is then devoted to an examination of a premise
of the managerial theory regarding the manager–shareholder relationship. The
shareholder–manager interaction conceived by the managerial theorist is a simple
one: the source of the shareholders' countervailing power *vis-à-vis* managerial
discretionary power is to be found only in the transferability of shares, which
makes the threat of a take-over by investors wishing to replace the existing
management a constant possibility. This managerialist premise will be examined
in the light of recent theoretical and factual developments.

Essentially, the neoclassical theory on the possibility of shareholders' unanimity will be surveyed, and its implications to the managerial theory will
be examined. This theory, although neoclassical in its theoretical framework,
holds that it is only in rare circumstances that shareholders having different
expectations and different risk attitudes form a unanimous opinion regarding
the corporate policy of their portfolio corporations. This conclusion may be
thought of as conceding to the managerialist contention that the role of the
manager in the corporate firm is never passive; for the aggregation of divergent
shareholders' opinions will be at best a political process in which the manager
must play the active role of interest mediator–administrator. More likely, the
manager will have to, and be able to, exercise his own judgement in corporate
policy-making in the face of shareholders' disagreement. On the other hand, this
theory may be thought of as casting some doubts on the managerialist premise as
well. For, as the theory indicates that the share price is not necessarily the focal
point of aggregating shareholders' diverse interests, the managerialist view that
the share price will constitute the only discipline imposed on the management
by the shareholders may be questioned.

The recent development of shareownership patterns reinforces this query.
The managerial theory was formulated in response to the phenomena observed
in the first half of the century, that shareownership was becoming progressively
more widely dispersed and thus shareholders seemed to be losing grounds to
professional managers. However, recently there has been a noteworthy change in
the mode of shareholding. Through the growth of institutionally managed funds,
the voting rights to stock in large corporations – if not the ownership thereof –
are being concentrated at a remarkable speed, reversing the earlier trend, and
bringing a closer nexus between a relatively few financial institutions and large
corporations. In light of this factual development, too, the fundamental premise
of the managerial theory regarding the shareholder–management relationship
must be re-assessed.

The organizational nature of the managerial utility

The business corporation is a legal 'person' who is organized for the purpose of
conducting economic activities; and this person, like a natural person, may

become an object or subject of legal action, may employ factors of production, may own assets, and is subject to taxation. The control of action of the corporation is legally vested in the board of directors except for decisions on structural matters, such as merger and dissolution, which fall directly into the shareholders' province.

A common view held by economists is that the board is set up as a trustee of the shareholders who possess collective rights *de jure* to select directors at shareholder meetings, and that the board, in turn, effectively controls the activities of employees of the corporation including those of its executive officers. The conventional neoclassical notion, which regards the corporate manager as an agent of the shareholders, is based on this view. Legally, however, the officers are agents not of the shareholders but of the board, while the board itself is not really an agent of the shareholders, but an independent institution.

For example, while the authority of an agent can normally be terminated by his principal at any time, directors are normally removable by shareholders only for good cause shown. Similarly, while an agent must normally follow his principal's instruction, shareholders have no legal power to give binding instructions to the board on matters within its powers. (Eisenberg, 1976, pp. 2–31)[4]

Furthermore, a closer look at the workings of the board would never fail to recognize that a small group of directors plays a decisive role in corporate decision-making. We can, of course, observe cases in which these 'in-groups' are identifiable with persons who own large blocks of shares. In many instances, however, the executive officers who operate actual businesses and control the internal organization of employees, but who do not necessarily own shares of the corporation in substantial amounts, are represented on the board and are very influential. By combining the functions of policy-making and operating, they often assimilate directorial systems to a considerable extent. Furthermore, the substantial number of directors is frequently nominated by the existing members from among employees subordinate to the top management, or from outsiders lacking effective information to oversee the managers, so that managerial power appears self-perpetuating to a great extent.

The managerial theorist argues that it is, therefore, valid to distinguish the management from the shareholders as a separate element in the corporate system. Marris elaborates this position:

Precisely, we define 'the management' as the particular in-group, consisting of directors and others, which effectively carries out the functions legally vested in the board. This does not mean that shareholders and management are necessarily opposed, or that policy will necessarily differ from that which might be pursued in a system where managers were immanent. All we are saying is that the two groups are sufficiently distinct, and the managers sufficiently autonomous, for the existence of a harmony of interests not to be regarded as axiomatic. Therefore, in order to understand the economic system of the corporations, it is essential to assess the factors determining the relative influence of, or balance of power between, these two forces operating within them. (Marris, 1964, p. 15)

This view gives an important insight into an aspect of the corporate firm, although Marris himself did not elaborate on the *intra*-organizational process of achieving a balance of power between management and shareholders. Instead, he posits, as we will see in greater detail, that corporate behaviour can be understood and predicted in terms of utility maximization of the manager subject only to a certain constraint imposed *externally* through the share market. But it seems quite reasonable to presume, from the quotation above, that the corporate objective is possessed of an organizational character.

In order to prepare for a discussion on this, let me begin by illustrating as simply as possible the structure of policy alternatives available to the manager in resolving the potential conflict of interests between himself and the shareholders. Suppose that time extends indefinitely through periods of equal duration. Let R be the maximum revenue net of current costs expected for the present period by the corporate firm. In order to increase revenue from one period to the next at a growth rate g, the firm must spend a fraction $s(g)$ of its current revenue on sales promotion, new equipment, personnel training, and the like, where $s(\cdot)$ is supposed to be an increasing convex function of g; that is, the firm can achieve a larger growth rate by devoting a higher proportion of revenue for that purpose, and the proportion increases ever faster as the growth rate increases. It is supposed that the expenditure for growth is financed out of retained earnings. Then the dividends that would be distributed to shareholders at the end of the current period will be $\{1 - s(g)\}R$.

The total end-of-period returns to a new investment in the stock of the corporation is composed of two elements, dividends and capital gain. Suppose that the investors on the current financial market believe, on average, that the firm's policy decision, particularly as to sales growth, will continue for ever. If the dividend is expected to grow at a steady rate g, then that is the rate of capital gain. In the absence of market uncertainty, the competitive valuation V of the firm's stock must satisfy the following condition:

$$\{1 - s(g)\}R + gV = \rho V$$

where ρ is the one-period interest rate prevailing in the money market. The left-hand side represents the total end-of-period returns to investments in the stock of the firm, and the right-hand side represents the interest income that the investment of the same amount in a one-period bond would yield. In equilibrium no arbitrage possibility may exist, so that the two must be equalized. Therefore, after suitable arrangements, we have

$$V = \frac{\{1 - s(g)\}R}{\rho - g} \quad .$$

V represents the aggregate wealth that the current shareholders are interested in. It is assumed that $s(\hat{g}) = 1$ for some $\hat{g} < \rho$, so that the value of V would not explode.

If g is increased continuously from zero (I ignore the possibility of negative growth), then at first V gradually increases, because the denominator decreases at a higher rate than the numerator decreases. But eventually the latter effect catches up, and V approaches a maximum value and then falls until it reaches zero at $g = \hat{g}$. Expenditure for growth is a necessary cost for the increment of shareholders' wealth up to a certain amount, but beyond a critical level it becomes too costly for them and the growth rate can be increased only if V is permitted to decline. In other words, if the management is interested solely in higher growth rates, then managerial utility can be enhanced at the expense of the stockholders' wealth. However, the shareholders may find some counter-vailing power in the transferability of shares, which could result in a take-over raid.

A take-over raider is a person or corporation who intends to acquire sufficient stock to be able to replace the existing management, to realize the quick capital gain obtainable by reducing g and letting V rise, or to amalgamate with other firms controlled by the raider. If excessive pursuit for growth lets the value of the stock drop too low, then the existing shareholders, becoming disenchanted by the current policy of the firm, may be induced to sell their shares to the raider at an offered price that is usually better than the market price. Thus, in striving for higher growth, the manager must strike a balance between his own increased utility and the increasing risk of a take-over.

Marris formalized the take-over discipline imposed on the managers by the shareholders in two ways: the first formulation is to treat a certain level of the market valuation of the corporation relative to the book value of its assets, called the 'valuation ratio',[5] as an exogenous constraint on growth maximization by the manager; the second formulation is to include the valuation ratio as a proxy variable for take-over risk in the managerial utility function together with the growth rate of the firm.

The growth rate variable in the utility function, as can be seen in Fig. 3.1, represents the collective interests of employed managers organized into a hier-archical system. On the other hand, the valuation ratio, which signifies the risk of a take-over raid as assessed by the manager, directly represents the interest of current shareholders. Therefore the utility function, with two variables, each reflecting the interest of a different element of a corporate system, may be considered as a representation of the top manager's perception of the intra-organizational balance of power between the internal organization of salaried managers and the shareholders' body. If we conceptualize the 'organizational' utility function as that criterion on which the interests of participants are weighted in corporate decision-making according to their respective bargaining power, the managerial utility function *à la* Marris has that flavour; although a more satisfactory internal theory of the firm needs to deal explicitly with the analytical construction of the organizational utility function from more elementary data, such as individual utility functions of members, rather than taking its given form as a datum.

Fig. 3.1

I consider that the relative failure of economic managerialism to offer a reasonable and consistent theory explaining the behaviour of the firm as a coalition of various participants is due partly to the nature of the problem itself. While manipulating the problem of maximizing a certain objective function, such as the profit function or the managerial utility function, subject to certain constraints is relatively easy mathematically, an appropriate analytical tool for analysing interactions among many rational agents who are aware of the rationality of other agents was not fully developed, or at least was not known to managerial economists, before the time of Mason's writing (1950s). But now, around a quarter of a century later, the developed game-theoretic apparatus is at hand for analysing such a problem. This development, combined with impressions gained by observing what has been happening to large corporations in industrialized economies, has led me to adopt the following views, as contrasted to Mason's diagnosis, which I will present in subsequent chapters.

1   The modern firm is in fact managed by a balancing of interests of various participants, such as shareholders, employees, and possibly others.
2   The failure of economists to analyse the workings of the firm as an associational coalition could possibly be overcome through the game-theoretic approach.
3   The failure of management (or the institutional framework of decision-making structures of the firm) to strike a 'proper' balance of interests among different participants of the firm will result in internal inefficiency.

Why growth?

The power, prestige, and status that are associated with the size of the firm that they command are doubtless objects of personal aspiration to top managers.

Moreover, Marris (1964) argues, the growth of the firm becomes a collective objective, supported unanimously by members of the internal organization of managers – not only its chief executive officers but its junior managers as well, for their salaries can be expected to increase if the growth rate of the firm accelerates. In this reasoning, Marris relies on the theory of salary developed by Herbert Simon (1957). Let us examine the reasoning in greater detail.

First, suppose that the employed managers of a firm are organized into a hierarchical pyramid, having discrete and finite levels. More specifically, assume that the 'steepness' of hierarchy, defined as the ratio of occupants in a particular hierarchical level to the occupants in the level immediately below, is a constant, say n, from the top of the pyramid to its bottom. Inter-organizational transfer of personnel is limited to the bottom level, because managers combined in a team are more productive in the firm in which the team was developed, so that vacancies in the upper levels are filled by promotion. Then opportunities for the personal advancement of an individual manager will vary directly with the growth of his firm.

Following Simon, assume that the manager's salary depends upon his position in the hierarchical organization. The higher the position he occupies, the more he receives. Only the salary paid to new entrants at the bottom level is market-determined;[6] otherwise salary does not reflect the marginal product of an individual manager. More specifically, assume that there is a constant rate of salary gradation in the following sense: the salary assigned to any hierarchical level but the bottom is greater than the salary of the level just below by a constant proportionality factor, say β. Simon proved from these assumptions that, on a logarithmic scale, a manager's salary is linearly related to his responsibility, measured by the number of subordinates controlled by him directly or indirectly. Specifically, let C_N be the total compensation of a manager commanding N subordinates; then we have the following equation to determine C_N:

$$\log C_N = \frac{\log \beta}{\log n} \log N + \text{constant}.$$

This theory is said to fit the empirical data well.[7]

Thus, Simon's theory seems to indicate that the growth of the firm would be supported not only by the top managers, but also by all income-oriented members of the internal organization. For the expected sum of future salaries (discounted at an appropriate interest rate) of a manager at any level will be increased if he has a better chance of promotion, provided that the internal pay structure remains invariant.

But is a fixed pay structure sustainable regardless of the speed at which the firm grows? We need to be careful about translating Simon's static theory into a dynamic one. The increased growth of the firm is normally possible only through higher expenditure in order to overcome the external and internal constraints on its expansion. It is recognized by Marris that an increase in growth expenditure would eventually reduce benefits accruing to the shareholders. But what is reduced by the increase in growth cost may not be limited to the share value.

First, we observe that the inter-organizational transfer of personnel is limited and that managers of apparently equal responsibilities are paid differently, depending upon where they are employed. These facts seem to suggest the possibility that managers' salaries do have an aspect of participation in the organizational rent, as conceptualized at the end of the previous chapter. Theoretically, this argument for rent-sharing derives from aforementioned propositions that managerial efficiency involves a team element (pp. 25-6 above), and that managers can exert a bargaining power over the disposition of the organizational rent through the threat of collective withdrawal of their efforts (p. 31).

I would now contend, further, that rent-sharing would entail a sharing of growth cost as another side of the same coin. A higher growth target would require an increased expenditure for advertising, training personnel and workers, capital costs, and so on. An increased expenditure that signifies a strain on the limited resources of the firm would reduce the total sum of organizational rent, net of growth cost, currently available for distribution between shareholders and managers. Therefore, if the managers' relative bargaining power for a share in the organizational rent remains constant, a higher growth rate must be accompanied by smaller salary funds today to support the given number of employed managers; accordingly, the level of the average salary must be lowered.[8] Of course, the bearing of the growth cost today would be compensated by expected gains from future promotion and consequent salary increases, but only to a certain extent. This is similiar to the aforementioned situation in which the bearing of the growth cost by the shareholders is compensated by capital gains to a certain degree, but not without a limit.

Of course, as noted already, managers' motives may not be limited to the narrowly defined pecuniary one. They may derive enjoyment also from performing their unique roles of exploring, planning, and organizing new activities of the enterprise. Still, the above argument seems to remain valid in that managers are not likely to give unreserved approvals to ever-higher growth for the firm. The managerialist growth maximization was in some sense considered *ad hoc* in nature, which appeared more reasonable in the period of relatively high growth in the 1950s and 1960s. As we have now passed that happy era, this hypothesis needs to be subjected to a more rigorous scrutiny. It suffices to hold, however, that managerial interest in corporate growth is not limitless, and that the manager is facing a more delicate task in balancing the time preference of the body of shareholders and that of the internal organization.

A digression – shareholders' non-unanimity

The managerialist theory posits that shareholders and management confront each other regarding a level of share price. Implicit in this assumption is that shareholders are unanimously interested in share-price maximization: a presumption with which neoclassical economists would not normally disagree. The difference between rigidly neoclassical and rigidly managerial theories of the firm lies in which of the two actors — the management or the shareholders — is assumed to hold the reigns.

There is however a new development on this subject on the neoclassical side. In rather a digressed form, this section surveys this new development, which holds, through a rigorous analysis typical of neoclassical economics, that it is only under rare circumstances that shareholders have a unanimous opinion on corporate policies, specifically in favour of share-price maximization in a world of uncertainty. The difference of opinions between, and possibly the lack of information possessed by, shareholders creates room for management to play an autonomous role. Thus the divorce between rigidly neoclassical and rigidly managerial theories may be thought of as somewhat artificial.

Once it is assumed that all factors of production are priced on the market or through bargaining, then, in the absence of uncertainty, all the shareholders would agree that the firm should maximize total revenue after payments for those factors, that is to say, should maximize profit. Even if they were diverse in their tastes, they would be unanimous in favouring a policy of profit maximization, for profits would be distributed among them on a *pro rata* basis and the greater profits would always increase their utilities.

But this happy consensus can break down in the presence of uncertainty. Profits are not uniquely determined by a firm's action in this case; at best, only a set of profits across possible states of nature is determinable. Let us assume that there is at least an agreement among investors concerning the classification of events, each identifiable with different profitabilities. However, suppose that they do differ as regards expectations; that is, each of them may have his own subjective estimate on the probabilities of occurrences of events. They may also differ in their attitude towards risk. (Their differing expectations and differing attitudes towards risk may be summarized in the form of different utility functions, defined on the set of dividends configuration across possible states of nature.)

In these circumstances, it is nonsensical to speak about profit maximization, for profits will now depend on an unknown state of nature, as well as on a managerial decision. Then what should be the objective of the firm from the viewpoint of the shareholder? Given rates of compensation to other factors, should management maximize shareholders' utilities? But then whose expectation, and whose taste towards risk, should be used in order to assess the desirability of alternative production plans? Should the management adopt a production plan that maximizes the market value of shares? Can the shareholders agree on it unanimously? These are the questions that have been intensively investigated in recent years, and some of the important results can be summarized as follows.[9] (The discussion will proceed based upon the neoclassical presumption that rates of remuneration to other factors are predetermined.)

Suppose that, given a set of announced managerial production plans of firms, each investor arranges his optimal portfolio in a competitive financial market. Consider a body of investors who become the shareholders of a firm through diversified individual portfolios. They are called the *ex post* shareholders.[10] They are likely to have differing expectations, attitudes towards risk, and portfolios. The value of the stocks has been determined on the market jointly with those of other financial assets.

Now suppose that the *ex post* shareholders of the firm gather at a shareholders' meeting and discuss the possibility of changing the managerial production plan that was a basis of their portfolio selection. Although, *given* the managerial plan of production, shareholdings of the firm have been optimal to them, their utilities may still be increased by a proper change in the managerial plan. Will there be a unanimous approval or a rejection of changes in the managerial plan?

If the *ex post* shareholders have arbitrary utility functions, then a necessary and sufficient condition for them to be unanimous in their opinions on possible (local) changes of production plan at the financial equilibrium is that the so-called 'spanning condition' holds relative to that plan. This rather technical condition implies that any decision to change the production plan of the firm locally would not alter the aggregate possibility set of state-distributions of profits already available in the whole market. In other words, a state-distribution of profits expected by any change in the production plan of the firm could have been realized by a proper combination of the stocks of other firms already available in the whole economy. Otherwise proposed changes in the firm's state-distribution of profits may be met with a divided response among the shareholders.

This spanning condition seems to be very restrictive. Marginal changes in returns resulting from changes in investment projects or other corporate decisions often have *firm-specific* risks which are not spanned by currently marketed stocks. Therefore, there are likely to be cases in which the shareholders cannot agree at their meeting, although all of them consider it optimal to include the stocks of the firm in their portfolios, provided that the managerial production plan remains unaltered.

So far we have been assuming that the shareholders meet when their portfolios are optimal relative to the market and that they discuss whether a further change in the production plan of the firm is beneficial for them. Now consider an alternative case in which the investors' portfolios are arbitrary. The case arises, for instance, if the once-optimal mix of stock in investors' portfolios becomes inappropriate because of changes in their expectations and/or tastes, technological changes, new stock issues elsewhere, and so on. Those shareholders whose portfolios are not optimal are called the *ex ante* shareholders. In this case, there are two different strategies that shareholders of a firm can pursue. First, they can go straight to the financial market and rearrange their portfolios individually. This type of behaviour is known as the 'Wall Street Rule' in the investment community: if you disapprove the management of a company, sell your shares of that company's stock. We will discuss this option in the next section.

An alternative for the *ex ante* shareholders of the firm is to meet together before resorting to trading on the financial market, and discuss the possibility of voting collectively for a change in the managerial plan of the firm or for a change in management team proposing more attractive policies. Is there any plan to be adopted unanimously by the *ex ante* shareholders? If so, can it be characterized as a plan that would maximize the share value of the firm?

Ex ante unanimity requires, in addition to 'spanning', a further condition. This is that the capital market must be completely competitive in the following senses:

1   share values are 'perceived' to be independent of the portfolio selections by individual investors;
2   the share value of the firm under consideration is 'perceived' to change equiproportionally in response to equiproportional changes in profits across the states of nature.

Under these conditions, the value maximization as 'perceived' by investors will coincide with the shareholders' collective interests. In general, however, production decisions, if any, that are unanimously supported *ex ante* by the shareholders will not maximize 'actual' market value. The argument for value maximization is that this will push the investor's budget constraint up and outward, thus unambiguously increasing his welfare. But if a firm is large, relative valuation of profits in different states implicit in the share price (the slope of the budget line) may be affected by the decision perceived, and value maximization is not necessarily the best policy. Also, if a new investment by a firm involves a unique risk which is very hard for individual investors to assess, shareholders may be, to a non-negligible extent, influenced by an opinion of the manager who has an informational advantage regarding the investment. This suggests that the manager of the corporation is not a passive agent of the shareholders — though he may not be completely independent of them. This seems to render support for the managerialist contention that the role of manager in the modern corporation is more than a mere agent of shareholders.

On the other hand, there is another important implication of the neoclassical model of shareholders' unanimity counter to the managerialist contention: that is, the share price may not be the sole interest of shareholders if the corporation is characterized by its non-smallness and uniqueness relative to the economy. The conventional wisdom holds that shareholders can impose an effective discipline on the management through the market. If investors do not agree with the management of portfolio corporation, it is told, they can sell their shares of that corporation's stock. The sale of shares is a 'no' vote, and if it occurs on a large scale it will affect the share price substantially, leading to a corrective action by the board or to a take-over raid. Therefore, the existing management will be always alerted to movements of the share price.

Under the condition of non-smallness, however, since the demand curve for a firm's shares will be downward-sloping, it is clear that a premium over the current market share price must be paid in order to buy sufficient shares to take over the corporation. The market share price measures only the valuation of the marginal shareholders, whereas the price relevant to a raider is that of the intra-marginal shareholders. We should not be surprised, therefore, to find that a corporation that is large and unique relative to the economy operates below the 'maximum' share price. (This argument is more thoroughly treated in King, 1977, pp. 131–52.)

Intra-marginal shareholders may rather wish to preserve some influence on corporate policy through the more direct route of corporate machinery. But as Berle and Means (1932) ardently argued, if shareholders are diverse and relatively small, it might be very difficult for them to do so. However, in this respect too, there seems to be a noteworthy new development, which I shall now take up.

The shareholders' counter-revolution?

The managerial economic theory was preceded, as noted above, by the development of an empirical thesis on the separation of control from ownership in the seminal classic by Berle and Means (1932). They described in detail the wide dispersal of shareownership of big corporations that had been taking place in the United States since the turn of the century and stressed the diminishing role of individual shareholders as an influence in corporate decision-making and the parallel growth of decision-making power of corporate management – a phenomenon that came to be called the 'managerial revolution' (Burnham, 1941). But in the last two decades or so, a trend reversing the atomization of shareownership has developed in all major capitalist countries and is expected to continue; we are witnessing the dramatic growth of institutional shareholding.

Shareholding by institutional investors in the United States, for instance, accounted for nearly one-third of the market value of stock outstanding at the end of 1980. Among the institutional holdings, by now the largest and fastest growing are pension funds (11.2 per cent of the market value of total stock in 1980), followed by personal trust funds (8.4 per cent). Relying on this development, Peter Drucker maintains, on the basis of his own rather inflated estimates, that 'the employees of America are the only true "owners" of the means of production', and that 'through their pension funds they are the only true capitalists around, owning, controlling, and directing the country's capital' (Drucker, 1976, p. 3). But the statistics of nominal ownership do not tell the whole story.

Actually, most pension funds are not self-administered. Management of pension assets, including the authority to buy, sell, and vote equities, is concentrated among banks, insurance, and investment companies. Combined with the management of personal and common trust funds and that of insurance funds, these institutions have an enormous concentration of the stock voting rights in large US corporations. The subcommittee of the Senate Committee on Government Affairs, headed by late Senator Lee Metcalf, undertook a very interesting study on *Voting Rights in Major Corporations*, the results of which were published in

1978. The subcommittee studied voting rights in 122 major corporations, the market value of which amounted to two-fifths of the market value of all outstanding common stock in the United States at the end of 1976. The study found that:

> In 19 of the 122 corporations a single institutional investor controls more than 5 per cent of the voting rights in the corporation. In 24 other corporations a combination of five or fewer investors control more than 10 per cent of the voting rights. In 13 additional corporations a family group controls more than 10 per cent of the voting rights. (US Senate, 1978, p. 1)

Particularly noteworthy is the power of a few large banks. Morgan Guaranty Trust Co. of New York is identified as one of the five largest stockvoters in 56 corporations out of the 122 corporations studied. Trust departments of the other ten major banks rank among the five largest stockvoters as many as 127 times. It appears that the trend identified by Berle and Means and their followers in the 1930s and 1940s of the wide dispersal of shareownership among many investors may now be giving way to a new trend towards control of the voting of the substantial blocks of stock in major corporations held by relatively few financial giants. This phenomenon of the close business–bank nexus has been more conspicuous in Japan and Germany for some time, as we will discuss in Part III.

One of the important consequences of this concentration of stockholdings by major financial institutions is the fact that they cannot quietly or readily liquidate their investment without seriously lowering its price to their disadvantage. Neoclassical folklore tells us that investors take share prices on the market as parametric signals and adjust their portfolios continuously in the best possible way. This behavioural pattern was also elevated to a maxim known as the 'Wall Street Rule', once almost universally followed within the investment community. But it is said that a rigid adherence to the 'Wall Street Rule' is now being abandoned.[11] The advantage of attempting to influence management by proxy votes, directorate holdings, and informal consultations rather than by selling stock seems to be, in some cases, greater for financial institutions that have enough shares of corporate stocks. The ability of those financial institutions, particularly commercial banks, to gain influence over other corporations may be reinforced by the borrowing of large sums of money by the latter from the former.

Is increasing institutional shareholding restoring an element of shareholders' control over the management? Are we witnessing the 'shareholders' counter-revolution'? Answering these questions is not easy. However, at least, the managerialist view that the fear of raiders constitutes a major discipline imposed on the management by shareholders seems to need modification. The interplay between the management of the corporation and its outside institutional shareholders is becoming more direct and self-sustaining. (This claim will be taken up again in chapter 11.) As indicated above, there are cases in which an institution's position is too large to be liquidated except at a substantial loss, so that it would be better for it to try to change managerial policy more directly. On the other hand, substantial blocks of stock held by the institutional shareholders might have given the management of the corporation the security from take-over, at least to some extent, and an organizational objective other than the value maximization may now be safely pursued – provided that it would not seriously harm the interests of the institutions. We have already seen, in the previous section, that value maximization may not necessarily coincide with the interest of at least a part of the shareholder body, when the firm is relatively large and unique in the economy.

Berle recognized the fact of enormous concentration of shareownership by financial intermediaries in his Preface to the revised edition of *The Modern Corporation and Private Property* published in 1962, but his conclusions were as follows. First, because of an accompanying increase in internal financing of corporate investments, the share markets have lost their significance as allocator of new investments. They have become only 'the mechanism of liquidity' (Berle and Means, 1932 (1962 edn, p. xxi)), redistributing wealth among individuals. Second, the financial intermediaries remove individuals more and more from the control of the modern corporation.

However, Berle seems to be preoccupied with implications of growing institutional assets to the classical notion of 'private property', while we are interested in its implications to the working of the modern corporate firm. Since institutional shareholders will no doubt have more potential power to influence the management of portfolio corporations than individual investors, institutional shareholders' surveillance over the management may not be reduced to the bare minimum. The time preference of outside pension and trust managers, who at least partially represent beneficial owners' interests, may not be completely coincidental with that of the inside managers. How then is this difference resolved? It seems more reasonable to recognize the body of shareholders, albeit not homogeneous, as an active element of the firm, and the direct interplay between management and shareholders as constituting an important mechanism of the firm.

A digression – relevancy of the agency theory to the corporation

Another important theoretical development of relatively recent vintage which may be thought of as bridging the gap between the neoclassical theory and the managerial theory is found in the agency–principal theory. In this theoretical framework, the separation of control and risk-bearing (residual-taking) between the manager and the shareholder is explicitly recognized. Eugene Fama, one of the contributors to this development, declares that '[T]he attractive concept of the entrepreneur (who is taken to be both manager and residual risk-bearer) is . . . laid to rest at least for the purposes of the large modern corporation' (Fama, 1980, p. 289). The two functions usually attributed to the neoclassical entrepreneur are treated as two separate factors within it.

In this respect, the principal–agency theory parallels the managerial theory. However, the principal–agency theory trails a neoclassical trait in another important respect. That is, the manager, albeit recognized as an autonomous entity having his own goal such as effort minimization, is presumed to be an agent who should act in the interest of the shareholders' body – the principal. The problem is then set as a principal's of how to control and discipline the manager to perform this task properly in spite of the likely divergence of a managerial goal from shareholders' interests. We have already seen that, in legal theory, the board of directors, as well as executive managers, is not regarded as precisely an agent of the shareholders' meeting (p. 37 above). The reason why neoclassical economists none the less stick to this out-of-date notion may be due to their belief that shareholders' sovereignty would contribute to an efficient resource allocation as well as an efficient risk-shifting. In challenging the opinion current among orthodox economists, I submit that employees (which include managers) would constitute firm-specific resources not entirely transferable through the market. A ramification of this claim is that interactions between the shareholders and the employees should not be conceived as a unilateral hierarchical control from the former over the latter, but that the two types of resource-holders may be treated as engaging in a bargaining game in the context of the modern corporation. Yet it may be worthwhile to discuss some of the important contributions within the framework of the principal–agency theory in their own merits and demerits.

The principal problem, as first formulated by Stephen Ross (1973), is whether there exists any class of reward schedule for the agent (the manager) such as to yield a Pareto-efficient solution for any pair of utility functions both for the agent and the principal. Some random factor uncontrollable by the agent is assumed to bear upon the outcome of agent's action, but the principal is assumed not to be able to distinguish the effect of the random event from that of agent's effort. Therefore reward schedules must depend upon observable outcomes alone. Of course, the agent is supposed to act so as to maximize his own expected utility subject to an agreed-upon reward schedule. In general, there is a solution to this problem only for a particular, albeit 'quite important and likely to emerge in practice' (Ross, 1973, p. 138), class of reward schedules.

But the solution implies that the reward to the behaviour pattern of the agent is perfectly known to the principal. In other words, the principal must hold perfect information concerning agent's preference. In such a case, it might be thought that the principal could simply instruct the agent what to do instead of stimulating the agent towards desired behaviour through the roundabout method of pecuniary incentive. Upon this reflection, the later development of the principal–agency theory has been directed towards an inquiry into possible mechanisms of monitoring and disciplining the manager in the absence of perfect information regarding managerial preference on the side of the shareholder. As for such mechanisms, the market for managers, the market for corporate control (an outside take-over), and the market for product have been proposed.

Fama imputes efficiency in information-processing to a managerial labour market. Suppose that a manager's contract is written so that his wage is set equal to the expected value of his marginal product, with shareholders accepting the noise in the *ex post* measurement of the marginal product. Fama was able to show that, if future expectations regarding a manager's marginal products (that is, future wages) are revised on the basis of past deviation of marginal products from the expected values in the manner of the Muth's rational expectations hypothesis (1960), the marginal product today and the sum of its contribution to future revisions in wages would be exactly matched. That is, if the manager shirks today and his marginal product does not keep up with his contract wage, it is fully accounted for in the stream of future wages, and the sum of his future wages will be reduced exactly by the difference between the current wage and marginal value product. 'The manager need not be charged *ex ante* for presumed *ex post* deviation from contract since the weight of the wage revision process is sufficient to neutralize his incentive to deviate' (Fama, 1973, p. 297).

This theory is cunning in the light of neoclassical tradition, although whether Fama's result can be carried through in the absence of the assumptions of the zero discount rate and the risk neutrality of the manager remains problematical. Therefore my comment on his theory boils down to the fundamental. Fama's approach is extremely individualistic in that managers' productivities are presumed separable and individually appropriable. On the contrary, I have emphasized that, since there are team as well as firm-specific aspects in managerial productivity, the market valuations of their marginal products in isolation may not add up to their true collective values as a team built up over a period (see Chapter 2). If this is so, the competitive managerial market may not be perfectly efficient in information-processing.

I will not deny, as I shall discuss towards the end of the book, that the evaluation of managers in the market plays a certain role in disciplining managers; but I would maintain that it would be more in terms of their reputations as organizational men, the precise meaning of which I shall develop in the course of subsequent discussions.

The efficiency and effectiveness of the market for corporate control as a disciplinary device has already been discussed to some extent and I will have more to say about this in Part III. Therefore for the moment I shall pass on to still another market mechanism, i.e. the product market. Oliver Hart (1983) built an interesting product market model in which two kinds of firms exist: entrepreneurial and managerial. Entrepreneurial firms are assumed to be run by and in the interest of owners, whereas managerial firms are run by managers who have goals of their own, in particular effort minimization. Suppose that owners of managerial firms are uncertain about their firms' costs and so do not know whether a bad performance of managerial firms is due to mismanagement or to a bad luck in cost. Therefore, when a firm's costs are low, the manager may be able to engage in discretionary behaviour and still fulfil his profit target. However, if the firm's costs are interrelated, lower costs would lead to the expansion of the entrepreneurial firm and the price will be lowered. As a result, managers who must fulfil a profit target will have less opportunity to engage in managerial slack to the extent that costs are interrelated. Thus, the product market may act as a sort of incentive scheme. The relevancy of this model hinges, however, upon the plausibility of the assumption that, while entrepreneurial firms have a noticeable effect on the price of outputs, the managerial firms are price-takers. But, in reality, the managerial firms are likely to be large corporations having price-setting powers, whereas owner–manager firms play only a marginal role in price formation. If that is so, the role of the product market as an incentive and disciplinary device may be limited.

Chapter 4

The Theory of the Worker-controlled Firm

Creeping worker control

The managerial theory is innovative, in that it throws analytical light into the neoclassical 'black box' to reveal the internal structure of the corporate firm. In Marris's (1964) theory, however, the internal structure of the corporation is identified with the pyramid of managers, and manual workers remain exogenous factors of production. In this respect, the managerial theory goes beyond neither the neoclassical nor the Keynesian doctrine.

As is well known, Keynes built his own model of unemployment by first rejecting the so-called second fundamental postulate of the 'classical' theory: 'the utility of the wage when a given volume of labour is employed is equal to the marginal disutility of that amount of employment.' This may be taken to imply that the determination of the real wage and employment is off the supply curve of labour. Keynes regarded the wage unit (the money wage rate) as one of the ultimate independent variables given from outside his economic system. It was determined by the supra-enterprise bargains, presumably between the trade union and the employers' association. In addition, for the purpose of explaining the then-prevailing unemployment, he regarded it unnecessary to question the first fundamental postulate of the 'classical' economics: the determination of employment according to the profit-maximizing principle.

Since the time of Keynes's writing, however, situations surrounding industrial relations and corporate decision-making have been considerably altered in Britain and elsewhere. In Britain unions are not organized on the enterprise basis as in Japan; nor is collective bargaining traditionally as decentralized at enterprise and plant level as in the United States; further, workers' participation in the management of the corporation has not been statutorily instituted as in Germany. But, as I will show in greater detail in Part III below, authority on industrial relations has been substantially transferred from the national- and regional-level bargaining units – trade unions and employers' associations – to the enterprise and plant level after passing an interim period during which the national and regional agreements were supplemented by fragmented workshop bargains. The joint steward committees that represent the bodies of workers on the plants or enterprises have some characteristics of Japanese enterprise-based unions, locals of American trade unions, or German works councils in that they are confined to one firm.[1] This localization trend in the bargaining system is congruent with that in wages. The traditional market-oriented or centrally bargained wage system is gradually giving way to the firm-specific pay structure in so far as jobs are tending to be evaluated more in relation to other jobs in the same firm and less with similar jobs in other factories (see, e.g., Brown and Sisson, 1975).

Pensions and career progression within the firm, once characteristic features of white-collar employment in Britain, have now been extended to the employment conditions of manual workers, and this development tends to diminish differences in status between white-collar and blue-collar workers. *The Industrial Relations Code of Practice, 1972*, stated that 'The aim should be progressively to reduce and ultimately to remove differences . . . in the conditions of employment and status of different categories of employees and in the facilities available to them [which are not] based on the requirment of jobs' (para. 42). The increasing importance of white-collar workers, as well as the white-collarization of manual workers, has far-reaching impacts on corporate decision-making, for the employees cannot be treated entirely as an exogenous factor but to a considerable degree must be regarded as an integral element of the corporate firm.

Although the universal trend seems to be towards the firm-specific determination of employment conditions and the repercussion of this on corporate decision-making is felt everywhere ever more strongly, there are of course, differences in the degree of and institutional arrangements for incorporating workers' voices into the decision-making structure of the corporation among the different industrialized nations. But before entering into a discussion on this topic, it seems appropriate to take up the analysis of a highly stylized model recognizing an involvement of workers in the decision-making of the firm.

In response to the call for the analysis of the economic implications of worker participation, the theory of the worker-controlled firm has recently attracted the attention of economists. This theory, inspired by the Yugoslavian experiment of self-management of the firm, was originally developed to explain and predict the behaviour of the firm as a voluntary association of workers in the market economy.

In the neoclassical firm the organizational rent, as we defined it at the end of Chapter 2, is assumed to accrue exclusively to the entrepreneur as profit; whereas the theory of the worker-controlled firm, as developed by Benjamin Ward (1958), Evsey Domar (1966), Jaroslav Vanek (1970), and others, deals with the firm that is managed in the sole interests of the associated workers. More specifically, the objective of the firm is formulated as the maximization of per capita income of the associated workers under certain constraints. Needless to say, employed workers in the capitalist firm cannot reap the whole organizational rent for themselves without changing the fundamental character of capitalism. Hence, those economists who use this model for the purpose of predicting the impact of worker participation regard the distributive share of the shareholders' body in the organizational rent as exogenous data which comprise a constraint on the income maximization by the workers (see, e.g., Dreze, 1976). But this is not a satisfactory treatment, for exactly the same reason as the neoclassical assumption of profit maximization is not. Only the workers of the firm appear as recognized rational maximizers in the model, and the shareholders' interests appear only implicitly in the form of a fixed-dividends requirement to which the workers must adjust in finding a solution that is optimal to them. More

satisfactory treatment would require explicit recognition of the sharing of organizational rent between shareholders and workers.

Suppose that some proportion, say $1 - \theta$, of the organizational rent goes to
employees and the rest, θ, goes to shareholders. The value of θ is variable between
zero and one inclusive, and its determination is internal to the firm by the definition of organizational rent. Leaving until Part II the question of how the
equilibrium value of θ is determined, let us assume that a certain non-zero, non-
one value of θ is achieved as an internal equilibrium distribution of the firm. The
sharing of the organizational rent may then have repercussions on other corporate
policies regarding pricing, employment, growth planning, and financing. It may
be conjectured that policies that would be adopted by the rent-sharing firm if
the management is efficient can be understood in terms of some kind of weighted
average of optimal policies for the shareholder-controlled firm (the case in which
$\theta = 1$) and those for the worker-managed firm ($\theta = 0$), with θ and $1 - \theta$ as respective weights. It is my intention in the next Part to show, through an heuristic
construction of a bargaining model, that this conjecture is in fact confirmed
under certain conditions. The increasing employees' involvement in the decision-
making of the firm may thus be described as 'creeping worker control'. For this
reason, the theory of the worker-controlled firm can provide us with a proper experimental model in which we can dissect the impacts of employees' bargaining
power on corporate behaviour.

As will be seen, the model of the worker-controlled firm behaves qualitatively
differently than the neoclassical model of the shareholder-controlled firm in
certain respects; thus, familiarity with the workings of the model may give insight to certain types of corporate behaviour that has hitherto been regarded as
pathological by neoclassical orthodoxy or has been explained by the *ad hoc*
introduction of political and/or other non-economic factors. From this perspective, the following section indicates why Keynesian aggregate demand policy
may not be effective *vis-à-vis* the worker-controlled firm, and hence why the
phenomenon of stagflation in the capitalist economy may be due partly to the
increasing bargaining strength of employees.

Dilemma of industrial democracy

In almost all studies, the objective of the worker-controlled firm is assumed to
be the maximization of per-worker income, subject to proper market and technological conditions.[2] An interesting conclusion drawn from this assumption is
that the supply curve of the single product that the firm is producing is, under
competitive conditions, downward-sloping. This can be easily seen.

Let p be the price of the product determined on the competitive market, $f(x)$
the amount of output that the firm can produce if the number of workers
associated with the firm is x, and C a given overhead cost. It is assumed that $f(\cdot)$
is a monotone-increasing, strictly concave function; that is, decreasing returns
to scale with respect to labour input prevails. Income per worker is expressed by

$$\frac{pf(x) - C}{x} \; .$$

The maximization condition is given by

$$pf'(x) = \frac{pf(x) - C}{x} \; .$$

That is, the maximization of income per worker is realized if and only if the marginal value product of labour is equal to the average earnings per worker. If the value that an additional worker can contribute is greater than the average earnings of the existing workers, then it is beneficial for the existing workers to build up the association and vice versa.

With a fixed cost C, it is in the interest of the associated workers to have a larger association so that the overhead cost per worker may be sliced more thinly. On the other hand, with decreasing returns to an additional unit of labour applied to a given amount of capital, it is desirable to have a smaller association so that the value added per worker may be high. The maximization would obtain by striking a balance between these conflicting influences. A rise in selling price of the product will increase the second effect and therefore work in the direction of a smaller association and smaller output. Thus, the supply curve of the product would be backward-sloping, provided that the dismissal of workers is permissible.

Suppose that the worker-controlled firm is in equilibrium and the market price of the product then rises relative to those of other goods and services. From the inference above, it is seen to be to the advantage of each worker to reduce the level of output and 'employment' of the firm, provided he is not the one to be dismissed. Under worker-management, however, associated workers may not be 'fired'. In that case, the firm will simply maintain the employment of existing workers. In any case, the improved market condition will not give an incentive to the worker-controlled firm to increase its employment. At best, all the gains from it will accrue to the existing workers; at worst, it might lead to a reduction in the firm's employment.

The essential picture does not change even if we incorporate the possibilities of joint production and imperfect competition into the model. In the case of joint production, the rise in the selling price of one product may lead not to a reduction of that product, but to the contraction of other outputs and of labour input (see Domar, 1966). Under the condition of imperfect competition, an upward shift of the demand curve for the product would very likely lead to a higher selling price and lower output except for a minor case (see Meade, 1974). The implication of the above results is rather far-reaching. In the economy composed of worker-controlled firms, Keynesian macro-policy to reduce unemployment through an expansion of effective demand may not be so effective as the neoclassical synthesis indicates.[3]

As is well known, Keynes adopted the conventional postulate regarding the determination of employment: 'The wage is equal to the marginal product of labour.' From this postulate he derived an important conclusion, namely that, given the money wage rate, a rise in the market price of the product would lead to the expansion of output and of employment by the firm. What led him to accept the money wage rate as one of 'ultimate independent variables' of his system was probably the British reality of his time, in which wages were typically settled at levels contracted between national trade unions and employers' associations so that the money wage rate was exogenous from the viewpoint of individual managements.

But if the determination of employees' earnings is internal to the firm, the bargaining power of the body of employed workers may be such that the neoclassical as well as Keynesian postulate of the equality of the marginal product of labour with the wage rate, available on the external labour market or determined at the supra-enterprise collective bargaining level, would not hold, and that employment would tend to be curtailed at a level less than what these postulates would predict. In other words, the mixing of the shareholders' interest with that of the employed workers may make the firm more insensitive to an improved market condition of the product. A general rise in the effective demand may result, therefore, in higher sales prices and a sluggish improvement in employment in the short run, unless employed workers are altruistic.

Recently greater than proportional attention has been paid to the monetary aspect of stagflation. But it is at the firm level that actual employment, wages, and prices are set. There must be some internal driving force for limiting employment as well as raising wages and prices, and part of that force may be identified with the increasing bargaining powers of incumbent employees at the sacrifice of outsiders and new entrants. Thus, the recent phenomenon of stagflation may be said to have an aspect of a 'dilemma of industrial democracy'.

Summary of Part I

The first part of this book has reviewed the orthodox theories of the firm as a way of introduction to my own model of the firm. Those theories have a common feature in identifying the objective of the firm with the utility-maximizing objective of a single type of actors: either the shareholders, the managers, or the workers. The other actors enter into the theories only implicitly, and only as passive conditions to which the 'firm' must adjust in finding the solution that is optimal to it. The construction of our model will be based upon an antithesis of this orthodox view.

As summarized at the end of Chapter 2, which reviewed the neoclassical theory, the firm can generate gains of its own, namely the organizational rent, by serving as a nexus for co-operative relationships between the employees and the shareholders which makes possible the optimal redistribution of risk as well as the efficient collective use of skills, knowledge, and funds. Therefore, it may be more insightful to treat the participants of the firm in a more symmetrical fashion. Specifically, it seems reasonable to conclude from what was stated in Chapter 2 that the body of employees acquires certain bargaining power over the disposition of the organizational rent by making the all-or-nothing choice of participation or non-participation in the firm.

It was suggested above and in Chapter 3 that the firm that strikes a balance between the interests of the employees and the shareholders may adjust itself to market environments in different fashions. Part II below is engaged in a rigorous conceptualization of the organizational equilibrium between the participants of the firm and the verification of this conjecture. Also, in the organizational framework the manager of the firm whose task is to maintain its operation is expected to play a more autonomous role than the neoclassical counterpart who is obliged to act in the interests of shareholders. But saying so does not necessarily mean, as was seen in Chapter 3, that the manager maximizes his own utility, treating the firm as a vehicle for satisfying his own interest. A somewhat heterodox view of manager will be developed in the next Part.

Part II

The Co-operative Game Model
of the Firm

Chapter 5

The Organizational Equilibrium

Introduction – the manager as a referee

In Part I it was repeatedly argued that the large corporate firm, internalizing its own employment structure, is likely to obtain gains of its own through a co-operation between the body of shareholders and the team of employees, and that this gain – the organizational rent – is distributed between them through bargaining internal to the firm. Part II will formulate this bargaining as a simple co-operative game between two players – the body of shareholders and the representative employees – and examine its outcomes.

Formally speaking, a co-operative game is defined as a game in which the players can conclude a binding agreement as to what outcome will be chosen to exploit the possibility of common interests. Co-operation in the sense of game theory does not mean that either party sacrifices its own interests for the sake of the other, only that each communicates and co-ordinates its actions for the purpose of furthering its own interests. A slightly modified application to our model of a simple yet most fruitful paradigm in co-operative game theory, the pure bargaining game, yields a reasonable concept of unique organizational equilibrium (co-operative solution) characterized by a power balance between the participants of the game and internal efficiency.

Those readers who are absorbed in specific bargaining situations, especially in Anglo-American collective bargaining, may have some difficulty in drawing an exact analogy between the bargaining process as described in this Part and the one with which they are familiar. But the bargaining game herein is constructed as a purely heuristic device for finding a reasonable concept of outcome that would stabilize the firm–organization's state in reaction to changing environments. Whether or not the actual decisions that would emerge out of some of the more concrete frameworks of the firm would approximate to such an outcome is a topic to be pursued in Part III.

In formulating the bargaining game, I will start with the simplest case in which there is neither market nor technological uncertainty and in which all shareholders and all hired employees are homogeneous in their respective tastes, risk attitudes, and status. Since there exists no environmental uncertainty, all shareholders are unanimously interested in obtaining a greater value for the shares that they hold, and all employees are interested in greater amounts of (lifetime) earnings. In spite of the absence of environmental uncertainty, however, we still need an additional assumption regarding players' risk attitudes, since there is an important indeterminacy left regarding the internal distribution of the organizational rent, namely players' attitudes towards the risk of *internal* conflict (failure to reach a co-operative agreement). As we will see, this assumption plays a very important role in the determination of rent distribution.

The homogeneity assumption is a heroic one indeed, but it provides a useful starting-point for defining such fundamental concepts as the bargaining power of players, organizational equilibrium, and so on. But note that, as is obvious from the discussion in Part I, it is implicit in our intra-firm model that all hired employees, albeit homogeneous within themselves, are idiosyncratic *vis-à-vis* outside workers. The homogeneity assumption will be relaxed with respect to employees in the following chapters. In Chapter 6 I shall consider the possibility of differentiation in the employment status in the firm-specific labour pool caused by lay-offs. In Chapter 7 I allow for the intergenerational turnover of employees and their stratification based upon the tenure in the hierarchical internal organization. Shareholders, on the other hand, will be treated as homogeneous throughout. Some implications of shareholders' differences in preference are treated in the 'theory of shareholders' unanimity' which was surveyed in Chapter 3 (pp. 42–6), so I shall confine myself to occasional comments on the robustness of my model as regards the assumption of shareholders' homogeneity.

The treatment of the manager in the present study bears comment. Managers in the real world, who are making their living either as shareholders, salaried managers, or possibly both, certainly have their own pecuniary and other motives. However, I will abstract from this personal aspect of the manager and conceptualize the essential function of the manager as one of mediating between the body of shareholders and the employees, who have a mutual interest in finding a co-operative game solution. In other words, in the parable to evolve below, the manager may be characterized as a 'referee' of the co-operative game. One may note a strong analogy between our concept of the mediating manager and the managerialist notion of 'a purely neutral technocracy' (Berle and Means, 1932, p. 312). There would be arguments as to whether this concept of manager has already been actualized, or is yet to be actualized for realizing the internally efficient operation of the firm, or is only a fantasy. In Part III I will argue in favour of the first two possibilities, depending upon actual situations. In this Part, the 'neutral' manager may be thought of as a mere personification of intra-firm equilibrating process like the Walrasian auctioneer.

Impersonal as he may be, the manager in the model is neither passive nor simple. On the contrary, in formulating managerial policy on, for example, pricing, employment, growth target, and financing, he must perform more complicated tasks than his neoclassical counterpart, who is a mere agent of the shareholders, or his 'managerialist' counterpart, who maximizes his own utility function. In anticipation of what is to come, let us tentatively define the organizational equilibrium of the firm as that state in which neither bargaining party can expect to raise its utility any further without risking higher losses caused by a breakdown of co-operation, assuming that the other party exercises the maximum advantageous threat of withdrawing co-operation. The attainment of this organizational equilibrium generally requires that the distribution of organizational rent must be determined in conjunction with the formulation of managerial policy, which, given market conditions and stocks of firm-specific resources, shapes a stream of organizational rents available for internal distribution over periods.

The conventional neoclassical view, as we saw in Chapter 3, is to regard the complex of the firm's decision-making processes as simplifiable by dichotomization: first, settle on the distributional share (i.e., wages) of the employees, either utilizing the external market mechanism or through collective bargaining apparatus, and then let the manager formulate the managerial policy unilaterally so as to maximize the residual. It turns out that this 'residual maximization rule' is efficient from the viewpoint of the participants of the firm only in 'classical' circumstances, and that, under the progressively prevalent employment structure as described in the Introduction (pp. 3-6), it is likely to result in an inefficient outcome which may be thought of as a micro-source of stagflation. This will be shown in the next two chapters.

This chapter takes up two other rules for dichotomizing the dual management–distribution decisions: the 'max-pie rule' and the 'weighting rule'. As we shall see, only the latter serves as a convenient rule for locating the organizational equilibrium in the rent-sharing firm.

At any rate, we wish to characterize not only the settlement of conflicting distributional claims put forth by the participants of the firm, but also the managerial policy of the firm towards markets, as outcomes of the organizational equilibrium. Thus, the manager in the model performs the combined roles of policy-maker and distributional mediator. In this sense, he is very much akin to the 'Arrovian firm' referred to in Chapter 2 (pp. 12-13), in which he plays the dual roles of Walrasian entrepreneur and Walrasian auctioneer. But the Arrovian firm executes those dual roles in a purely market milieu, whereas the manager of our model does the same within an organizational context, although his policy options and distribution possibilities are conditioned in important ways by the external markets.

The bargain possibility frontier

As noted already, the main purpose of this chapter is to conceptualize a notion of the bargaining power of participants of the firm (shareholders and employees) and its organizational equilibrium. For this purpose, let us begin with a description of the opportunities open to the participants under the assumption of no environmental uncertainty. We will formalize this description by drawing up the set of efficient combinations of the firm's share value and total earnings for the existing employees. I shall call this the bargain possibility frontier. Its shape is determined by the endowments of firm-specific resources as well as by market conditions facing the firm.

It is assumed that time extends indefinitely, through periods of equal duration. At the beginning of the current period, the firm is equipped with a certain stock of productive assets whose output capacity is at most x_{max} units of its product. At the beginning of the current period, the firm's sales price is assumed to be fixed in conjunction with the planned sales growth from the current period to the next. To realize the target growth, 'growth expenditure' for research and development, sales promotion, new equipment, personnel training, and the like must be made over the current period. The effects of these expenditures will not be realizable until the next period, when the market demand for the firm's product will expand in response to the firm's sales efforts and when its investment in human and physical capital will become productive. The manager is guided in his price-setting and growth expenditure decisions by his expectations as to market conditions. His expectation for the current period is called short-term and that which covers future periods is called long-term.

The manager's short-term expectation is summarized in the subjective demand function for the firm's product in the current period:

$$x = \alpha p^{-(1/\eta)} \qquad (0 < \eta < 1) \tag{5.1}$$

where x is the amount of sales expected in the current period under the sales price p; α is a parameter that represents the level of demand (business cycle), with the convention that an increase in α increases the demand for the product; and η is the inverse of price elasticity, which is conventionally regarded as representing the 'degree of monopoly' (Lerner, 1933-4) of the firm. To put it a slightly different way, η signifies the 'degree of specificity' of firms' output to customers.

In the organizational paradigm as conceptualized by Herbert Simon (1952-3), the customers are explicitly recognized as coalitional members of the firm, whereas in the traditional approach to the firm the customers appear only implicitly in the form of a demand function to which producer-members of the firm must adapt in finding a solution suitable to them. In this respect I shall follow, albeit reluctantly, the traditional approach to avoid premature complication.[1]

The manager's long-term expectation is summarized by what I will call the *growth cost function*, defined, *à la* Hirofumi Uzawa (1969) and Robert Solow (1971), as follows.[2] Let us assume a simplified situation in which physical equipment is subject to complete depreciation within a period. In this situation, a decision about investment in new equipment can be made only with regard to a planned growth rate, independently of the amount of existing stocks. Then we may assume that there is a simple correspondence between a planned growth rate g of sales from the current period to the next period (with price being fixed at the current level) and the average growth expenditure, T per unit of current sales, being that supposedly necessary to realize the growth rate. Thus we have

$$T = \phi(g) \tag{5.2}$$

where $\phi(\cdot)$ is a monotone-increasing, convex function. That is, the faster the firm wants to grow, the more increasingly it must expend. The elasticity of the growth cost function $g\phi'(g)/\phi(g)$ measures the degree of relative difficulty the firm faces in its attempt to grow and may be considered as inversely related to the amount of firm-specific resources that can be devoted to growth.

It is assumed that there is no new equity issue to finance growth and that actual growth expenditure is completely written off from current sales revenue.[3] Complications that may arise from the existence of fixed durable equipment are treated in the appendix on pp. 82–4 below.

In this chapter, I assume that the employees are all homogeneous and are remunerated equally. Payment w to the employees is composed of two parts:

$$w = \bar{w} + \Delta w. \tag{5.3}$$

One part, $\bar{w}$, is equal to the wage that any worker can earn for the same period of time in the competitive external labour market (in alternative employment) and is treated as given in the model. The residual Δw, which I will call the *premium earnings* of the hired employees, represents participation in the organizational rent, as conceptualized on pp. 30–2, and is an endogenous variable in the model.

Let us denote the average constant prime cost of output, which includes the (competitive) labour cost net of the payment of premium earnings, by c. The organizational rent in the current period may be defined as the total revenue net of the prime cost, $px - cx$. This rent is divided between growth expenditure, dividends to the shareholders, and employees' premium earnings. Let us denote the organizational rent after the payment of growth expenditure by

$$\pi = (p - c - T)x \tag{5.4}$$

and refer to that cash flow as the 'organizational rent a.g.e.'.

Let θ be the shareholders' share of the organizational rent a.g.e. and l the number of employees necessary for a unit of product. Then average premium earnings Δw of the employees is given by

$$\Delta w = \frac{(1 - \theta)\pi}{lx} \qquad (0 \leqq \theta \leqq 1). \tag{5.5}$$

Here it is assumed that the amount of employment can be adjusted exactly to the requirement of expected short-term demand at the beginning of the current period. For the sake of simplicity, it is also supposed that the employees exert an effective constraint on the management for the continued employment of the N employees already in the firm. (The possibility of lay-offs will be considered in the next chapter.) Then, together with capacity of physical equipment, the manager is constrained in his choice of sales price by the condition:

$$(x_{\max} \, \alpha)^{-\eta} \leqq p \leqq (N/\alpha l)^{-\eta} \tag{5.6}$$

or, equivalently,

$$(N/l) \leqq x \leqq x_{\max}.$$

It is assumed that the hired employees are interested in the amount of their lifetime earnings at the employing firm. (If an outside opportunity looks better, then the employees can of course switch to it.) For the sake of simplicity, economies of scale in production and technological progress are assumed away throughout this Part. Then, as far as the employees' relative share, $1 - \theta$, is expected to remain unchanged over periods, so is the average premium earnings per employee. Since hired employees are remunerated equally, given a discounted rate ρ of future earnings and an expected length H of remaining working periods of an employee, the discounted sum of his lifetime premium earnings at the firm would be equal to the current premium earnings Δw times

$$\left\{ 1 - \left(\frac{1}{1+\rho} \right)^{H} \right\} / \rho.$$

Therefore, levels of lifetime well-being of employees may be ordered according to the amount of current premium earnings Δw.

Let us now turn to the shareholders' side. Suppose that a fixed number of shares is owned by the *ex ante* shareholders before the beginning of the current period. At the beginning of this period an implicit or explicit agreement concerning employees' earnings is made between the management and the representative employees in a manner described in the next section, and corporate decision-making regarding sales price and growth expenditure is then made. Only after this agreement is reached, but before current production takes place, does the share market open, allowing shareownership to be freely traded. Those who become the shareholders after corporate decision-making are called *ex post* shareholders.

After current production ends, the residue of the organizational rent over the growth expenditures and over the payments to the employees is distributed as dividends to the *ex post* shareholders. In addition to this, returns to the *ex post* shareholders include capital gains realizable before production in the next period. In general, the rate of share appreciation depends upon investors' expectations about those factors that determine the future stream of dividends, such as the state of the internal organization, managerial policies, and market conditions. Therefore there is no simple, satisfactory theory of capital gains. I avoid this difficulty here by assuming that investors replace their uncertain knowledge of future events by a simple convention; that is, they believe that, on average, the existing state and the firm's policies will continue indefinitely.[4] Then the expected rate of share-value appreciation will be equal to the growth rate, g, currently aimed at by the manager of the firm. The dividends at the end of the current period will equal $\theta \pi$. In the absence of market uncertainty, the competitive valuation S of the firm's stock in the current share market must satisfy the following relation through arbitrage:

$$gS + \theta \pi = \rho S$$

where ρ is the one-period interest rate. The left-hand side represents the total returns to the investment in the stock of the firm that accrue to the *ex post* shareholders after the current production, and the right-hand side represents the interest income that investment of the same amount in one-period bonds would yield. After a suitable arrangement, we can derive

$$S = \frac{\theta \pi}{\rho - g}. \tag{5.7}$$

The *ex ante* shareholders, i.e. those who own shares at the time of the firm's policy-making and bargaining with the representative employee, are interested in the larger value of S realizable in the current share market.

Summarizing, decision variables of the firm are the sales price p (implicit in it is the amount of employment $\alpha l p^{-(1/m)}$), the growth rate g, and the shareholders' share θ in the organizational rent a.g.e. With each choice of p and g, there will be associated a given level of the organizational rent a.g.e., and its possible allocations between the shareholders and the employees can be represented by a straight line trade-off relation between the share value and total premium earning for the existing employees,

$$W = \Delta w N. \tag{5.8}$$

By considering all possible choices of g and p subject to the constraint (5.6), there is a frontier curve in the space (W, S) as depicted in Fig. 5.1. Let us call the curve the *bargain possibility frontier* and denote it by

$$S = \psi(W). \tag{5.9}$$

The point Σ, with null employees' premium earnings ($\theta = 1$), represents the maximum share value subject to the market constraints (5.1) and (5.2) that is potentially realizable for the firm that is under the full control of its shareholders; it thus corresponds to the neoclassical equilibrium. The point Ω, maximizing the employees' average earnings ($\theta = 0$), represents the outcome for the worker-controlled firm, subject to the same constraint. In between on the frontier, we observe employees' participation in the organizational rent, which is efficient from the standpoint of the participants of the firm.

The next problem is: which point on the bargain possibility frontier has the most stabilizing effect on the organizational state of the firm? Before entering upon the direct examination of this issue, it is worth noting a trivial matter: any particular point on the bargain possibility frontier entails a particular choice of price and growth expenditure which yields the straight line tangent to the frontier at that point. This line never touches the frontier at any other point except in the case of a linear frontier. In other words, the managerial policy that supports one efficient distribution generally does not remain efficient for other distributions. Therefore, the distributional decision and the managerial decision cannot be dichotomized without spoiling internal efficiency in such a way that the managerial policy is formulated so as to maximize the present-value sum of the series of cash flow (organizational rent a.g.e.) first, and the settlement of distribution afterwards. This rule, to maximize the size of the pie prior to division, may be referred to as the 'max-pie rule'.

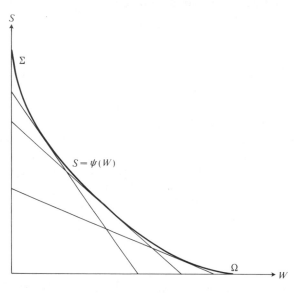

Fig. 5.1

George deMenil, who studied a model of bilateral monopoly between the employer and the union, points out, however, that 'movement to the contract curve (our bargaining frontier) can be viewed as a maximization of the joint surplus of employer and union', and that 'the interests of the employer and the union are not in conflict in all of the areas of activity of the firm. In this model, their common interests encompass capital plans, the determination of employment, and pricing policy' (deMenil, 1971, pp. 26, 28).

Why is the max-pie rule valid for deMenil's model and not for ours? The inefficiency of the max-pie rule in our model arises from an important asymmetry in participants' preferences for the growth of the firm. Although the internal bargaining will be modelled as a two-person game between the body of shareholders and the representative employees, each party actually contains or represents many members, and the future number of its membership will be affected by managerial policy in different ways. The body of shareholders has options as to the membership size; that is, shareholders are free to choose whether new shares should be issued or not in order to finance investment of the firm. Actually, the shareholders' body is indifferent, under an idealized condition such as we are presently dealing with, between those options, as the Modigliani and Miller (1958) theorem indicates.[5] On the other hand, the efficient number of employees is determined uniquely by the technological requirement, yet the existing employees are not indifferent to the future size of their body. Specifically, if sales are planned to grow at a certain positive rate, the number of employees must grow at the same rate in our model. Meanwhile, the existing employees must bear the cost of growth in the form of reduced current organizational rent after growth expenditure available for internal distribution. Thus, existing employees must sacrifice some share of pie today in order to make a bigger pie tomorrow — but then there will be a proportionally larger number of colleagues wanting to share it. In contrast, the shareholders are willing to trade off the size of pie today for that tomorrow up to a certain point in the expectation of capital gains (see pp. 38–9).

This asymmetry in participants' preferences for growth of the firm is the fundamental source in making the max-pie rule inefficient within the framework of our model, except for the case in which the bargain possibility frontier becomes a straight line. But this exceptional case arises only in a stationary state in which no growth possibility exists for the firm and the number of employees remains constant over periods. In deMenil's model, capital plans are admitted as an element of the model, but investment is essentially a one-shot action for adjusting the stocks of capital to the current market condition, and decisions that have implications extending over more than one period are not explicitly incorporated into the model. This implicit stationarity assumption is responsible for the applicability of the max-pie rule.

The bargaining process and its equilibrium

Although employees' and shareholders' opinions differ about the desirable time pattern of the organizational rent stream, as well as about its distribution, they cannot injure each other unless they cease to co-operate and incur the cost of open conflict. They have, therefore, a mutual interest in reaching an explicit or implicit agreement on the policy of the firm, and on the internal distribution of organizational rent, before actual production starts. This is considered to be a typical co-operative game situation.

In order to find a reasonable concept of a solution of the co-operative game, which will be called the 'organizational equilibrium' in this book, let us construct a model of the bargaining process as an heuristic device. The following formulation of a bargaining process owes a great deal to Frederick Zeuthen (1930) and John Harsanyi (1956, 1977), although a movement on the bargaining possibility frontier in our model, i.e. any change in internal distribution, must involve a simultaneous adjustment of the managerial policy on sales price and growth expenditure. Accordingly, the implications of the model are rather rich.

Imagine that, before an actual production period starts, bargaining on employees' premium earnings takes place between the representative employees and the manager, who also formulates the managerial policy in order to equilibrate the balance of interests between the employees' body and the shareholders' body; and that the agreement reached between the representative employee and the manager is turned into a binding contract after having been ratified by its constituents, the body of employees and the body of shareholders. This may sound a little fancy, but the parable that is to evolve will hopefully reflect an essential aspect of efficient *collective bargaining*. Alternatively, the following model may be interpreted as describing a process of managerial calculation to stabilize the organizational state of the (non-unionized) firm. I will refer to such process as the *implicit bargaining*.

The representative employee is supposed to be risk-averse, and his risk attitude is represented by a concave von Neumann–Morgenstern (N–M) utility indicator $U(\cdot)$, defined on the domain of possible total premium earnings for the existing employees, W. Note that premium earnings are uncertain until an agreement is reached even if there is no market uncertainty. The N–M utility indicator represents the employees' *collective* risk attitude towards the uncertainty of their premium earnings arising from a possible failure of the co-operative agreement with the body of shareholders. (I will comment on the nature of the collectiveness later.) In the case of implicit bargaining, the utility indicator is interpreted as representing the manager's subjective assessment of the employees' risk attitude.

The other game-player is essentially the body of shareholders who participate in sharing the organizational rent. However, the shareholders themselves neither negotiate with the representative employees directly nor formulate managerial policy on sales price and growth expenditure. Such duties are relegated to the manager. The manager is assumed to be guided in the bargaining process by a single concave utility function $V(\cdot)$, defined on the domain of share value, S. The utility indicator is supposed to represent the manager's view as to the collective risk attitude of the body of shareholders towards the uncertainty of share value arising from the possible failure of a co-operative agreement with the employees.

Imagine that bargaining takes place preceding a production period, but that wage negotiations, as well as associated managerial policy adjustments, can be repeated as many times as desired, and that no production takes place until an equilibrium of the process, as defined below, obtains.

Suppose that at bargaining time τ, the total of premium earnings for the existing employees, W^τ, is an agreed base for wage negotiation. If the manager is an efficient policy-maker, the corresponding share value then is $S = \psi(W^\tau)$. If the employees decide to withhold their co-operation in production, however, the share value will decline from that value. The representative employee can use this possibility as a threat in making demands for higher premium earnings. But the situation is symmetrical with respect to the body of shareholders: they too can withhold their co-operation if an agreement satisfactory to them is not reached. In general, the bargaining parties will have a choice between several possible threats, each involving a different degree of non-cooperativeness.[6] However, let us assume for simplicity that each party's threat is uniquely given and that. in a situation of conflict, the total of employees' premium earnings for the existing employees is $\hat{W}$. The value of $\hat{W}$ could be zero at the worst, which is the case when the employees are guaranteed earnings only at the rate available on the external labour market. However, we do not restrict possibilities to this extreme case and allow for cases in which $\hat{W} > 0$. Denote $U(\hat{W})$ by $\hat{U}$.

Imagine that, at bargaining time τ, the representative employee contemplates whether or not to make a demand for premium earnings h/N per employee in addition to the W^τ that is an agreed base for negotiation at that time. In order for the demand to be worth making, the expected collective utility gain

$$(1-q)\{U(W^\tau + h) - U(W^\tau)\}$$

must exceed the expected collective utility cost $q\{U(W^\tau) - \hat{U}\}$ of open conflict, where q is the employee's subjective estimate of the probability that the shareholders will withhold their co-operation when the representative employee insists upon the additional premium of h/N per employee. In other words, the maximum probability per h of open conflict that the representative employee can tolerate at W^τ is given by equating the two and solving for q/h:

$$\frac{q}{h} = \frac{U(W^\tau + h) - U(W^\tau)}{h\{U(W^\tau + h) - \hat{U}\}}$$

and as $h \to 0$, $q/h \to U'(W^\tau)/\{U(W^\tau) - \hat{U}\}$. This ratio is interpreted as representing the employees' 'firmness' in making a demand for infinitesimally small increases in their earnings from W^τ (see Harsanyi, 1956).

The above ratio often comes up also in the theory of employment contracts, and its meaning can be clarified in that context as well (see, e.g., Azariadis, 1975). Consider the risk premium k that is required by the body of existing employees when their total earnings are W and the possibility of internal conflict is q. By the definition of a risk premium,

$$(1-q)U(W+k) + q\hat{U} = U(W).$$

Expanding $U(W+k)$ about W and neglecting terms of orders higher than the first, we obtain

$$\frac{k}{q} = \frac{U(W) - \hat{U}}{(1-q)U'(W)}.$$

Letting $q \to 0$, the ratio tends to the inverse of

$$\frac{U'(W)}{U(W) - \hat{U}} \equiv B_u(W). \qquad (5.10)$$

In words, $B_u(W)$ is the reciprocal of the marginal risk premium needed to compensate the employees for risking an infinitesimally small probability of internal conflict when their attained total earnings are W. It is implied that the larger the value of $B_u(W^\tau)$, the bolder will be the employees in demanding higher earnings than W^τ. Call $B_u(W)$ the employees' *boldness* at W (Aumann and Kurz, 1977, p. 1147).[7]

Turning to the shareholders' side, let the share value when employees withdraw co-operation be $\hat{S}$, which is exogenous to the model. If the manager rejects the employees' demand for additional earnings h/N per employee at time τ without causing their withdrawal of co-operation, the shareholders' net gain would be $V\{\psi(W^\tau)\} - V\{\psi(W^\tau + h)\}$; whereas if he fails to reach an agreement, and if the employees withdraw their co-operation, the shareholders' loss would be $V\{\psi(W^\tau + h)\} - V(\hat{S})$. By reasoning symmetrical to that for the employees' case, the maximum risk per h of open conflict that the shareholders can tolerate is

$$\frac{V\{\psi(W^\tau)\} - V\{\psi(W^\tau + h)\}}{h[V\{\psi(W^\tau + h)\} - \hat{V}]}$$

where $\hat{V} = V(\hat{S})$. As $h \to 0$, this ratio tends to

$$- V'\{\psi(W^\tau)\}\psi'(W^\tau) / [V\{\psi(W^\tau)\} - \hat{V}].$$

This expression represents the degree of shareholders' firmness (as assessed by the manager) to withstand the employees' demand for infinitesimally small increase in their earnings from W^τ. Alternatively, by applying exactly the same reasoning as in the case of the employee, we understand the expression

$$\frac{V'(S)}{V(S) - \hat{V}} \equiv B_v(S) \tag{5.11}$$

as representing the reciprocal of the marginal risk premium needed to compensate the body of shareholders for risking an infinitesimally small probability of internal conflict when their attained share value is S. Call $B_v(S)$ the shareholders' *boldness* at S.

The essence of Zeuthen's (1930) construction is to suppose that each party will make a concession to its opponent when it finds that the latter's readiness to bear the risk of open conflict is firmer. In mathematical notation,

$$h \gtreqless 0 \quad \text{according as} \quad B_u(W^\tau) \gtreqless - B_v{}^\tau\{\psi(W^\tau)\} \cdot \psi'(W^\tau).$$

Harsanyi (1977, p. 12) refers to the relation as the 'Zeuthen principle'. Another way of writing it is

$$\frac{dW^\tau}{d\tau} = B_u(W^\tau) + B_v\{\psi(W^\tau)\}\psi'(W^\tau). \tag{5.12}$$

This may be read as follows. *The manager of the firm mediates internal distributional claims and formulates managerial policies in the direction of increasing* $B_u(W)W + B_v(S)S$; *i.e. of increasing the weighted sum of total earnings of the* *existing employees and the share value of the firm, with the respective measures of parties' boldness B_u and B_v as parametric weights.*

The process (5.12) reaches an equilibrium when the right-hand side becomes zero. I will call this the *organizational equilibrium*. This is the state in which neither of the game-players (the participants of the firm) can raise its utility without risking a higher expected loss of utility owing to the possible withdrawal of co-operation by the other player. Therefore 'rational' players will not dare to disturb such a state by making a demand for a larger share in the organizational rent. From the viewpoint of the manager as mediator, it is also characterized as the state in which the weighted sum of employees' earnings and the shareholders' wealth, with the parties' boldness at that state as parametric weights, is perceived to be unraisable by any *marginal* change in either the managerial policy or the internal distribution.[8,9]

Since we have assumed that the shareholders are homogeneous in every respect, the body of shareholders will ratify the equilibrium distributional agreement made by the manager, and the managerial policy implicit in it, if they are rational. However, in a more general situation, the investors who became shareholders of the firm through portfolio selection in the financial market possibly differ in their preferences. Then an interesting question arises of whether the manager's actions can ever be approved unanimously by the shareholders, if the manager is guided by his own assessment of the collective utility function of the share-holders' body. To put it differently, if the collective utility indicator $V(\cdot)$ is replaced by a private utility function $v(\cdot)$ of any shareholder, will the same bargaining outcome emerge? In the process of bargaining, the shareholders' marginal gains from rejecting the employees' demand for higher earnings must be evaluated relative to the total losses they may incur in the event of a failure to reach an agreement with the employees. The manager's evaluation is represented by the measure

$$- B_v(S) \cdot S = \frac{- V'(S) \cdot S}{V(S) - \hat{V}}$$

where $S = \psi(W)$. Measurement would be different if the utility indicator $v(\cdot)$ of an arbitrary shareholder were substituted, unless all the shareholders had the same utility indicator (i.e., unless they had the same risk attitude towards internal conflict) and the manager correctly perceived it.

Thus, in effect, we are assuming situations in which either the manager be-haves paternalistically (the manager's preference is imposed) or the preferences of the shareholders are aggregated through majority voting at a shareholders' meeting. Specifically, suppose that the manager is to be guided by the collective boldness function defined by

$$B_u(\cdot) = \Sigma_i \theta_i b_i(\cdot)$$

where $b_i(\cdot) = v_i'(\cdot) / v_i(\cdot)$ is the boldness function, defined on the domain of S, of the ith individual whose share in the firm is θ_i. Individual boldness functions are all monotone-decreasing; for

$$\frac{db_i}{dS} = \frac{-(v_i')^2 + v_i v_i''}{(v_i)^2} < 0 \qquad (5.13)$$

provided that $v_i'' < 0$, i.e. that every shareholder is a risk-averter. Since the number of *ex ante* shareholders is fixed, the collective boldness function is also monotone decreasing, and thus managerial behaviour in collective bargaining guided by the majority voting principle will not exhibit any inconsistency.[10] When an agreement is reached with the representative employee, the desires of the voter in the median of the distribution of shareholders by their boldness represents the desires of the shareholder body.

The same kind of aggregation problem will arise on the employees' side. The situation is even a little more complicated, since the number of employees is variable depending on the managerial policy adopted. For instance, suppose that the wage demand is raised. As will be seen in the next section, the amount of employment must be reduced accordingly in order for the outcome to remain on the bargain possibility frontier. How is the trade-off between the amount of employment and the wage to be evaluated by the 'body' of employees? In this chapter, by assuming away the possibility of lay-offs and regarding the body of N employees existing prior to collective bargaining as the constituency of the representative employee, we shall evade this issue. We are assuming that the preferences of the existing employees are aggregated through majority voting at a union meeting in the case of collective bargaining, or that the manager behaves paternalistically in the case of implicit bargaining. I shall take up the more complicated problem of aggregating the preferences of employees in the possibility of lay-offs in the next chapter.

The weighting rule

Any change in market and technological conditions (and/or managerial expectations regarding them), as summarized in the product demand function (5.1) and the growth cost function (5.2), modifies the shape of the bargaining possibility frontier, and the location of the corresponding organizational equilibrium must involve simultaneous adjustments of managerial policy and internal distribution. In general, these two adjustments need to be correlated. The task seems rather complicated. Is there any method of simplifying the solution of the organizational equilibrium by dichotomizing the managerial decision and the distributional decision? We have seen that the 'max-pie' rule, or the 'joint surplus' maximizing rule, almost always leads to an inefficient outcome: the rule in which the managerial decision precedes the distributional decision. Will the reversal of the order of decisions be helpful? One simple dichotomization rule along this line is the neoclassical residual maximization rule; I will discuss this in the next chapter. Another conceivable method along the same line is what I will call the 'weighting rule', the rule for deciding on the relative shares of participants in the organizational rent independent of (product) market conditions, and for adapting managerial policy to changing environments by averaging the currently most desirable policies for both the participants using the respective shares as weights. In this section I will show that, under certain conditions, this method is indeed workable for locating the organizational equilibrium sequentially, thus confirming the conjecture stated in Chapter 4 (pp. 53-4).

First, let us recall that the organizational equilibrium is characterized as the stationary point of the weighted sum $B_u W + B_v S$, with B_u and B_v taken parametrically. Now, substituting (5.5) and (5.8) into W and (5.7) into S in the expression, differentiating the result with respect to θ, and noting the possibility of a corner solution, we have the following necessary condition for the organizational equilibrium:

$$\frac{B_u(W^*)W^*}{1-\theta^*} - \frac{B_v(S^*)S^*}{\theta^*} \left.\begin{matrix} \geq \\ = \\ \leq \end{matrix}\right\} 0 \quad \text{for} \quad \left\{\begin{matrix} (\theta^* = 0) \\ (0 < \theta^* < 1) \\ (\theta^* = 1) \end{matrix}\right. \tag{5.14}$$

where the asterisks indicate the equilibrium values. (We have an analogous condition with respect to the variables p and g, which is discussed later.) The search for a workable 'weighting rule' shall be started from the following question: In what case can this relation alone determine the equilibrium value of θ prior to the determination of equilibrium values of other variables p and g? In order to find a solution to this question, we must proceed somewhat in a roundabout way.

To begin with, note that the levels of B_u and B_v represent the relevant parties' boldness in the small. Conceptually, the measure of boldness of the representative employee (the body of shareholders) comprises two components: his attitude towards risking open conflict in the organization (the denominator of the boldness function), and his attitude towards small gains (the numerator of the boldness function). The measure declines as his premium earnings (the share value) increase (see expression (5.13)). This is because his inducement towards small gains declines rapidly as his income (his wealth) increases if he is risk-averse. To cancel out the component that measures his attitude towards small gains and to obtain a meaningful measure of global boldness, let us divide the measure of his boldness by the Arrow-Pratt measure of absolute risk aversion in the small, $U''/U'(-V''/V')$ at the corresponding income (wealth). The resulting ratio (or zero, if the ratio is negative),

$$\xi_u = \max\left\{\frac{-(U')^2}{U''(U-\hat{U})}, 0\right\} \qquad \xi_v = \max\left\{\frac{-(V')^2}{V''(V-\hat{V})}, 0\right\}$$

may be interpreted as measuring the *pure boldness* of the representative employee (of the body of shareholders), as Aumann and Kurz (1977) called it. The concept may appear rather arbitrary, but it turns out to be very meaningful, as will be seen below.

If the measure of pure boldness of the representative employee is a strictly positive constant ξ_u over a relevant range of premium earnings, then $U'/U = -\xi_u U''/U'$. (The utility indicator is normalized in such a way that $U(\hat{W}) = 0$.) Exponentially integrating, we have $U = cU'^{-\xi_u}$. Integrating again,

$$\log U(W) = \frac{\xi_u}{1 + \xi_u} \log (W - \hat{W}) + C_u$$

is obtained where C_u is a constant. If the measure of pure boldness of the shareholders perceived by the manager is a strictly positive constant ξ_v, then

$$\log V(S) = \frac{\xi_v}{1 + \xi_v} \log (S - \hat{S}) + C_v$$

where C_v is a constant. Let us call utility functions of this type constant-pure-boldness (CPB) utility functions.

If the utility functions of the representative employees and the body of shareholders are of the CPB type, equation (5.14) can be rewritten as

$$\frac{(1 - \theta^*) \pi^* - (1 - \hat{\theta}) \hat{\pi}}{\theta^* \pi^* - \hat{\theta} \hat{\pi}} = \frac{1 + \xi_v^{-1}}{1 + \xi_u^{-1}} \equiv \xi \tag{5.15}$$

where $(1 - \hat{\theta})\hat{\pi} = (lx^*/N)\hat{W}$ = employees' share in the organizational rent in the absence of an agreement, and $\hat{\theta} \hat{\pi} = (\rho - g^*)\hat{S}$ = shareholders' share in the organizational rent in the absence of an agreement. It is implied by (5.15) that the share of the employees in the net gains in the organizational rent from co-operation (inclusive of the newly employed), relative to those of the body of shareholders, is proportional to their relative bargaining power *vis-à-vis* the shareholders measured by ξ.

Solving (5.15) explicitly for Δw, we have

$$\Delta w = (\hat{W}/N) + \frac{\xi}{1 + \xi} \left(\frac{\pi^*}{lx^*} - \frac{\hat{\pi}}{lx^*} \right).$$

That is, the employees' premium earnings are equal to the earnings available in the absence of a co-operative agreement plus $\xi/(1 + \xi)$ times gains in the average labour productivity from the co-operation.

Finally, let us consider the case in which given threats by both players represent such a serious degree of non-cooperation that, if they were actually put into action, the organizational rent would disappear completely so that $\hat{W} = \hat{S} = 0$. This is the case in which, without an agreement to be reached, the employees can earn only at the rate available on the external competitive market and no surplus is produced for the shareholders. This appears as an extreme bargaining situation, but the supposition hopefully provides us with an appropriate vantage-point for identifying the most fundamental factors determining the equilibrium distribution.

If $\hat{W} = \hat{S} = 0$, and if both the utility functions are of the CPB type, then equation (5.15) can be reduced to the following simple sharing rule:

$$\frac{1 - \theta^*}{\theta^*} = \frac{1 + \xi_v^{-1}}{1 + \xi_u^{-1}} \equiv \xi. \qquad (\Theta)$$

That is, the relative shares of the employees and the shareholders in the organizational rent a.g.e. remain invariant regardless of the product market condition and growth potential of the firm. We will refer to this rule as the 'constant sharing rule'.

The class of CPB function has been constructed heuristically in the search of an appropriate concept for the 'global' power of bargaining partners who make an all-or-nothing choice of participation or non-participation in a co-operative agreement. It is interesting to note, however, that the class of CPB functions is a subset of a class of utility functions that can be constructed from a certain postulate regarding agents' attitudes towards risk 'in the small': the class of utility functions that exhibit constant relative risk aversion. A function $f(\cdot)$ is said to belong to this class if $-xf''(x)/f'(x) = $ constant R for all $x \geq 0$, where the left-hand side is proportional to risk premium per the variance of x relative to the expected value of x and is considered to represent the degree of an agent's risk aversion.[11] Those functions in this class for which $0 \leq R < 1$ are the CPB functions, and the pure boldness derived from them is given as $(1 - R)/R$. Specifically, if the body of shareholders is risk-neutral, i.e. if $R = 0$, then ξ_v becomes infinite and, in turn, $(1 + \xi_v^{-1})/(1 + \xi_u^{-1})$ becomes $(1 + \xi_u^{-1})^{-1}$: the employees can still enjoy a surplus over the competitive rate available on the external market, provided the pure boldness of the representative employee is strictly positive. When does this pure boldness become zero? Only if the employees are so risk-averse that $R \geq 1$, in which case they will not dare to face any risk involved in making a demand for earnings higher than the competitive rate. The whole gains from co-operation accrue to the shareholders. One may say that this precisely corresponds to the situation that the neoclassist supposes to be generally true (see, for instance, pp. 15-16, 20, 31-2).

Equilibrium conditions other than (Θ) can be found by seeking the values of p and g for which the expression $B_u W + B_v S$ attains a stationary value, with B_u and B_v taken parametrically. Then we have

$$p^* = \begin{cases} (N/\alpha l)^{-\eta} & (0 \leq \theta^* \leq \eta) \\ \min\left[\dfrac{\theta^* \{c + \phi(g^*)\}}{\theta^* - \eta}, \left(\dfrac{N}{\alpha l}\right)^{-\eta} \right] & (\eta < \theta^* \leq 1) \end{cases} \qquad (P)$$

and

$$\frac{\theta^* \{p^* - c - \phi(g^*)\}}{\rho - g^*} = \phi'(g^*). \qquad (G)$$

If the constant sharing rule applies, conditions (P) and (G) can be solved for p and g in terms of the equilibrium value of θ *predetermined* by (Θ). If not, conditions (P) and (G) still serve as conditions for the organizational equilibrium, but in this case the equilibrium value of θ must be solved simultaneously with those of p and g from a system of equations consisting of (5.14), (P), and (G). Also, it may be added that (P) and (G) together provide the conditions for *efficient* managerial policy, whenever the relative shares of participants in the organizational rent, θ and $1 - \theta$, are predetermined somehow, even if we do not rely upon our concept of organizational equilibrium. Such may be the case when the relative shares are determined by a managerial notion of fairness, historical intertia, etc.

To give an intuitive interpretation of the conditions above, let us imagine the shareholder-controlled firm facing the same technological and market conditions (5.1), (5.2), and (5.7), with $\theta \equiv 1$; and the worker-controlled firm facing the same technological and market conditions (5.1), (5.2), and (5.5), with $\theta \equiv 0$. Refer to them simply as the Σ-firm and the Ω-firm, respectively. Refer to our rent-sharing firm as the *-firm, for which the value of θ^* is predetermined according to (Θ). Consider the average of the marginal benefit (alternatively, cost) from a marginal policy change for the Σ-firm and that for the Ω-firm multiplied by the number of employees, with distributional shares θ^* and $1 - \theta^*$ in the *-firm as respective weights, and call it the 'marginal organizational benefit (alternatively, cost)' for the *-firm from the same marginal policy change. As we will see immediately below, corner solutions aside, conditions (P) and (G) are nothing but the conditions of the equality of the marginal organizational benefits with the marginal organizational costs from an extra current sale (in quantity terms), and from an extra 1 per cent increase in growth rate, respectively. Therefore, policy-making according to (Θ), (P), and (G) may be called the 'weighting rule', for obvious reasons.

As is well known, the marginal net revenue from an extra current sale for the Σ-firm is given by

$$(1 - \eta)p - c - \phi(g). \qquad \text{(P-}\Sigma)$$

The marginal per-employee cost from an extra current sale for the Ω-firm is zero, as the number of employees will increase equiproportionally with current sales by the assumption, and the marginal per-employee revenue is $-\eta p / lx$. Therefore the marginal net earnings times the number of employees is given simply by

$$-\eta p. \qquad \text{(P-}\Omega)$$

Averaging (P-Σ) and (P-Ω) with θ^* and $1 - \theta^*$ as the respective weights, and evaluating the result at $p = p^*$ and $g = g^*$, we arrive at condition (P). In Fig. 5.2, the curve P represents the graph of condition (P).

Next, consider an extra 1 per cent increase in the growth rate of the firm. The marginal increase in the share value for the Σ-firm then is given by

$$\left[\frac{\{p-\phi(g)-c\}x}{(\rho-g)^2}-\frac{\phi'(g)x}{(\rho-g)}\right]\frac{1}{100} \qquad (\text{G-}\Sigma)$$

where the first term represents the marginal increase in the present value of a series of dividends arising from a 1 per cent decrease in the 'effective discount rate', defined as the difference between the rate of interest ρ and the rate of capital gain g. The second term represents the present value of the series of marginal growth cost. Multiplying by the effective discount rate $\rho-g$ transforms the marginal share value increase into the marginal net benefit for the Σ-firm in flow terms.

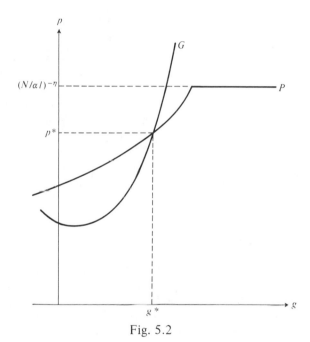

Fig. 5.2

The marginal per-employee benefit for the Ω-firm from an extra 1 per cent growth is zero and its marginal cost is $-\phi'(x)/100l$. Therefore, the marginal net benefit times the number of employees is given by

$$-\phi'(g)\frac{x}{100}. \qquad (\text{G-}\Omega)$$

Averaging (G-Σ) in flow terms and (G-Ω), with θ^* and $1-\theta^*$ as respective weights, and evaluating the result at $p=p^*$ and $g=g^*$, we get condition (G). The curve G in Fig. 5.2 represents the graph of the condition (G).

Condition (G) is reminiscent of the Keynesian 'marginal efficiency of capital'.

Let the discount rate that equates the present value of the additional 1 per cent dividend stream to the marginal cost of an extra 1 per cent growth be called the 'marginal efficiency of growth'. Condition (G) states that growth expenditure should be expanded until the marginal efficiency of growth becomes equal to the effective interest rate, $\rho - g$.

Still another way of reading condition (G) is possible in terms of the Tobin's 'q'. Multiplying both sides of equation (G) by $g^*/\phi(g^*)$ and using (5.7), we have

$$\frac{g^* S^*}{\phi(g^*) x^*} = \frac{g^* \phi'(g^*)}{\phi(g^*)}. \tag{G}$$

The left-hand side is 'the ratio of the increment of market valuation to the cost of the associated investment', i.e. 'the q ratio on the margin' (Tobin and Brainard, 1977, p. 243). The right-hand side tells what extra percentage of growth expenditure is necessary to realize a 1 per cent increase of sales growth, i.e. the elasticity of the growth cost. Condition (G) then reads: Growth should be pursued until the q ratio becomes equal to the elasticity of growth cost. As the elasticity of growth cost is greater than one for a positive growth rate, by our assumption on the growth cost function, so is the equilibrium value of the q ratio. It must be stressed here that condition (G) gives an equilibrium condition only for the case where employees do not benefit from the growth of the firm. We will modify condition (G) later by taking into account the employees' gains from growth made possible through their promotion in the expanding internal organization.

The equilibrating behaviour of the firm

The determination of the equilibrium sales price p^* and the equilibrium planned growth rate g^* is illustrated in Fig. 5.2 and is given by the point where the curve G intersects the curve P from below. Table 5.1 summarizes how the curves shift and how the equilibrium market policies p^* and g^* change in response to an upward shift of various parameters (or functions) of the model indicated in the first column.

For example, from the table we can see that the strengthening of bargaining power of employees *vis-à-vis* shareholders will definitely increase the sales price, thus aggravating the monopolistic exploitation by the firm more than under the pure shareholder-controlled firm. This sales price increase will be accompanied by a very small increase in the growth rate when the employment of existing employees is not a binding constraint. However, if it does become a binding constraint, the strengthening of employees' bargaining power will lead to the slowing down of the growth rate. This is seen as follows. Consider the case in which the intersection of curve P and curve G occurs at $p^* < (N/\alpha l)^{-\eta}$. If the balance of bargaining power is tilted in favour of the employees, the equilibrium markup margin will increase and curve P will shift upward. This will have the indirect effect of improving the marginal efficiency of growth. But the decline in the shareholders' share associated with a strengthening of the employees' relative bargaining power will have the direct effect of worsening the marginal efficiency of growth, shifting curve *G* leftward. Both these shifts have the effect of raising the equilibrium sales price, but they have conflicting effects on the planned growth rate. Between them the former effect is proved to be a little stronger (see the mathematical appendix on pp. 90–1 for the proof). If the sales price reaches the maximum $(N/\alpha l)^{-\eta}$, then a corner solution obtains and a further strengthening of the workers' bargaining power entails the slowing down of the planned growth rate.

Table 5.1 *Behavioural responses of the firm to parametric changes*

d($\cdot$)	Shift of *P*	Shift of *G*	$\dfrac{dp^*}{d(\cdot)}$	$\dfrac{dg^*}{d(\cdot)}$
α (level of product demand)	$\cdot$, ($\uparrow$)	$\cdot$	0, (+)	0, (+0)
η (product demand elasticity)	$\uparrow$	$\cdot$	+	+0
ξ (relative bargaining power of employees)	$\uparrow$	$\leftarrow$	+	+0, ($-$)
c, ϕ (cost level)	$\uparrow$	$\leftarrow$	+	$-$
$g\phi'/\phi$ (growth cost elasticity)	$\cdot$	$\leftarrow$	$-$	$-$
ρ (the interest rate)	$\uparrow$	$\leftarrow$	?	$-$

Notes: Dots $\cdot$ indicate no shift in response to a change in the parameter indicated in the parameter indicated in the corresponding row of the left-hand column.
+0 indicates a small positive change.
Symbols in parentheses indicate changes when the equilibrium price p^* is a corner solution.

A change in the level of product demand will have a positive effect on sales *p* only when the employment of existing employees is a binding condition. In other words, when the demand level is very low, a marginal rise in the demand level will lead to a higher sales price. Otherwise, the firm will respond to a change in the demand condition by the adjustment of output (and that of employment).

In order to assess the effect of the interest rate on market behaviour, we need to consider the possible fixity of durable equipments, which would cause the dead-weight cost in depressed phases. Introduction of this possibility would complicate the model, however, so I treat it in the following appendix, meanwhile recording only the result: an increase in the interest rate will not only shift the *G* curve leftward, but will also shift the *P* curve upward. The combined effect will be a slowing down of investment, but its effect on sales price is unambiguous. The firm may shift the burden of excess capacity to a higher sales price.

In sum, *equilibrating behaviour of the firm is more prone to the phenomenon of stagflation than is that of a pure shareholder-controlled firm. The sales price will be more downwardly rigid.* This tendency will be confirmed further in the analysis of Chapters 6 and 7.

Appendix: Fixity of durable equipment

In this appendix, we shall consider how the equilibrating behaviour of the model of a rent-sharing firm is affected by the introduction of a more realistic assumption: the existence of fixed durable equipment.

Let us start with an imaginary situation in which the amount of equipment inherited from the previous period is somehow exactly equal to the requirement of current production, x. In this situation, if g is the planned rate of sales growth and if one period is necessary to install new equipment, then the amount of new investment needed to meet demand in the next period is $(g + \delta)kx$, where δ is the rate of depreciation and k is the price of the equipment with 1 unit output capacity. However, if the current endowment of fixed equipment K_0 differs from the current requirement kx, the investment needed will differ from this amount, and instead will equal $(1 + g)kx - (1 - \delta)K_0$, where it is assumed that $kx \leq K_0$. The difference,

$$\Gamma_\delta(x) = (g + \delta)kx - \{(1 + g)kx - (1 - \delta)K_0\} = (1 - \delta)(K_0 - kx),$$

may be interpreted as the saving of investment cost owing to the initial endowment of stocks of durable equipment. Consider that the growth cost function $\phi(\cdot)$ relates a planned growth rate to the amount of growth expenditure, such as is needed for sales promotion, per expected sales *net* of the investment cost. The organizational rent at the current period is now defined as

$$\pi^0 = \{p - c - \phi(g) - (\delta + g)k\}x + \Gamma_\delta(x).$$

Let

$$\pi = \{p - c - \phi(g) - (\delta + g)k\}x.$$

If the firm is supposed to be in a steady-state growth path from now on, it expects the organizational rent at period $t (= 2, 3, 4 \ldots)$ to be $\pi(1 + g)^t$.

If this firm is shareholder-controlled, then the share values will equal

$$S_\Sigma = \left\{ \frac{\pi}{\rho - g} + \frac{\Gamma_\delta(x)}{1 + \rho} \right\}$$

and the marginal benefit to the shareholders from an extra sale in flow terms will be the marginal share values times the effective discount rate $\rho - g$:

$$(1 - \eta)p - \{c + \phi(g) + (\delta + g)k\} + \Gamma'_\delta(x)\frac{\rho - g}{1 + \rho}$$

$$= (1 - \eta)p - \left\{c + \phi(g) + \frac{(1 + g)(\rho + \delta)}{1 + \rho}k\right\}. \quad \text{(PF-Σ)}$$

If the planned growth rate is g, then an amount $(1 + g)k$ per unit product must be fixed in durable equipment until the next period, and the opportunity interest cost and depreciation cost incurred will amount to $(1 + g)(\rho + \delta)k$, which will then be discounted to the present period at the rate ρ. However, the term does not include K_0, and the rate of operation of the existing stocks of equipment does not count from the shareholders' point of view.

If this firm is controlled by workers who will be associated with this firm permanently, their utilities will be related to the present value of lifetime premium earnings:

$$\Delta w_\Omega = \frac{1}{lx} \left\{ \frac{\pi}{\rho} + \frac{\Gamma_\delta(x)}{1 + \rho} \right\}$$

where the premium earnings are supposed to be paid at the end of the production period and the discount rate used by them is equal to that used by the shareholders. Then the marginal per-worker benefit from an extra sale times the number of workers is, in flow terms,

$$\left[-\frac{\eta p}{lx} + \frac{\rho}{1 + \rho} \left\{ \frac{\Gamma_\delta(x)}{lx} \right\}' \right] lx = -\eta p - \frac{\rho}{1 + \rho} \cdot \frac{(1 - \delta)K_0}{x} \quad \text{(PF-}\Omega\text{)}$$

and includes K_0. The second term indicates that the endowment of durable equipment is sliced more thinly if there are more workers, so that it is in the interests of the existing workers to restrict the output. It is interesting to note that the shareholders are forward-looking in the sense that they are concerned with the opportunity cost of new investment, whereas the workers are backward-looking in the sense that their interests are tied to the mode of using the endowed stocks of durable equipment.

An equilibrium condition for the rent-sharing firm is given by the weighted sum of the marginal benefits at the shareholder-controlled firm and at the worker-controlled firm, with the shareholders' and the employees' shares in the *-firm as respective weights being set equal to zero. After rearrangement, this can be written as

$$p^* = \frac{1}{\theta^* - \eta} \left[\theta^* \left\{ c + \phi(g^*) + \frac{(1 + g^*)(\rho + \delta)}{1 + \rho} k \right\} \right.$$
$$\left. + (1 - \theta^*) \frac{\rho}{1 + \rho} \cdot \frac{(1 - \delta)K_0}{x^*} \right]. \quad \text{(PF)}$$

The other equilibrium condition is now modified to become

$$\frac{\theta^* \{ p - c - \phi(g^*) - (\delta + g^*)k \}}{\rho - g^*} = \phi'(g^*). \quad \text{(GF)}$$

Assuming that the constant sharing rule applies, (PF) and (GF) jointly determine the equilibrium growth rate g^* and sales price p^* for a given value of θ^* predetermined according to (Θ). The examination of (PF–Ω) indicates that the marginal benefit of sales expansion from the employees' point of view is always negative, so that it is in the interests of existing employees to restrict output. This was so even in the absence of a fixed durable equipment (see (P–Ω) on p. 78), but this tendency is accentuated by the introduction of fixed equipment, for reasons cited above. Therefore we conclude that the sales price of the rent-sharing firm tends to be higher if there is a large endowment of fixed equipment as compared with the shareholder-controlled firm.

Next, let us examine the effect of an upward change in the interest rate on the equilibrium values of the managerial policy. The effect can be decomposed into a long-run effect represented by a shift of curve G and a short-run effect represented by a shift of curve P (see Fig. 5.3). If the interest rate is raised, the marginal efficiency of growth deteriorates relative to the interest rate, and curve G shifts leftward $(G' \rightarrow G'')$. Growth must be restrained, and the sales price can be lowered because of the lessened need for growth financing $(I \rightarrow M)$. This long-run effect, however, may be cancelled, at least to some extent, by the short-run effect if there is fixed durable equipment. As is seen from condition (PF), an increase in the interest rate raises the marginal opportunity cost of new investment, or the dead-weight cost of existing equipment, from the shareholders' point of view as well as the marginal investment cost saving from the employees' point of view: the curve P shifts upward $(P' \rightarrow P'')$.

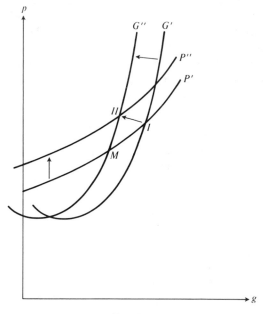

Fig. 5.3

This shift exerts upward pressure specifically on sales price, if the elasticity of the growth function is high so that the curve G is relatively steep. In this case, the increase [decrease] in the interest rate may discourage [encourage] new investment without a noticeable effect on the sales price, or even with a rise in sales price.

Financing of investment

This section, as an application of the weighting rule, discusses how our rent-sharing firm would choose a method of financing its investment. First, we summarize the recent development of the theory of corporate finance under the neoclassical assumption of value maximization. Then we discuss which method of financing is most beneficial to the employees in the framework of the theory of the worker-controlled firm. We predict that a method of investment financing in the rent-sharing firm would have a characteristic of the combination of the optimal financial choices of the two embryonic firms, the shareholder-controlled firm and the worker-controlled firm. Although the weighting rule provides a scientific method simplifying the analysis of behaviour of the hybrid firm, the rent-sharing firm, the discussion to follow may be rather intricate because of the nature of the problem. Therefore, those readers who do not have any specific interest in the financial aspect of the firm may skip this section, and go directly to the next chapter without losing touch with any material necessary for future discussion.

One of the most interesting but not so obvious results drawn from the orthodox postulate that the firm is completely controlled by the shareholders may be found in the Modigliani–Miller theorem (see Modigliani and Miller, 1958). This states that, given the production plans of firms, the individual opportunity sets of returns to financial investments remain invariant regardless of the way production plans are financed, provided there is no tax, transaction cost, or barrier to free competition on the financial market. This is so because the individual opportunity sets of returns are completely determined by the technological possibilities of production plans of firms and investors' initial endowments of assets. There is therefore no compelling reason for a firm to choose any particular method of raising finance from new share issue, external debt, and internal retention of profit: they all serve the shareholders equally well.

The content of the Modigliani–Miller theorem is well known, but for the sake of subsequent comparative discussion of the financial policy of the worker-controlled firm, let us summarize briefly the essence of reasoning leading to the theorem. Suppose that a firm decides to substitute external financing for internal financing and that the proportion of its profit released from the retention is now to be distributed among the shareholders as dividends. The external debt will incur interest payments in future periods and thereby reduce future cash flow to the shareholders. But capital losses arising from the expected reduction of cash flow is exactly matched by the receipt of higher dividends. Thus, current stock-holders are indifferent between debt financing and internal financing. A financial choice of the firm between external debt and internal retention of profits will not have any impact on the value of the firm, defined as the sum of share values and debts.

Compare, next, the floating of new shares and internal financing by retained profit. Share flotation will make it possible for the present shareholders to enjoy higher dividends in the current period, as in the case of external financing. How-ever, they will have to share future profits with the new shareholders. If there is no uncertainty, the present gain and the present value of the future losses of dividends from the new share issues to the existing shareholders will be exactly balanced again. Even if there is uncertainty as to future profits, the present shareholders might as well subscribe to new shares in the expectation that the same income prospect could be reproduced as under internal financing. Thus, the present shareholders cannot gain by choosing one method of financing over another.

The introduction of a tax system would complicate the picture slightly. In the original discussion of the tax effect Modigliani and Miller were concerned only with corporate income tax. Since interest payments are usually tax-deductible at corporate level, the method of external financing appeared advantageous from the capital cost point of view. Modigliani and Miller thought that the obvious risk of insolvency through excessive debt financing would check an indefinite increase in the debt–equity ratio, however. But many financial economists, including Miller (1977) himself, have come to believe that the exclusive concern with corporate tax is not adequate to analyse the effect of taxes to investors' welfare (see Auerback and King, 1982); the combined effect of taxes at a per-sonal level must be taken into account as well. For instance, a heavy reliance on debt commits the corporation to paying out a substantial proportion of its revenue in the form of interest payments, which may be tax-deductible at corporate level but are taxable at investor level under the personal income tax system (unless the investor is a tax-exempt institution such as a pension fund). On the other hand, if the corporation retains that portion of earnings, the in-vestor may be subject only to the low capital gains rate. Therefore the gains to investors from retention may be greater.

To see this analytically, assume no uncertainty and the usual 'perfect' market. Let t_c be the corporate tax rate, t_e the personal tax rate applicable to capital gains, and t_d the personal tax rate applicable to interest incomes. Interest pay-ments by the corporation are deductible for corporate tax purposes. Imagine that the shareholder-controlled firm substitutes internal retention of earnings for debt financing and saves interest payments to the amount of $1 million, which costs the investors $$(1 - t_d)$ million of net interest incomes and the corporation t_c million of corporate tax. But the investor can now receive an amount $\{(1 - t_c)(1 - t_e)\}$ million in the form of after-tax capital gains. Therefore if $(1 - t_c)(1 - t_e) > (1 - t_d)$, the optimal policy from the investors' viewpoint is to let the firm finance investment from retained earnings and to use any excess retentions to redeem debt and vice versa. Only when the equality

$$(1 - t_c)(1 - t_e) = (1 - t_d) \tag{5.16}$$

holds will the investors become indifferent as to a choice of corporate financing between external and internal financing. It is also proved that new equity issue is always an inferior method of financing as compared with debt financing and external financing when interest payments are tax-deductible at corporate level (see King, 1977, pp. 92–102).

Actually, there is a gradation in personal income tax rate. Since the personal income tax is progressive, for those investors in higher tax brackets the gain from internal financing (the left-hand side of (5.16)) may exceed the cost of giving up external financing (the right-hand side), whereas for those investors in lower tax brackets the reverse inequality may hold. But this creates little problem. As Merton Miller observes,

Companies following a no-leverage or low-leverage strategy (like IBM or Kodak) would find a market among investors in the high-tax brackets; those opting for a high-leverage strategy (like the electric utilities) would find the natural clientele for their securities at the other end of the scale. (Miller, 1977, p. 269)

Only an equilibrium *aggregate* debt–equity ratio will exist, and this will equal the relative wealth of those with a tax preference for debt as opposed to equity.

Now let us turn to the worker-controlled firm. Does the same kind of the indifference property as the original Modigliani–Miller theorem hold for this firm? That is, given an investment plan of the firm, are the existing workers indifferent as to whether it raises its finance by external debt or by internal retention of earnings of the firm? (Note that it is not obvious that share issue is compatible with the institutional set-up of the worker-controlled firm — so let us exclude this possibility from the consideration.)

An investment in new equipment is likely to require the employment of new workers to operate the equipment. Suppose that they have equal rights in future earnings along with existing members of the firm. Assume now that the firm decides to finance the new investment internally. This means that the entry of new workers is financed at the sacrifice of existing members in the form of reduced current earnings, whereas future fruits from the investment will be shared equally by new entrants and existing workers. In the case of external debt, on the other hand, future interest payments will be born equally by the new entrants and existing members. Therefore it is to the advantage of existing workers to finance the new investment by external debt, provided that the investment makes it necessary to increase the membership of the firm.

In the case of the shareholder-controlled firm, the existing shareholders can choose at will whether to admit new entrants who will have claims to future dividends, and if they decide to do so they are compensated by requiring the new entrants to pay entry fees, so to speak, in the form of share subscription.

But in the case of the worker-controlled firm, the new entry of workers is determined by the technological nature of the new investement, and it is to the benefit of the existing members to make new entrants share the interest cost of investment. A little reflection will reveal that the introduction of personal income tax would not change the picture in any essential way.

Of course, this argument needs some qualification. If an investment reduces the required future input of labour through the introduction of labour-saving technology, there is less opportunity, at least on the part of existing employees, to mitigate the burdens of cost-bearing by putting off the actual payment of the capital cost. Since there will be a smaller number of new entrants than the number of outgoing employees in the future period, the employees who have prospects of longer tenure with the firm are better off by sharing the capital cost currently with the relatively larger number of existing employees. Therefore, even the worker-controlled firm may rely more on internal financing if an introduction of substantial labour-saving technology is involved.

The weighting rule tells us that the equilibrium financial policy for the rent-sharing firm would be characterized as a weighted sum of the two optimal policies for investors and employees respectively. Therefore we would predict that those firms whose shareholders are in a relatively higher income bracket and whose employees are relatively weak in their bargaining power will finance more of their investments by internal retention of organizational rents. On the other hand, those firms in which shareholding is diverse among many small investors and in which the internal employment structure is well established will rely more upon external debt.

A normative aspect of the organizational equilibrium

The organizational equilibrium was defined as a state of power balance between the body of employees and the body of shareholders in the sense of the equality of the parties' boldness, while meeting the efficiency requirement of being on the bargain possibility frontier. This organizational equilibrium can be characterized in an alternative way as suggested by Harsanyi (1956). By definition of the parties' boldness functions, the equilibrium condition, $B_u(W) + B_v \{\psi(W)\}\psi'(W) = 0$, is equivalent to the condition:

$$\mathrm{d} \log\{U(W) - U\} \{V(\psi(W)) - \hat{V}\}/\mathrm{d}W = 0.$$

This is a necessary condition for the Nash product $\{U(W) - \hat{U}\} \{V(S) - \hat{V}\}$ to be maximized on the bargain possibility frontier. The Nash product is, in fact, locally maximized at the organizational equilibrium, unless the process (5.12) happens to start from an equilibrium that is a non-maximum stationary value of the Nash product, if any. This is so because process (5.12) describes a gradient method that purports to 'climb up' the hill, the height of which in any point in the (W,S) plane is defined by the value of the Nash product at that point. Therefore, the bargaining process always improves the value of the Nash product until the process reaches an equilibrium. The bargaining process always converges to an equilibrium. There may be an equilibrium that is not a Nash product (local) maximum, but such equilibrium can be avoided by employing the perturbation routine around it (see Hori, 1975). In sum, *the organizational equilibrium is almost always a Nash product (local) maximum.*

The original formulation of the bargaining problem by Nash (1950) and the subsequent development of it presupposes the convexity of the bargain possibility set. If the bargain possibility set is of this 'classical' type, then a Nash product maximum is the only bargaining outcome that satisfies 'normative' conditions as specified by Nash, and that may be called the 'co-operative' solution. Although the bargain possibility set in our model (transformed in terms of U and V) is not necessarily convex, it can be proved that a Nash product maximum, if unique, also satisfies the Nash conditions. Paraphrased liberally, the set of Nash conditions are stated as follows:

1 *Efficiency*: the bargaining outcome must be on the bargain possibility frontier.
2 *Information economy*: the outcome of bargaining depends only on the relationship of the outcome to the conflict point, and does not depend on other alternatives in the bargaining possibility set. Put another way, slight modifications in irrelevant alternatives should not alter the bargaining outcome.
3 *Fairness*: the outcome should be independent of the labels of players. If the players were placed in completely symmetrical positions, the outcome should yield them equal utility gains.[12]

The organizational equilibrium, if unique, may be thus thought of as having normative properties as specified above. It may be considered that this alternative characterization of the organizational equilibrium as the co-operative solution provides a logical foundation for using the present model as a basis of normative diagnosis (to be developed in Part III) of various decision-making structures of the firm. From now on, I shall use the expressions 'co-operative solution' and 'organizational equilibrium' interchangeably.

Mathematical Appendix

Derivation of the equilibrium condition

As noted above (p. 88), the organizational equilibrium is alternatively characterized as a stationary point of the Nash product $\{U(W) - U\}\{V(S) - V\}$ subject to $S = \psi(V)$, or equivalently to the conditions defined by (5.1)-(5.6) and $0 \leq \theta \leq 1$.

Taking the logarithm of the Nash product and forming the Lagrangean L, we have

$$L = \log \left[U \left(\frac{(1-\theta)\{p-c-\phi(g)\}N}{l} \right) - \hat{U} \right]$$

$$+ \log \left[V \left(\frac{\alpha\theta\{p-c-\phi(g)\}p^{-(1/\eta)}}{(\rho-g)} \right) - \hat{V} \right] + \mu(p_{\max} - p) + \lambda(1-\theta)$$

where μ and λ are Lagrangean multipliers.

Differentiating the Lagrangean expression with respect to p, g, and θ, and setting each at zero, we have

$$\frac{B_u(1-\theta)p\eta N}{l} - \frac{B_v\theta x\{(1-\eta)p - c - \phi(g)\}}{(\rho-g)} \leq 0 \quad (0 \text{ if } p < p_{\max})$$

$$\frac{B_u(1-\theta)N}{l} + \frac{B_v\theta x\left[(\rho-g)-(1/\phi')\{p-c-\phi(g)\}\right]}{(\rho-g)^2} = 0$$

$$\frac{B_u N}{l} - \frac{B_v x}{(\rho-g)} = 0 \qquad (0 < \theta < 1)$$

where $B_u = \dfrac{U'}{(U-\hat{U})}$ and $B_v = \dfrac{V'}{(V-\hat{V})}$.

Solving the three equations for p, T, and θ, we can get the equilibrium solution of the bargaining game, i.e. (P), (G), and (5.14).

The sign of dg/dθ

Differentiating formulae (P) and (G) with respect to θ, we have

$$\begin{bmatrix} m_{11} & m_{12} \\ m_{21} & m_{22} \end{bmatrix} \begin{bmatrix} dp/d\theta \\ dg/d\theta \end{bmatrix} = \begin{bmatrix} \dfrac{\eta p}{\theta} \\ -r \end{bmatrix}$$

if $p < p_{\max}$, where

$$r = p - c - \phi$$
$$m_{11} = -(\theta - \eta)$$
$$m_{12} = \theta\phi'$$
$$m_{21} = \theta$$
$$m_{22} = (1-\theta)\phi' - (\rho-g)\phi''.$$

Because the matrix $M = (m_{ij})$ is proportional to

$$\begin{bmatrix} L_{pp} & L_{pg} \\ L_{gp} & L_{gg} \end{bmatrix}$$

evaluated at the equilibrium in the direction defined by $L_\theta = 0$, M is negative definite from the local maximization of the Lagrangean. Hence $m_{22} < 0$ and $|M| > 0$. Solving for $dg/d\theta$, we have

$$dg/d\theta = -\{m_{11}r + m_{21}(\eta p/\theta)\}/|M|$$
$$= -\{-(\theta - \eta)r + \eta p\}/|M|$$
$$= -\eta r/|M| \leq 0$$

where $dg/d\theta = 0$ only if $\eta = 0$. If $p = p_{\max}$, then

$$dg/d\theta = -\phi'(\rho - g)/\theta m_{22} > 0.$$

Chapter 6

Equilibrium Bargain and Inefficient Bargain I: The Case of Lay-offs

The model constructed in the last chapter is still not too far removed from its neoclassical counterpart except for the fact that employees' earnings, apart from managerial policy-variables such as sales price and expenditure for sales growth, are treated as endogenous variables. If the bargained wage is viewed hypothetically as being predetermined *outside* the model, conditions (P) and (G) in Chapter 5 appear to be identical with the optimal policy for the neoclassical firm that, facing the same technological and market conditions, maximizes the share values. This can be seen as follows. Substituting (5.5) into (P) and rearranging the equilibrium sales price of our model is seen to satisfy the relation

$$p = \frac{1}{1 - \eta} \{l\Delta w + c + \phi(g)\}.$$

Viewing Δw as predetermined, the relation is identical with the familiar markup pricing formula for the monopolistically competitive firm *à la* Abba Lerner (1933–4); the sales price of the monopolistic firm is set at a level that equals marginal cost marked up by the inverse of one minus the degree of monopoly. We have also seen (p. 80) that condition (G) is equivalent to Tobin's 'marginal q ratio' condition, a well-known neoclassical rule for the investment decision that is optimal from the viewpoint of shareholders. In these circumstances, the market behaviour of the rent-sharing firm towards the external market appears to be indistinguishable from that of the shareholder-controlled firm, and the role of the manager as a referee of the co-operative game within the firm is not transparent.

   This quasi-equivalence between the equilibrium policy for the rent-sharing firm and the optimal policy for the shareholder-controlled firm is a natural consequence of assuming that the employees' welfare depends only on the level of current earnings, as in the neoclassical model, although in our model the current earnings are treated endogenously. However, once we allow employees' welfare to be affected, even indirectly, by other managerial policy variables, such as employment and sales growth, the apparent similarity between the models disappears. Such cases arise when the employment status and the associated earnings of the employees are differentiated and affected by managerial policies. In this and the next chapter we will consider two possible sources for such differentiation – the possibility of lay-offs and the hierarchical nature of the internal organization supported by the seniority principle of promotion – and will examine how the behaviour of the co-operative game model departs in these cases from the neoclassical prediction. In other words, we will see how the neoclassical policy prescription to maximize the share value subject to the predetermined level of wage will lead to internal inefficiency.

The McDonald–Solow model

Since Leontief's classic paper (1946), it has been known that, if a body of workers is interested in the amount of employment as well as the wage rate, then efficient bargaining cannot be supported by agreeing on an average wage first and then letting the employer choose the amount of employment unilaterally so as to maximize profit subject to this wage. Recently, interests in this proposition have been revived, and explorations into possible modes of efficient (or equilibrium) bargains under insufficient demand conditions have been pursued by Hall and Lilien (1979) and McDonald and Solow (1981). Such bargains may entail employment of less than the total number of workers that constitutes a bargaining party. In this section I will expound the latter's contribution, relating it to our own framework.

For the purpose of dealing with the possibility of lay-offs, let us modify our own model in three respects. First, in order to concentrate on the effects of insufficient current demand for the product which will necessitate the lay-offs of existing employees, suppose that there is no possibility of sales growth over periods and that the firm is in a stationary state. Thus we eliminate the growth variable from the model. Second, it is most convenient to deal explicitly with the number of workers employed L and the average earnings w of employed workers as primary variables of the model rather than to treat them as being implicitly determined by the sales price and the employees' share in the organizational rent. Third, we drop the constraint (5.6) and deal only with cases in which

$$L < N$$

at equilibrium, where N is the number of workers, all alike, in the specific labour pool of the firm. We may consider N as the number of workers represented by a union in the collective bargaining situation. A certain exogenous level of income $\bar{w}$ is available to the unemployed as an unemployment compensation benefit inclusive of the possible shadow value of not holding a job or in the form of earnings from other employment in the external market.

If L workers are actually employed at random out of the labour pool N, each member has a probability L/N of having a job and a probability $1 - (L/N)$ of not being employed by the firm. Suppose that each worker has a *private* utility function $u(\cdot)$ of the von Neumann–Morgenstern type which is concave. Then the expected utility of a worker is

$$\frac{L}{N} u(w) + \left(1 - \frac{L}{N}\right) u(\bar{w}) = \frac{L}{N} \{u(w) - u(\bar{w})\} + u(\bar{w}). \qquad (6.1)$$

It is to be noted that the private utility function $u(\cdot)$ represents the individual worker's attitude towards the risk of lay-offs. By the same reasoning as on p. 71, the expression

$$b_u(w) = \frac{u'(w)}{u(w) - u(\bar{w})} \qquad (6.2)$$

can be interpreted as the inverse of the individual 'marginal risk premium of unemployment' when earnings from the employment are w. It is easy to see that the increase in the (shadow) unemployment compensation $\bar{w}$ decreases the marginal risk premium.

The indifference map of individual workers is derived by setting (6.1) equal to constants. It has the usual shape in the (L,w) space which is convex to the origin. In addition, the indifference curves are all asymptotic to the horizontal line at $w = \bar{w}$. The curves u', u'', u'''. . . in the order of higher utilities are shown in Fig. 6.1

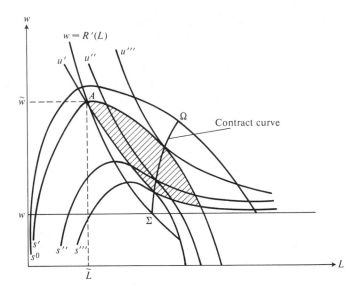

Fig. 6.1

Let the technology of the firm and the demand for its product be jointly summarized by a revenue function $R(L)$ giving dollar revenue net of material costs as a function of total employment L. It is assumed that $R(L)$ exhibits decreasing returns to scale; that is, $R'(L) > 0$ and $R''(L) < 0$. The profit of the firm is given as

$$s = R(L) - wL. \qquad (6.3)$$

The profit-earner (the body of shareholders) is indifferent to any (L, w) combination that leaves $R(L) - wL$ constant. The isoprofit curves have the shape depicted as s°, s', s'', s''', ... in the figure. For any L, isoprofit curves have a positive slope until w reaches $R'(L)$, then become negative. For any L, a smaller w allows a larger profit, so lower isoprofit curves are better for the profit-earner. Let s° represent the zero profit curve.

Suppose that wage bargaining is settled at $w = \bar{w}$. If we let the manager of the firm choose the amount of employment unilaterally so as to maximize profit subject to this wage, he seeks the lowest isoprofit curve that touches the horizontal line at $w = \bar{w}$ where the usual profit-maximizing condition of the equality of marginal revenue with the wage is satisfied. But, clearly, the employment–wage configuration $A(\bar{L}, \bar{w})$ chosen by this two-step decision-making is not efficient. There are employment–wage points at which both parties are better off, as Leontief's classic paper has shown. The lens-shaped area enclosed by the isoprofit curve and the indifference map passing through point A is the set of outcomes Pareto-superior to A. The two-step residual-maximizing leaves the employment 'too low' and the wage 'too high'.

The inefficiency of the two-step decision-making results from the fact that, although the workers' utilities depend upon the amount of employment, there is no means allowed for them to trade wages for higher probabilities of employment, and the manager, as an agent of the profit-earner, chooses the amount of employment unilaterally. In order to achieve efficiency, the union must be able to exert some influence over the employment, and/or the manager must act as an arbiter to induce the profit-earner to agree upon an outcome that does not maximize profit for a given wage.

Obviously, efficient outcomes are points of tangency between an isoprofit curve and an indifference map. We call the locus of such points the 'contract curve'. From the tangency condition, points on the contract curve satisfy the following condition:

$$R'(L) - w = -\frac{1}{b_u(w)}. \tag{6.4}$$

In other words, *the wage must be equal to the marginal revenue product of labour plus the marginal risk premium of unemployment*.[1] By differentiating (6.4) with respect to w,

$$\frac{dL}{dw} = \frac{1}{R''(L)} \cdot \frac{\{u(w) - u(\bar{w})\}u''(w)}{\{u'(w)\}^2} = \frac{-1}{R''(L)\,\xi_u(w)} > 0$$

so that the contract curve is upward-sloping, where $\xi_u(w)$ is the measure of pure boldness as defined on p. 75. Furthermore, the bolder the individual worker is, the higher will the contract curve be located. Ignoring the possibility of negative profit, the end-points of the contract curve, Σ and Ω, represent the familiar equilibrium point for the two embriotic firms, i.e. the shareholder-controlled firm and the worker-controlled firm. At the former point, the employees do not have the internal bargaining power to extract anything above the level available outside. At the latter point, the employees extract all the organizational rent producible.

Which point on the contract curve between the two extremes has the equilibrium property in the sense conceptualized in Chapter 5? In order to investigate this problem, let us first transform individual workers' prospects of uncertain incomes into corresponding certainty equivalents. When the wage is w with a probability of employment of L/N and the unemployment compensation is $\bar{w}$ with a probability of $1 - (L/N)$, the certainty equivalent, $\hat{w}$, of this prospect is

$$\hat{w}(w, L) = u^{-1}\left[\frac{L}{N}\{u(w) - u(\bar{w})\} + u(\bar{w})\right]. \qquad (6.5)$$

This is the sure income that gives the same utility level as given in (6.1). Since there are N workers represented by the union, the total certainty equivalent of members' earnings is simply

$$W = \hat{w}N.$$

In the absence of a collective bargaining agreement, the body of workers is assumed to receive $\bar{W} = \bar{w}N$ in total. Now we can derive the bargain possibility frontier in the (W, s) space, in a similar manner as Fig. 5.1.

Let a function $U(\cdot)$, defined on a feasible region of W, be the *collective* utility function of the union. As in the previous chapter, this function represents the attitude of the union (leadership) towards the risk of a failure to reach an agreement with management, whereas the private utility function $u(\cdot)$ represents the attitude of individual member-workers, all alike, towards the risk of lay-offs. In other words, the private utility function of member-workers, together with the profit function (6.2), defines the contract curve to which the union (leadership) is subject, whereas the collective utility function of the union, jointly with the utility function of profit-earners as defined below, determine a choice (the bargaining equilibrium) from the contract curve.

In distinguishing the two, we depart slightly from the original McDonald–Solow model. Later, we will see why it seems more reasonable to do so theoretically. However, it may be worth remarking here that, by the widely accepted models of trade union behaviour, the union leadership is recognized as a distinct element from the union rank-and-file. By this view, the objectives of the leadership are: (1) the survival and growth of the union as an institution and (2) the personal political survival of the leaders.[2] Given these objectives, the risk of failing to reach an agreement with management must be of central importance to the union leadership.

Let $V(\cdot)$ be the utility function of the profit-earner, whose domain is the set of feasible profits. The function represents the attitude of the profit-earner towards the risk of failure to reach an agreement with the union. In the absence of an agreement, profit is assumed to be $\bar{s}$.

The boldness functions of the union, B_u, and of the profit-earner, B_v, are now defined as

$$B_u(W) = \frac{U'(W)}{U(W) - U(\bar{W})}$$

and

$$B_v(s) = \frac{V'(s)}{V(s) - V(\bar{s})} .$$

To repeat, these represent the risk limits of an internal conflict that the union and the profit-earner can tolerate respectively.

Now we are ready to apply the same logic as developed in the last chapter to obtain the organizational equilibrium, defined as the outcome (W^*, L^*) for which the following condition is satisfied: the weighted average of total certainty equivalent W of the workers' uncertain earnings and profits s, with the boldness of the union and of the profit-earner as respective parametric weights, must be unraisable by any marginal change in either wages or employment. Specifically, the marginal change in the employment must be unable to raise the weighted average so that

$$B_u(W) \, N \frac{\mathrm{d}\hat{w}}{\mathrm{d}L} + B_v(S) \frac{\mathrm{d}}{\mathrm{d}L} \{R(L) - wL\} = 0 \qquad (6.6)$$

which, together with (6.4), constitutes the sufficient condition.[3] Since it follows by the definitions of w and $b_u(w)$ that[4]

$$\frac{\mathrm{d}\hat{w}}{\mathrm{d}L} = \frac{1}{Lb_u(\hat{w})} ,$$

(6.6) can be transformed into

$$w = R'(L) + \frac{B_u(W)}{B_v(s)} \cdot \frac{N}{Lb_u(\hat{w})} . \qquad (6.7)$$

Expressions (6.4) and (6.7) can now determine the organizational equilibrium.

In order to investigate the nature of the organizational equilibrium, let us first assume a very special case in which: (*a*) the profit-earner is risk-neutral (his utility function is linear in profit) towards internal conflict, and profit in the absence of a collective agreement is zero, so that

$$B_v(s) = \frac{1}{R(L) - wL} , \qquad (6.8)$$

and (*b*) the union's boldness is identically equal to the reciprocal of the sum of the members' marginal risk premiums of unemployment, so that

$$B_u(wN) = 1 / \left\{ \frac{N}{b_u(w)} \right\} . \tag{6.9}$$

This second assumption is implicit in the McDonald–Solow model, which does not distinguish between the collective utility function and the private utility function, and leads to the following result. Substituting (6.8) and (6.9) into (6.7),

$$w = \frac{1}{2} \left\{ R'(L) + \frac{R(L)}{L} \right\} . \tag{6.7MS}$$

The marginal productivity of labour, $R'(L)$, defines the profit-maximizing wage for given employment, whereas the average productivity of labour, $R(L)/L$, gives the maximum average income for a given number of workers at the worker-controlled firm. Expression (6.7MS) specifies the equilibrium wage at our rent-sharing firm as the arithmetic mean of the two. Since $R'(L)$ and $R(L)/L$ are both decreasing functions of L, the graph of (6.7MS), which may be referred to as the 'power curve', is downward-sloping as depicted in Fig. 6.2 so that the equilibrium is achieved at $w = w^*$ and $L = L^*$.

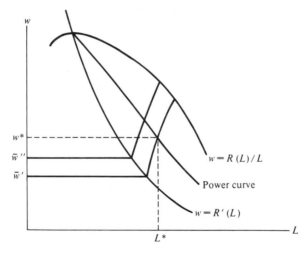

Fig. 6.2

An increase in $\bar{w}$ decreases the individual marginal risk premiums of lay-offs; and this, in turn, increases the collective boldness of the union under the assumed condition and shifts the contract curve upward. Therefore, if the unemployment compensation or forgone alternative earnings increase, *ceteris paribus*, the equilibrium wage rises at the sacrifice of employment. On the other hand, an improvement of the product market shifts both the contract curve and the power curve to the right. It is obvious from crude geometry that these combined shifts make employment strongly cyclical and wages rather sticky. Therefore, simultaneous improvements in the labour market, reflected by an increase in $\bar{w}$, and the product market produce offsetting effects. The net effect of the two opposing forces is uncertain. If the effect of the improvement in the product market dominates that in the labour market, then 'efficient bargain will make employment, more than the wage, bear the brunt of cyclical adjustment' (McDonald and Solow, 1981, p. 904). On the other hand, if current wages in other industries have an important influence on the new wage negotiation while the current state of product demand has little impact, then the wage is more pro-cyclical and employment is rather insensitive to the business cycle.

The effect of relaxing assumption (*a*) of the profit-earner's risk-neutrality, or of zero profit in the event of internal conflict, is easy to visualize. The decrease in the profit-earner's boldness shifts the union power curve upward so that both the equilibrium wage and employment increase, as expected. If both the union and the profit-earners have utility functions of constant-pure-boldness, and if employees' relative bargaining power, as defined in expression (5.15) above, is represented by ξ, then the power curve is expressed as

$$w = \frac{1}{1+\xi}\left\{R'(L) + \xi\frac{R(L)}{L}\right\} . \tag{6.7*}$$

The weight on the average productivity in determining employees' earnings increases as their relative bargaining is enhanced.

The leadership–membership relation in the union

Going back to assumption (*a*), let us enquire into its meaning. Integrating (6.9) with respect to w, assumption (*b*) is seen equivalent to the postulate, in terms of the original utility functions, that

$$U(wN) - U(\bar{W}) = C\{u(w) - u(\bar{w})\} \qquad \text{for any } w, \tag{6.9*}$$

where C is a constant. This equivalence of the collective utility function and the members' utility functions (up to the affine transformation) appears to be innocent from the individualist viewpoint, which regards the union as a magnified mirror-image of rational individuals who constitute it. However, there is a purely theoretical reason to doubt whether the equivalence assumption is a proper one.

Let us first note that condition (6.7MS) can be restated as

$$wL = R'(L)L + \frac{1}{2}\{R(L) - R'(L)L\} .$$

That is, the wage bill is equal to the employees' products (marginal value products) plus half of the net revenue (the organizational rent) over their products. Why is their relative share in the rent equal to exactly 50 per cent regardless of whether the number of employed workers is 1 or 1000 or any other number? This rather odd result is an example of what Harsanyi called the 'joint-bargaining paradox' (Harsanyi, 1977, pp. 203–5). The paradox occurs in our model as a result of the combined effects of two factors implicit in (6.1) and assumption (*a*). First, as is seen from (6.9*), the game under the assumption (*a*) is equivalent to a two-person game between the profit-earner and any *single* union member who represents the body of employees. Second, this union member, given a wage rate, is risk-neutral towards changes in the rate of employment (i.e. the private utility function is linear in *L*). If two players who are both risk-neutral play a co-operative game, the Zeuthen–Nash–Harsanyi solution dictates that net gains from the co-operation must be divided evenly between the two. Therefore, if more workers form a coalition (union) for bargaining purposes, and if the union's collective attitude towards internal conflict is a mere mirror-image of individual members' attitudes towards risk as regards lay-offs in the sense formulated in (6.9), then each worker's share in the rent will become smaller. In order to avoid this peculiar result, it seems appropriate to assume that the collective utility function of the union is *not* a simple mirror-image of members' private utility functions, but is possessed of its own collective characteristics.

An interesting model of collective bargaining is proposed by Ashenfelter and Johnson (1969) in which possible discrepancies between the objectives of union leadership and the desires of individual member-workers are explicitly recognized. For instance, when unemployment compensation or alternative opportunities are good, individual union members may attribute relatively lower risk premiums to the risk of unemployment from the firm. However, failure to reach a contract with the management may be very costly to the union as an institution. In these circumstances, the membership's expected wage increase may be greater than the level that the union leaders consider reasonable to bargain for. How is this gap resolved? Of course, the union leadership can sign an agreement that is less than rank-and-file expects. But this will deplete the political stock of the union leadership. Ashenfelter and Johnson made the interesting point that one aspect of a strike may be its use by union leaders as an instrument to persuade the rank-and-file to accept a lower wage. The outbreak of a strike has the shock effect arising from the management's resistance and the resultant loss of normal income, thus lowering the rank-and-file's 'firmness'. With the passage of time, the leadership may feel that the wage increase expected by the rank-and-file will be lowered sufficiently that it can safely sign a contract with the management for a lower wage. Thus, the leadership's preference prevails in the choice of final bargaining outcome.

One should probably not go so far as to generalize the Ashenfelter–Johnson argument and hold that every occurrence of a strike can be understood as a result of leadership–rank-and-file conflict. There may be cases in which their description reasonably approximates reality, while in other cases rank-and-file members may vote for strikes with warranted expectations of achieving their aspiration. However, the point should be well taken that the union is not a mere agent of employees,[5] and that the preference and the opinion of union leaders are not necessarily identical with those of members. The analysis of dynamic interactions between the union leaders and the rank-and-file is far beyond the scope of this book, but it is important to recognize that it is the collective utility function of the union (employees), however it may be aggregated, that plays a decisive role in the determination of the bargaining equilibrium; while the desires of member-employees remain only to define the bargaining situation (i.e. the contract curve from which a contract is chosen).

Chapter 7

Equilibrium Bargain and Inefficient Bargain II: The Case of Employees' Hierarchy

The model of Chapter 5 is rudimentary as an internal model of the firm, in the sense that the employees are assumed to be homogeneous and are remunerated equally; differences in experience and responsibilities among employees in the internal organization, as well as the associated earnings differential, are not explicitly recognized. But this is not a satisfactory treatment, particularly in our context; for the fundamental premise of the co-operative game approach is that the incumbent employees derive their bargaining power at least partly from their firm-specific skills, particularly the collective efficiency of teamwork fostered over periods of time. There are obviously differences in experience, and hence in the degree of skill aquisition, among the employees.

This chapter constructs a model of the firm internalizing a hierarchical employment structure in which hired employees are differentiated by their tenures and ranks. An important consequence of this assumption is that a positive rate of return from the growth of the firm accrues to the employees owing to their expectations of the promotional gains made possible from such growth. However, the rate of return from a given growth rate to the employees will be shown to be not as large as that accruing to the shareholders. As a result, a strengthening of employees' bargaining power would lead to a slow-down of corporate growth, the phenomenon that I referred to in Part I as the 'dilemma of industrial democracy'. Furthermore, the two-stage decision-making, in which the wage rate is predetermined and a growth rate is chosen afterwards by the manager so as to maximize the share price, will be shown to lead to internal inefficiency characterized by a lower growth rate than that at the organizational equilibrium (the co-operative solution).

The model of employees' hierarchy

The link of employees to the corporate firm is never permanent because of the limits of working years, even if we set aside voluntary quits and discharges. An older generation of employees must be replaced by a new generation. When a new generation of employees arrives at the 'port of entry' to the firm from the 'ocean' of external markets, either to replace an older generation or as an addition to the expanding work-force of the firm, the new workers are equipped only with general skills and are not effectively organized. Only after acquiring firm-specific skills by working as a member of the team can the incumbent employees, as a collectivity, become effective 'players' of the co-operative game.

I wish to enrich the co-operative game model of the firm by treating the inter-generational turnover of employees explicitly.

It is a common fact of observation that employees of large firms are internally organized into promotional hierarchies, and that the principle of seniority is widely used as a basis for promotion. It has recently been argued, and statistically verified by Freeman and Medoff (1979) and Koike (1984), among others, that the principle of seniority is not necessarily counter-productive; for its adoption as a basis of promotion reduces the feeling of rivalry among the employees, and may solve the prisoner's dilemma of the 'rat race' (Akerlof, 1976) among employees to outdo fellow workers. Also, in a less rivalrous atmosphere, the amount of assistance that older workers are willing to provide to younger workers may be greater, thus leading to a greater intergenerational transmission of skills. Furthermore, the system of seniority serves as an incentive device to reduce quits of employees. Since employees' turnover is costly, the reduction of quits is one way in which the seniority rule raises productivity.[1]

As a gradation of pay accompanies the promotional hierarchy, prospects of employees' lifetime earnings depend upon the rate of promotion. Employees will not then be indifferent as to the rate of growth that the corporate firm will pursue: a higher growth rate will entail the expansion of the internal organization, hence a higher rate of promotion. From this possibility Marris (1964) has inferred, as we have seen in Chapter 3, that the employed managers, organized hierarchically, would unanimously support the maximization of the growth rate of the corporate firm. His argument seems to make sense, however, only if a system of internal salary gradation is rigidly maintained regardless of the growth rate of the corporate firm. Actually, growth of the firm is not possible without cost in terms of advertising, investment in new equipment, research and develop-ment, training of personnel, etc. As expenditures to carry on such activities constitute a competitive claim for the current organizational rent, it is unlikely that only benefits from growth will accrue to the employees, and not costs. Also, if the rate of promotion is higher, a new generation of work-force in the external market may accept an employment offer of a lower starting salary/wage in prospect of higher earnings in the future. It seems more reasonable to assume that the determination of an internal gradation of earnings is interrelated to the choice of growth rate of the firm.

Keeping the above considerations in mind, let us construct a model of the corporate firm that is characterized by the intergenerational turnover of the employees, as well as by the hierarchical nature of their internal organization, and examine the equilibrium outcome of the co-operative game between the shareholders and the incumbent employees.

Let us suppose that time extends through periods of equal duration. Imagine a firm existing at the beginning of the current period with a team of employees who have one-period work experiences at the firm. Those employees are called the 'incumbent' employees, and the shareholders of the firm at the beginning of the current period are called the *ex ante* shareholders. All employees reach mandatory retirement ages after two periods of work experience. The firm operates with a two-level internal organization of the employees. Job openings at the upper level, created by the expansion of the internal organization and/or retirement of senior employees, are filled by promotion of the incumbent employees only; no recruitment from outside is made except at the lower level.

Timing of events is modelled as follows. At the beginning of the current period planning on sales growth is made. In conjunction with this planning, decisions about the promotion of incumbent employees and the hiring of new ones, as well as the rates of remuneration to be offered to employees of both levels, are made. In this decision-making process, the management of the firm must weigh the relative bargaining power as between the *ex ante* shareholders and the incumbent employees, in the manner described in the previous chapters. After the decision-making, the share market opens and shareownership may be freely traded. Those who become shareholders after the corporate decision-making are called the *ex post* shareholders. The employees from the previous period then become the senior employees and the newly employed become the junior employees. At the end of the period, the senior employees retire after the receipts of contracted compensation. The junior employees remain in the firm in prospect of possible promotion in the next period. All the operating costs, including expenditure for sales promotion and compensation for the employees, are written off from current sales revenue. The residue of current sales revenue after these disbursements forms dividends, payable at the end of the period to the *ex post* shareholders.

Let us now specify the model technically. Suppose, without loss of generality, that the sales of the firm at the previous period was equal to one, and let

$$y = \text{rate of sales planned for the current period.}$$

In other words, $y - 1$ is the growth rate of the firm's sales revenue. Growth of sales is not realizable without cost, however. The proportion of the sales cost to the total sales revenue realized within a period is represented by a monotone-increasing convex function $\phi(y)$. That is, the faster the firm wants to expand its sales, the larger proportion of current sales revenue must be retained to finance the sales promotion. The marginal effect on sales growth of an additional expenditure is, however, diminishing.

The sales revenue after sales expenditure $y\{1 - \phi(y)\}$ is to be divided between shareholders and employees. The shareholders' side of the model is retained as simple as in the previous chapter. Let

$$\theta = \text{the shareholders' share of sales revenue after sales expenditure.}$$

In addition to dividends amounting to $\theta y\{1 - \phi(y)\}$, returns to the shareholders include capital gains realizable before the next period's production. Suppose that investors on the share market believe that, on average, the current corporate policy will be sustained for ever. The current growth rate $y - 1$ is then also the rate of appreciation of share value. In the absence of market uncertainty, the rate of return to shareholding will be equated to the rate of yield of a one-period bond, denoted by $\rho - 1$, through market arbitrage. Therefore, letting

$$S = \text{total share value of the firm,}$$

we can derive, in the exactly same manner as we derive (5.7), that

$$S = \frac{\theta y \{1 - \phi(y)\}}{\rho - y} \tag{7.1}$$

where it is assumed that $\phi(\hat{y}) = \hat{y}$ for some $\hat{y}$ such that $\hat{y} < \rho$, so that the value of S will not explode.

Let us turn to the more complicated side of the model, the internal organization of employees. Assume that the ratio of members at the higher level to those at the lower level that is necessary for efficient operation of the internal organization, conventionally called the 'span of control', is technologically determined and denoted by n. It is assumed necessary for the firm to employ $1 + n$ employees to realize one unit of sales revenue (net of material cost). Let

w_l = the rate of pay per period for employees of the lower level

and

w_h = the rate of pay per period for employees of the upper level

where it is assumed that

$$w_l \leqq w_h. \tag{7.2}$$

We call 2 tuple (w_h, w_l) satisfying (7.2) the 'pay schedule' of the hierarchical firm. By the definition of θ, feasible pay schedules must satisfy

$$w_l + w_h n = (1 - \theta) \{1 - \phi(y)\} . \tag{7.3}$$

We assume that any opening at the higher level is to be filled through promotion of an occupant at the lower level. Only openings at the lower level are filled through recruitment from the external labour market. Let

N = the number of the incumbent employees at the beginning of the current period.

Every one of these was at a lower rank in the previous period, but either will be promoted to the higher rank or will remain at the lower rank in the current period. Let

q = the proportion of the incumbent employees to be promoted to the higher rank in the current period.

The number of jobs at the higher level to be filled is yn, so that

$$q(y) = \min \left(\frac{yn}{N}, 1 \right). \tag{7.4}$$

The number of incumbent employees in the current period remaining at the lower level is $N - yn$; hence $(n + 1)y - N$ is the number of jobs supplied to the external market at the beginning of the current period. Suppose that the newly employed believe that, on average, the present growth policy of the firm will be maintained in the next period. Then, letting

p = the average probability of the new employees' promotion in the next period,

it follows that

$$p(y) = \min \left\{ \frac{ny^2}{(n + 1)y - N}, 1 \right\} \qquad (7.5)$$

and $p(y)$ is graphed in Fig. 7.1. It should be noted that, in contrast to the incumbent employees' case, an acceleration of the rate of growth will not necessarily assure the new employees greater 'promotability'. Since, at a sufficiently low rate of growth, fewer employees would be newly employed in the current period, they would face less keen competition for promotion among themselves.

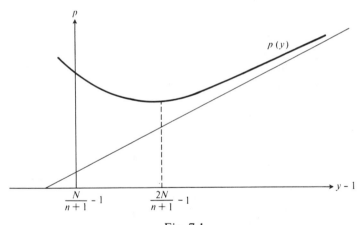

Fig. 7.1

Suppose that a representative new employee has a concave von Neumann-Morgenstern utility function $\sigma(\cdot)$ of per-period earnings and that he discounts his utility in the next period at a rate ρ. Also, being endowed with general skills acquired outside the firm, he is assumed to have a certain level of reservation earnings $\hat{\omega}$ such that, if the expected utility sum implied by an employment offer of the firm falls short of the utility sum derivable from the constant flow of those earnings, he would reject the employment offer. Then it must hold that

$$\frac{p(y)}{1 + \rho} \, \sigma(w_h) + \left\{ 1 + \frac{1 - p(y)}{1 + \rho} \right\} \sigma(w_l) \geq \left(1 + \frac{1}{1 + \rho} \right) \sigma(\hat{w}). \qquad (7.6)$$

Transform the probability p into a normalized pseudo-probability,

$$\hat{p} = \frac{1}{2 + \rho} p. \tag{7.7}$$

Then (7.6) can be simply written as

$$\hat{p}(y)\, \sigma(w_h) + \{1 - \hat{p}(y)\}\, \sigma(w_l) \geq \sigma(\hat{w}). \tag{7.8}$$

Expressions (7.2) and (7.8) define an admissible set of internal pay schedules $\{w_h(y,\theta),\ w_l(\theta,y)\}$ for given values of θ and y satisfying (7.3). Let us consult Fig. 7.2, in which the ordinate represents the value of w_h and the abscissa represents the value of w_l. Any pay schedule $(w_l,\ w_h)$ can be represented by a point in the space spanned by the two axes. The constraint (7.2) restricts the admissible pay schedule to the region lying above the $45°$ line which signifies $w_h = w_l$. The set of pay schedules satisfying (7.8) with equality for a given value of y is represented by the indifference map $\hat{\sigma}_y$ in the diagram. Regardless of the value of y, indifference maps always intersect the $45°$-line at $w_h = w_l = \hat{\omega}$; but as $\hat{p}(y)$ increases, the slopes of tangencies to the map at this point decrease. The constraint (7.3) is represented by a straight line $L_{y,\theta}$, with its slope equal to $-(1/n)$ and its intercept with the ordinate equal to $(1 - \theta)\,\{1 - \phi(y)\}$.

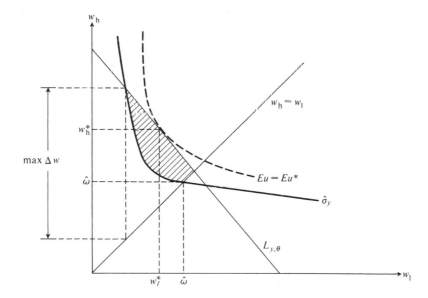

Fig. 7.2

Then, for given values of y and θ, the set of admissable pay schedules is represented by the area enclosed by $45°$-line, $\hat{\sigma}_y$, and $L_{y,\theta}$. For any given value of θ, the increase in y shifts $L_{y,\theta}$ towards the origin. In spite of this, it cannot necessarily be guaranteed that

$$\frac{d\,\{\max\;\Delta w(y)\}}{dy} < 0 \quad \text{for all } y,$$

where max $\Delta w(y)$ is the maximum admissible differential of earnings $\Delta w = w_h - w_l$; because an increase in y gives a higher probability of promotion $\hat{p}(y)$ for junior employees in a certain region (see Fig. 7.1), so that a wider earnings differential may be acceptable to them. However, if y increases sufficiently, then the effect of increasing sales expenditure, i.e. the shift of $L_{y,\theta}$, dominates, and the admissible differential is increasingly restricted. There is a maximum value of y beyond which no admissible pay schedule can be designed.[2]

Let us note that the variables of the model are w_h, w_l, y, and θ under the assumption that the shareholders and junior employees subjectively expect the current growth rate $y - 1$ to persist indefinitely. We will discuss in the next section how the subjective equilibrium values of these variables are determined. It is worth noting in advance, however, that, given the set of equilibrium values of these variables, the expected utility of individual senior employees,

$$Eu = q(y)\,u(w_h) + \{1 - q(y)\}\,u(w_l),$$

must be maximized at the equilibrium values of w_h^* and w_l^* in the admissible region, corresponding to the equilibrium value of y^* and θ^* where $u(\cdot)$ is a concave von Neumann–Morgenstern utility function. There is nothing in the model that prevents the indifference curve $(Eu)^*$, corresponding to the equilibrium pay schedule, from being tangent to $L_{y,\theta}^*$ at a point other than the corner point where Δw is maximized (see Fig. 7.1). In other words, the equilibrium pay schedule may be such that the constraint (7.8) is not binding. This implies that the organizational equilibrium may not be efficient from the viewpoint of the shareholder–senior employees coalition, because, by lowering the first-period wage of junior employees from w_l^* until (7.8) becomes binding and then distributing the resulting surplus between the shareholders and the senior employees as additional dividends and seniority premiums, we can make the existing members of the firm better off than at the equilibrium.

The possible inefficiency of the equilibrium outcome in the model is a consequence of our specifying a rate of compensation differentiated only by ranks, but not by tenures; so that the *internal* bargaining power of the senior employees has a spill-over effect of raising the utility level expected by junior employees to more than the level imposed by the *external* market. If constraint (7.8) is not binding, then rationing is likely to take place on the seller's side of the labour market. This rationing may be interpreted as a micro-source of the so-called 'classical unemployment' in the Malinvaud (1977) sense, in that it is caused not by the demand constraint, but by the strength of bargaining power of the incumbent employees.

Growth criteria in the hierarchical firm

In order to determine the organizational equilibrium for the model just formulated, we proceed in the same way as we did when dealing with the McDonald–Solow model. For simplicity, let us assume that the individual utility function of senior employees is of the constant relative risk aversion type,

$$u(w) = w^{1-R}.$$

where R is the degree of relative risk aversion and $0 \leq R < 1$ (see p. 77). Then the certainty equivalent $\hat{w}_s$ of uncertain earnings of senior employees in the hierarchical organization is given by

$$\hat{w}_s = \left[q(y)w_h^{1-R} + \{1 - q(y)\} w_l^{1-R} \right]^{1/(1-R)}. \tag{7.9}$$

From the viewpoint of individual employees who regard the rate of compensation w_h and w_l as exogenously given (although they are actually endogenous variables of the firm as a system), the percentage gain in the certainty equivalent arising from a 1 per cent increase in growth rate — that is, the marginal rate of elasticity substitution between current earnings and growth of the firm — is given as

$$\frac{1}{\hat{w}_s} \frac{d\hat{w}_s}{dy} = \frac{q'(y) \Delta u}{(1-R) \hat{w}_s^{1-R}} \tag{7.10}$$

where

$$\Delta u = w_h^{1-R} - w_l^{1-R}.$$

This marginal rate of elasticity substitution is the monetary rod for the incumbent employees' subjective assessment of the gains probable from the growth of the firm that would enhance opportunities of promotion. The marginal rate measures these promotional gains from an extra 1 per cent growth by a hypothetical percentage increase in current earnings, had the equivalent gains been achieved through sure compensation instead of uncertain promotion. Therefore the marginal rate is hereafter referred to as the 'marginal rate of promotional gains' to incumbent employees from an extra growth. This marginal rate is a strictly decreasing function of y until it reaches zero at $y = N/n$. That is, the increase in growth is perceived by incumbent employees as an opportunity to improve earnings, if $y < N/n$, but in diminishing degrees (see Fig. 7.3).

Total certainty equivalent of earnings by incumbent employees is simply

$$W = \hat{w}_s N.$$

Let $U(\cdot)$ be the collective utility function of the body of incumbent employees defined on a relevant region of W. For simplicity, let us assume that the collective utility function is equivalent to the individual employees' private utility function $u(\cdot)$ in the sense defined by (6.9*),[3] and that the utility level achieved by the incumbent employees in the absence of a co-operative agreement is zero.

Then the collective pure boldness of the incumbent employees towards the risk of internal conflict is given as

$$\xi_u \equiv \frac{1}{R} - 1.$$ (7.11)

On the other hand, suppose that the share value achievable in the absence of a co-operative agreement is zero and that the shareholders's body has the collective utility function $V(\cdot)$ with constant pure boldness ξ_v.

The internal balance of bargaining powers between the shareholders' body and the incumbent employees is achieved when the expression $B_u(W)W + B_v(S)S$, with local boldness B_u and B_v taken parametrically, is not raisable by changing w_h, w_l, y, and θ, satisfying constraints (7.1)-(7.3) and (7.8)-(7.9).

Details of the derivation of equilibrium conditions are relegated to the mathematical appendix to this chapter; here I shall describe some of the more important results. First of all, the equilibrium relative share must satisfy

$$\frac{1 - \theta^*}{\theta^*} = \frac{(1 + \xi_u^{-1})^{-1} + \hat{\mu}\epsilon}{(1 + \xi_v^{-1})^{-1}}$$ (7.12)

where ϵ is the junior employees' expected utility elasticity given by

$$\epsilon = \frac{\hat{p}(y)\sigma'(w_h)w_h + \{1 - \hat{p}(y)\}\sigma'(w_l)w_l}{\sigma(\hat{w})},$$

and $\hat{\mu}$ represents the increase in the expression $B_u(W)W + B_v(S)S$ made possible by a 1 per cent reduction in the junior employees' reservation utility $\sigma(\hat{w})$ when the internal allocation is appropriately rearranged. If constraint (7.8) is not binding (which is a non-negligible possibility, as has already been indicated on p. 108), then $\hat{\mu} = 0$. Expression (7.11) can then be reduced to the constant sharing rule (Θ). In other words, when the incumbent employees' collective bargaining power is such as to exert a spill-over effect of generating a higher utility level for the forthcoming employees than the market-constrained level, the relative share of the employees in the organizational rent, inclusive of the junior employees, is determined only by the relative bargaining power of the incumbent employees *vis-à-vis* the shareholders' body.

Assuming that the equilibrium conditions are solved for a pay schedule in terms of growth rate y, the equilibrium growth rate y^* must satisfy the following condition, if $\hat{\mu} = 0$:

$$\theta^* \left(\frac{1}{y^*} + \frac{1}{i - y^*} \right) + (1 - \theta^*)\frac{1}{\hat{w}_s^*} \cdot \frac{d\hat{w}_s^*}{dy} = \frac{\phi'(y^*)}{1 - \phi(y^*)}$$ (G-H)

where $(1/\hat{w}_s^*)/(d\hat{w}_s^*/dy)$ is the marginal rate of promotional gains to incumbent employees from an extra 1 per cent growth at the equilibrium growth rate.[4] The right-hand side (RHS) of (G-H) is the ratio of the marginal cost of an extra 1 per cent growth to the marginal benefit from that extra growth accruing to the firm viewed as an organization of the shareholders and employees. Its inverse may be called the 'marginal growth efficiency' of the firm. The term in the first parenthetic brackets in the left-hand side (LHS) of the equation is equal to the derivative of the logarithm of $\theta y/(i-y)$ with respect to y and the rate of appreciation of the 'value of the firm', defined as the discounted sum of future organizational rents *before* the payment of sales expenditure.

The condition (G-H) can now be read as follows. *The organizational equilibrium growth rate of the firm is achieved at that level under which the average of the rate of appreciation of the value of the firm before sales expenditure and the marginal rate of promotional gains to the incumbent employees, with the shareholders' and employees' shares in the organizational rent as respective weights, is equal to the inverse of the marginal growth efficiency of the firm.*

In Fig. 7.3 the equilibrium relation (G-H) is illustrated. Marginal growth efficiency decreases as the target growth rate increases; hence the graph of the RHS of (G-H) is upward-sloping. As noted already, $(1/\hat{w}_s^*)\,(d\hat{w}_s^*/dy)$, with the pay schedule fixed at the equilibrium value (w_l^*, w_h^*), is a decreasing function of y until it reaches zero at $y = N/n$, at which point the probability of promotion becomes certain for the senior employees. The rate of appreciation of the value of the firm decreases first and then rises as y approaches $\hat{y}$. The graph of the LHS of (G-H), being the weighted sum of the two, may be depicted as illustrated. The organizational equilibrium growth rate is represented at the familiar scissors' cross: $y = y^*$.

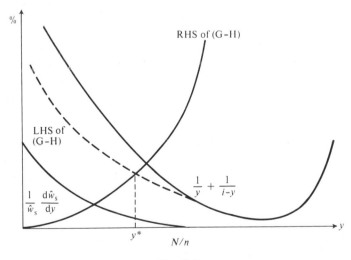

Fig. 7.3

Maximizing the share values (7.1) subject to the constraint that the pay schedule must equal the equilibrium one, $w_h = w_h^*$ and $w_l = w_l^*$ requires

$$\theta \left(\frac{1}{y} + \frac{1}{i-y} \right) = \frac{\phi'(y)}{1 - \phi(y)}.$$

Therefore, share values are *not* being maximized at the organizational equilibrium, given the wage bill. If the manager chooses a growth rate so as to maximize the share value after an agreement on a pay schedule with the incumbent employees, he neglects gains from the growth of the firm accruing to employees in the form of probable promotions, and ends up with too low a growth rate from the organizational point of view. He must consider the additional returns of growth to the employees in formulating the growth target of the firm, and/or the incumbent employees must exert some influence over the management so as to make their interest in the growth of the firm reflected in the corporate policy-making.

Finally, let us investigate the effect on the organizational equilibrium growth rate of a strengthening of the bargaining power of the incumbent employees. We stick to the case for which the constant sharing rule (Θ) holds so that θ^* is determined independently of y. It is straightforward to show that

$$\frac{1}{\hat{w}_s} \frac{d\hat{w}_s}{dy} < \frac{1}{y} + \frac{1}{i-y}$$

for all y such that $0 \leqq y < \hat{y}$. In other words, the benefit from additional growth is always appreciated relatively more highly by the shareholders than by the incumbent employees. Therefore, a decrease in the value of θ, i.e. more weighting on the preference of the incumbent employees, will always diminish the value of the LHS of (G–H) for any value of $0 \leqq y < \hat{y}$. On the other hand, the RHS of (G–H) is an increasing function of g. Therefore, a relative increase in the pure boldness of the incumbent employees *vis-à-vis* the shareholders' body always leads to a decrease in the organizational equilibrium growth rate of the firm.

With the analytical results thus far obtained, we have the following propositions.

Proposition 1 (*Allocative Dynamic Inefficiency*) The strengthening of the bargaining power of incumbent employees is likely to result in lower investment and a rationing of new jobs at the port of entry to the firm as well as an increase in the wage share.

Proposition 2 (*Internal Dynamic Inefficiency*) Value maximization subsequent to wage bargaining disregards the returns accruable to employees from the growth of the firm, and thus results in lower investment and less employment from an organizational point of view.

In recent years, macroeconomists have been paying increasing attention to a type of unemployment that is distinct from the Keynesian unemployment caused by demand constraints: namely, the situation in which firms are producing the notional supply — that is, the desired output that would emerge if firms are not rationed in their factor or output market — and the real wage is too high for full employment. Malinvaud called such unemployment 'classical unemployment' and remarked that it is likely to occur 'when anticipations or social tensions lead to an abnormal increase in real wages' (Malinvaud, 1977, p. 107). Although the set-up of the disequilibrium model that Malinvaud employs to examine its causes and implications is short-run, classical unemployment is also likely to be accompanied by a slow-down of capital accumulation. Kouri (1979) modelled a channel through which such association will emerge: a boom in real wages lowers the marginal value product of capital relative to the exogenously given world cost of capital and thus reduces investment incentives. Proposition 1 indicates, however, that a relatively lower growth benefit to employees is, in addition to the profit squeeze, a factor contributing to slower growth of the firm when employees' bargaining power is strengthened. It slows down the growth rate more than the theory of monopolistic competition would predict, thus aggravating dynamic allocative inefficiency. Furthermore, Proposition 2 suggests that there is a case in which even this lower growth benefit to employees is completely disregarded in investment decision-making. Disregard of employees' gains from growth may be said to be a source of internal dynamic inefficiency.

I conclude this chapter by suggesting a few ways in which my model may be extended. First, I adopted a model of simple two-level hierarchy, but the analytical results obtained therefrom are essentially robust even if the model is generalized so as to embody any fixed number of hierarchical levels. More interesting modelling, albeit complicated, would be to let the number of hierarchical levels depend upon the size of the firm. Second, I derived the equilibrium condition under a simplified assumption that the shareholders and junior employees expect the current growth rate $(y - 1)$ to persist indefinitely. However, under changing technological and market environment, this subjective expectation will not be fulfilled at the equilibrium solution in the *next* period except for the case of steady state. Therefore, I have assumed in effect the ideal situation in which the initial stock of incumbent employees somehow meets the steady-state requirement with $N = y (1 + n)/(y + 1)$; or else the assumed formation of expectation is a first approximation to a future environment of which the agents are completely ignorant. A better approach would require a more sophisticated notion of subjective equilibrium.

   Third, I assumed that, in the event of a failure of agreement, payoffs to the employees and shareholders are null. This assumption is, needless to say, very strong, but relaxing it to allow for non-zero disagreement payoffs complicates only the distributional rule (7.12) (see pp. 74–7). The important relation (G–H) remains intact in this case, although θ in that relation cannot be predetermined even if $\hat{\mu} = 0$ and must be simultaneously determined together with y.

Mathematical Appendix

Derivation of equilibrium conditions

By assuming the identity of the collective utility function with the private utility function in the sense as defined by (6.9*), and assuming homogeneity of degree $1 - R$ of the private utility function, the organizational equilibrium, characterized as a stationary point of the expression $B_v S + B_u \hat{w}_s N$, with B_v and B_u as parametric weights, is equivalently characterized as that of the utility product $V(S) \cdot (N\hat{w}_s)^{1-R}$ over the domain of $(\hat{w}_s, w_h, w_l, y, \theta)$ satisfying (7.1), (7.2), (7.3), (7.8), and (7.9). Forming the Lagrangean expression of $\log V(S) + (1-R) \log \hat{w}_s$ subject to (7.3), (7.8), and (7.9) (we ignore the possibility of (7.2) becoming binding, which is nothing but the case treated in the previous chapter), differentiating the expression with respect to those primary variables, and noting the inequality constraint (7.8), we have the following equilibrium conditions:

$$\frac{1}{\hat{w}_s^{1-R}} - \gamma = 0 \tag{A7.1}$$

$$-\lambda n + \mu \hat{p}(y) \sigma'(w_h) + (1-R)\gamma q(y) w_h^{-R} = 0 \tag{A7.2}$$

$$-\lambda + \mu \{1 - \hat{p}(y)\} \sigma'(w_l) + (1-R)\gamma \{1 - q(y)\} w_l^{-R} = 0 \tag{A7.3}$$

$$B_v \frac{dS}{dy} - \lambda(1-\theta)\phi'(y) + \mu \hat{p}'(y)\Delta\sigma + \gamma q'(y)\Delta u = 0 \tag{A7.4}$$

$$B_v \frac{S}{\theta} - \lambda\{1 - \phi(y)\} = 0 \tag{A7.5}$$

$$\mu[\hat{p}(y)\sigma(w_h) + \{1 - \hat{p}(y)\}\sigma(w_l) - \sigma(\hat{w})] = 0 \tag{A7.6}$$

where λ, μ, and γ are non-negative Lagrangean multipliers, each corresponding to constraints (7.3), (7.8), and (7.9), respectively, and

$$\Delta\sigma = \sigma(w_h) - \sigma(w_l).$$

(A7.1)–(A7.6), (7.3) and (7.9) constitute the system of eight equations with the five primary variables and the three Lagrangean multipliers. Solving for those primary variables, we can derive the equilibrium internal distribution and the equilibrium growth rate.

Multiplying w_h and w_l on both sides of (A7.2) and (A7.3), respectively, adding the results side by side, and using (7.3), (7.9), and (A7.1), we can derive

$$(1-R) + \mu\sigma(\hat{\omega})\epsilon = \lambda(1-\theta)\{1 - \phi(y)\} \tag{A7.7}$$

where ϵ is defined as in the text. Substituting (A7.5) into (A7.7) gives

$$\frac{1-\theta}{\theta} = \frac{(1-R) + \mu\epsilon\sigma(\hat{\omega})}{B_v S}. \tag{A7.8}$$

Using (7.11) and $B_\nu S = (1 + \xi^{-1})^{-1}$, and setting $\mu\sigma(\hat{\omega}) = \hat{\mu}$, we arrive at (7.12) in the text. Since μ is the Lagrangean multiplier corresponding to (7.8),

$$\hat{\mu} = -\frac{\text{d} \log V(S) + (1-R) \text{ d} \log \hat{w}_s}{\text{d} \log (\hat{\omega})}$$

evaluated at the equilibrium, and it can be given the interpretation cited in the text. If (7.8) is not binding, $\mu = 0$ from (A7.6); and

$$\frac{1-\theta}{\theta} = \frac{(1 + \xi_u^{-1})^{-1}}{(1 + \xi_v^{-1})^{-1}} .$$

Substituting (A7.5) and (A7.8) into (A7.4), we can derive the condition (G–H), as given in the text, if $\mu = 0$; or, more generally,

$$\theta \left(\frac{1}{y} + \frac{1}{i-y} \right) + (1-\theta) \frac{1}{\hat{W}} \frac{\text{d}\hat{W}}{\text{d}y} = \frac{\phi'(y)}{1 - \phi(y)} \tag{A7.9}$$

for $\mu > 0$, where

$$\frac{1}{\hat{W}} \frac{\text{d}\hat{W}}{\text{d}y} = \frac{q'(y)\Delta u + r\{p'(y)\Delta\sigma\}}{(1-R)\hat{w}_s^{1-R} + r\{\epsilon\sigma(\hat{\omega})\}} .$$

In this ratio, r is given as

$$r = \mu\hat{w}_s^{1-R} = -\frac{\text{d} \log V(S) + \text{d} \log u(\hat{w}_s)}{\text{d}\sigma(\hat{\omega})} \qquad u(\hat{w}_s) = -\frac{\text{d}u(\hat{w}_s)}{\text{d}\sigma(\hat{\omega})}$$

evaluated at the equilibrium, and is the marginal rate of utility substitution between the senior employees and the junior employees; $p'(y)\Delta u/\epsilon\sigma(\omega)$ is the growth elasticity of certainty equivalent to junior employees' earning perspective, as inferred analogously from (7.9). In other words, it measures the marginal rate of saving of labour costs made possible by giving higher promotability to the junior employees. By setting

$$a = \frac{r\{\epsilon\sigma(\hat{\omega})\}}{(1-R)\hat{w}_s^{1-R} + r\{\epsilon\sigma(\hat{\omega})\}}$$

we can decompose the term $(1/\hat{W})(\text{d}\hat{W}/\text{d}y)$ as follows:

$$\frac{1}{\hat{W}} \frac{\text{d}\hat{W}}{\text{d}y} = (1-a) \frac{1}{\hat{w}_s} \frac{\text{d}\hat{w}_s}{\text{d}y} + a \frac{p'(y)\Delta\sigma}{\epsilon\sigma(\hat{\omega})} .$$

This is the weighted average of the marginal rate of promotional gains to the senior employees and the marginal rate of cost-saving on the junior employees' wage bill, both made possible from extra growth. Relatively lower bargaining power of the incumbent employees (less R) would lead to more weighting on the cost-saving effect. Unless the time preference of the junior employees is substantially lower than that of the senior employees, the shifting of weight would not block the slow-down of growth of the firm.

Part III

Efficiency of Three Legal Models
of the Firm

Chapter 8

Institutional Efficiency

Summary of Parts I and II

Part I covered the origin and nature of organizational rent as produced by the formation of the firm (that is, by an enduring combination of firm-specific resources). In Part II we then examined the determination of managerial and distributional decision variables of the firm, as an outcome of a game between shareholders and employees. The solution of those decision variables, arising in a co-operative framework and characterized by the principle of internal efficiency-cum-power balance between the constituents of the firm, was defined as the state of organizational equilibrium. However, in some situations the firm might find itself in an inefficient equilibrium. More specifically, we derived the following propositions.

1   In the co-operative framework, a strengthening of the bargaining power of incumbent employees results in an unequivocal increase in equilibrium wages, lower equilibrium investment, and lower equilibrium employment (even the rationing of new jobs at the port of entry to the firm) in an expansionary period, and smaller equilibrium lay-offs in a depressed period, thus aggravating the exploitation of a monopolistic position by the firm more than under full entrepreneurial control.

2   Internally efficient bargaining (co-operative solution) cannot be supported by first agreeing on an average wage and then letting the management unilaterally choose the amount of employment and/or the target growth rate so as to maximize share value subject to this wage. In general, there are other combinations of decision variables characterized by lower current wage, higher employment (security of jobs for the employees), and higher investment (chances for the employees to improve their position) under which both the current shareholders and the incumbent employees are expected to be better off. The achievement of internal efficiency thus requires that internal distribution and managerial policy should be chosen conjunctionally.

3   If the external job opportunities (in terms of real wages) are more sensitive to business cycle fluctuations than are the product markets of the firm, the equilibrium amount of employment tends to be sticky and the internally determined equilibrium wage level will become procyclic. If the opposite is the case, the internally determined equilibrium wage level will tend to be sticky in real terms and the amount of employment will bear more of the burden of external fluctuations.

It is to be remembered that, in the above propositions, efficiency refers to 'internal' efficiency as viewed by the current shareholders and the incumbent employees. The concept of internal efficiency, as contrasted with allocative efficiency realizable through the perfectly competitive mechanism, was first conceptualized by Harvey Leibenstein (1966) as 'X-efficiency'. While our notion of internal efficiency is concerned with modes of *combination* of decision variables of the firm, Leibenstein's original notion of X-efficiency dealt with the variations of outputs for *given* amounts of inputs caused by motivational factors, non-marketable inputs such as managerial knowledge, and the like. Recently, however, Leibenstein (1982) came to regard the X-efficiency of production as a theory of games problem, played between the firm (which he identifies with the management) and the employees. Their mutual distrust and egoistic pursuit of self-interest, he argues, may trap them in a prisoner's dilemma situation, i.e. a mutually disadvantageous position. As a solution, conventions develop within the firm to co-ordinate decision-making, but actual conventions are likely to fall short of providing efficient outcomes. Thus, in focusing on modes of combinations of decision variables of the firm as a source of possible internal inefficiency, Leibenstein's notion of X-efficiency and our notion of internal efficiency tend to converge, although the following difference in approaches to the problem may be noted: Leibenstein attends more to the (inefficient) non-cooperative aspect of the game within the firm, whereas our main concern is with possibilities (and/or failures) of institutionalizing an efficient co-operative game within the firm. The control of decision variables may be more conducive to internally efficient choices in some institutional settings of corporate structure and industrial relations than in others. In other words, the achievement of internal efficiency seems to be decisively conditioned by the institutional choice as to the decision-making structure of the firm. Thus, we may legitimately question how the co-operative game can be institutionalized within the firm. It is to this problem that we shall now turn.

The classicist v. managerialist debate

Almost a quarter of century ago, Edward Mason edited *The Corporation in Modern Society* (1959), a now-classical collection of essays by prominent jurists, economists, political scientists, and others, which dealt with various aspects of the corporate system. Divergent views were expressed by the contributors regarding the (normative) nature of the corporation, but it seems reasonable to say that there were two threads of thought. One, which may be called the managerialist view, was to regard the corporate firm as a sort of coalition of associational groups such as shareholders, employees, suppliers, customers, and even the general public; and to visualize the manager of the corporation as harmonizing the objectives of those groups. The other view, more traditional among economists as well as jurists, was expressed, for instance, by Eugene Rostow, who argued:

As an abstract statement of the social duty of business enterprise in the middle of the twentieth century, I believe the 'rule'. . . of long-term profit maximization . . . conforms more concretely than any alternative both to the image of preferred reality for business behavior in public opinion, at this state in the evolution of our legal and economic order, and to the ends business enterprise is expected to fulfill as part of nation's system of law for governing the economy. (Rostow, 1959, p. 70)

Apart from the problem of aggregating divergent preferences of shareholders and the vagueness involved in the notion of 'long-term' profit maximization under uncertainties, the idea of identifying the corporate objective with the sole interest of shareholders is unmistakably clear. In contrast, the balancing of the claims of various interest groups within the corporate firm was not so easy to visualize. Abram Chayes in the managerial camp had this to say:

[Corporate members'] rightful share in decisions on the exercise of corporate power would be exercised through an institutional arrangement appropriately designed to represent the interests of a constituency of members having a significant common relation to the corporation and its power. It is not always easy to identify such constituencies, nor is it always clear what institutional forms are appropriate for recognizing their interests. The effort to answer those questions is among the most meaningful tasks of the American legal system. (Chayes, 1959, p. 41)

Almost a quarter of century after those sentences were written, this managerialist task does not seem to have been fulfilled in the United States to the same degree as in Western European countries and Japan, which have at least been moving towards an equivocal acceptance of the managerialist philosophy or even towards the institutionalization of employees' voices in corporate decision-making structures. What accounts for the relative failure of managerialism in the United States? Is it because, as Mason (1958, p. 9) indicated, the economy is not so managerial as the literature suggests? Or is it that the contention may be correct, but that the managerialists have not yet penetrated deeply enough into the system to explain how the corporation can, or does, satisfy its obligation to its constituencies? Or does the managerialist argument serve only as a shabby apology for the corporate management which is not accountable to any one and is enjoying its discretionary power? In Part III I aim to approach afresh the old, yet unsettled, debate between managerialists and traditionalists regarding the nature of the modern corporate firm. In order to carry out this task, however, I will limit the perspective of my discussion in a somewhat special way.

Institutional efficiency

In the ensuing discussion, I shall regard the corporate firm as consisting only of the shareholders' body, the employees' body, and management. The customers of the firm appear only implicitly, in the form of the demand function for the outputs. They are supposed to receive consumers' surplus, determined after decisions by the firm have been made and put into effect. Finally, the interests of the general public are abstracted away. Thus we have dispensed with the constituencies of the corporate firm that are the major concern of the jurists. One may argue that the general public is forced unwittingly to swallow pollutants emitted by corporate activities; that consumers may not know the quality and safety of what they are buying because of the high cost of information; or that the general public may be affected indirectly by corporate bribery of public officials at home and abroad; etc. Certainly, what is good for the shareholders, the trade union, the employees, and management combined is not necessarily in the public interests. Let me offer, however, a couple of excuses as to why I am confining the perspective of discussion in the above way in spite of the obvious limitations.

First, because economists have been so much engaged in the notion of 'shareholders' sovereignty' (as discussed in Chapter 2), even the impact of employees' voices on corporate policy-making has not been fully explored, to say nothing of the impact of the other constituencies. Mason once asked:

If profit maximization is not the directing agent, how are resources allocated to their most productive uses, what relation have prices to relative scarcities, and how do factors get remunerated in accordance with their contribution to output?'

And he complained:

[T] he 'philosophy of natural liberty' had a reasonable answer to these questions, but I can find no reasoned answer in the managerial literature. (Mason, 1958, p. 7)

It may be that the survival of the 'shareholders' sovereignty' doctrine is owed partly to the very absence of a convincing alternative economic explanation of corporate behaviour.

In Part II I provided my own answer to those questions posed by Mason, assuming that the objective of the firm is constructed as a result of a co-operative game resolution of partly conflicting, partly harmonizing, claims of shareholders and employees for firm-specific gains; furthermore, I indicated that 'long-run profit maximization' may fail to achieve efficiency under a certain employment structure and a certain bargaining framework. Now it is a time to mesh those economic results with judicial discussions on corporate structure and industrial relations, and to see if any new insight can be gained by a comparison of different legal structures of corporate firms involving the employees. Although the general public, customers, creditors, and so on are excluded from explicit consideration, since the employees' body is the most enduring and readily identifiable constituency of the firm, the inclusion of the employees in the model is a first step towards a more complete theory of corporate firms. Furthermore, since the topic of industrial democracy — that is, the question of how the employees' voice is to be recognized in the corporate decision-making —

has been discussed in earnest in the last decade, particularly in Europe, our approach in singling out the employees' body as a coalitional partner to the shareholders may have its own value and relevancy.

The second reason for restricting our nomenclature of corporate constituencies to employees and shareholders (and management, in a somewhat special way) is related more specifically to our notion of internal efficiency. A combination of decision variables of the firm is defined as being internally efficient if it cannot be improved in the Paretian sense from the viewpoint of the existing shareholders and the incumbent employees – that is, so as to increase the objective of the shareholders and/or that of the employees – without sacrificing either of them. In addition, an institutional framework for decision-making of the firm is said to be *institutionally efficient* if, for any market environment, an outcome of decision-making thereof is expected to be internally efficient.

As discussed in Part II (and summarized at the beginning of this chapter), the organizational equilibrium (internal efficiency) is, in general, accompanied by the exploitation of a monopolistic position by the firm in the sense of Edward Chamberlain (1962) and Joan Robinson (1934). The marginal organizational cost of an additional unit of output is equated, in the organizational equilibrium, to the 'marginal organizational revenue', but not to the sales price. The only difference from the orthodox parable of monopolistic competion is that the 'marginal organizational revenue (cost)' replaces 'marginal revenue (cost)'. The former is a weighted average of the marginal revenue (cost) to shareholders and the marginal earnings (cost) of the employees, whereas the latter is supposed to be accruable to the entrepreneur (the shareholders) alone. Because the marginal earnings of the existing employee from an additional unit of output is negative (see p. 78), the marginal organizational revenue curve is more steeply downward-sloping than the ordinary marginal revenue curve and the equality of the marginal organizational revenue with the marginal organizational cost will lower the equilibrium output level below the level predicted by the orthodox theory of monopolistic competition. In other words, the allocative inefficiency under the shareholder–employee coalition at the sacrifice of the consumers' surplus is higher than under full entrepreneurial control (see Chapter 6). Likewise, the shareholder–employee coalition will lower the equilibrium target growth rate below the level realizable under the full entrepreneurial control, thus resulting in dynamic allocative inefficiency (see Chapter 7). But the whole story has not yet been told.

A further problem is that *institutional inefficiency may become an extra source of inefficiency, in addition to allocative inefficiency*, by restricting the amount of output (and employment) and lowering the target growth rate below the levels given by the co-operative game solution. Allocative inefficiency results from the monopolistic position of the shareholder–employee coalition, while the institutional inefficiency is a result of the mis-arrangement of decision variables within that coalition under specific institutional set-ups. Therefore, given a monopolistic position of the firm, a separate treatment of institutional inefficiency may be warranted.

I do not pretend that it is possible to quantify the relative magnitudes of allocative inefficiency and internal inefficiency under a certain institutional framework for decision-making of the firm; but the impression gained by observing the divergent performances of firms having different national–institutional structures is that the relative magnitude of institutional inefficiency may be substantial.[1] Thus, there seems to be a good reason for concentrating on the unexplored problem of institutional inefficiency, taking the relatively well understood problem of allocative inefficiency as given. This is the second reason why we exclude from explicit consideration customers, for whom allocative efficiency is the most relevant, and consider only shareholders and employees, between whom internal efficiency is definable.

Even though it is admitted that internal efficiency is of practical significance, it may be still reasonable to wonder whether it is possible to remedy monopolistic allocative inefficiency without sacrificing internal efficiency. One conceivable method would be to subsidize the firm so as to realize the equality of sales price with marginal organizational cost, the well-known condition for maximization of public welfare (in the sense of maximizing the sum of the organizational rent and consumers' surplus). But the calculation of such an optimal subsidy rate would involve the collection of detailed managerial information and would not be possible without costly bureaucracy. The potential gain in allocative efficiency could well be offset by an information inefficiency in the public administration of a cumbersome subsidy system.

Is it possible, then, to approximate allocative efficiency by breaking up monopolistic firms and making the demand curves facing the individual firm flatter? The discussion of Part I is relevant here: the firm owes its own *raison d'être* at least partly to gainful, enduring combinations of firm-specific resources, and the breaking up of the firm may result not only in the siphoning-off of the 'monopolistic gain' by the corporate constituencies, but also in the destruction of consumers' surplus by dissolving socially useful combinations of firm-specific resources. Although eclectic, perhaps we must live with some sort of 'reasonable' competition among firms, in which only 'excessive' exploitation of monopolistic positions is appropriately held in check. How much competition is reasonable, and how much monopolistic exploitation excessive? This can not be answered without introducing a notion of 'fair' distribution between the corporate constituents, as rather narrowly defined here, and the public. Doing so is far beyond the scope of this book, however. It is only cautioned that a singleminded belief in 'pure' competition would not contribute to a better understanding of the efficiency problem in the corporate economy.

Models of the decision-making structure of firms

Now let us set out main issues to be discussed in Part III. There are two, mutually interrelated, issues. First, admitting that the employees are a constituency of the firm, what proper mechanism can be found to provide an outlet of the employees' voice into the decision-making process of the firm? More specifically, do current institutional frameworks of collective bargaining provide adequate scope for an efficient conciliation of conflicting claims of employees and shareholders? Should employees' representatives be recognized in the statutory structure of corporate governance in order to achieve efficient corporate planning? If so, how? Alternatively, can the management be a guardian of employees' interests without involving inefficient intervention by the unions and other employees' representatives?

The second issue is concerned with the objectives and responsibilities of the corporate management. What is, or shall be, the objective of management? To whom are they, or should they be, responsible? More concretely, should the board of directors provide a forum for the discussion of corporate planning to all corporate constituencies? Or should management exert independent judgements to balance the interests of the constituencies? If so, how can they be controlled and monitored so that they are responsible and accountable to corporate constituents?

In order to consider those questions, we begin by distinguishing between the management as a bundle of functions in the firm and the management as an institutional element in the decision-making structure of the firm. The bundle of *functions* comprises the following:

1 decisions on such fundamental actions as merger, dissolution, sales of substantial portion of corporate assets, or bylaw amendments;
2 decisions directly related to employees' earnings such as wages, pension plans, sick pay, etc., and decisions on distribution of corporate earnings;
3 decisions on managerial policy such as sales prices, employment, diversification, investment, financing, location, and the like;
4 implementation of the above decisions and the accompanying internal allocation of resources;
5 monitoring of the uses of resources within the firm, including rewarding and sanctioning employees' performances by such methods as promotions, demotions, transfers, disciplines, and discharges;
6 reporting corporate activities to the shareholders, unions, public authorities, media, and others entitled to know.

Of these six functions, the first one, *fundamental decision-making*, belongs to the realm of shareholders' authority (general meeting) in most corporate statutes, although the actual initiative of fundamental actions may, except for an outsiders' take-over, emanate from the board of directors, or even from the executive officer. The other managerial functions (2-5) are supposed to belong exclusively, or at least principally, to the management as a *structural element* of the corporate firm. In fact, the management as a structural element of the corporate firm may be defined as a team that is engaged in *all* of those functions. However, this definition does not preclude the possibility that the performance of some of the managerial functions listed above may be shared with the other elements of the corporate firm. Some corporate statutes provide that *managerial policy-making* (item 3 above) may be intervened by the shareholders' body, and that decisions on the distribution of corporate earnings (item 2) must formally be approved by it. Wage determination (item 2), and in certain circumstances even a part of managerial policy-making (item 3) may be subject to joint decision-making with the union (as the representative of employees) in the unionized firm. Items 4 and 5 are generally considered to be managerial prerogatives, but even here these tasks are usually performed according to relatively well-defined procedural rules, and it is not rare to find such rule-making shared by managements and unions.

We can then differentiate models of decision-making structures in firms by specifying the *motives* of the management team as well as the *modes* of sharing those managerial functions between the management team (M) and other elements of the firm, i.e. the shareholders' body (S) and the employees' body (E). Specifically, by restricting the scope of our explicit consideration to wage determination (item 2), managerial policy-making (item 3), and rule-making (item 5), we can distinguish three stylized models of the decision-making structure of firms (see Fig. 8.1):

1   the *shareholders' sovereignty-cum-collective bargaining model*, in which M, acting as a surrogate of S, determines some of decision variables jointly with the representative of E (the union), and the rest of variables unilaterally;

2   the *participative management model*, in which the representatives of S (directors) and E make decisions jointly, or in which M makes decisions under the joint supervision of S and E;

3   the *corporative managerialism model*, in which neutral M makes decisions to integrate and mediate the interests of S and E.

As a degenerate model, or a variant, of model 3, we may also consider:

3a the *managerial discretionary model*, in which an independent M makes decisions according to its own utility subject only to constraints imposed by S and E.

In reality, none of the pure models exists. For instance, even where collective bargaining and shareholders' surveillance are most developed, as in the unionized industries in the United States and Britain, management may enjoy a certain degree of discretionary power. In Germany, where workers' participation in management is statutorily institutionalized, regional collective bargaining on standard wage rates plays a significant, if not complete, role in the determination of actual earnings of workers. Also, as we shall see later, the German co-determination system at the corporate management level is usually supplemented by a system of works councils at shop and establishment levels which may be viewed as a statutorily provided collective bargaining apparatus; whereas a participative management model presented by the Bullock Committee to the

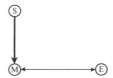

(1) The shareholders' Sovereignty-cum-Collective Bargaining model

(2) The Co-determination model

(3) The Corporative Managerialism model

(3a) The Managerial Discretionary model

Fig. 8.1

British Parliament in 1977 (now definitely shelved) may be viewed as a direct extention of collective bargaining into the board room. Thus, collective bargaining may coexist with, or extend into, participative management. In the Japanese firm, where the apparent function of the management team is to mediate between different constituents of it, enterprise-level wage bargaining and policy consultation with the enterprise-based union is an essential part of decision-making within it.

Thus, the above three stylized models should be regarded only as abstractions of certain dominant aspects of actual, diverse decision-making structures. However, to make the following discussion concrete, I shall illustrate the argument by referring to the statutory provisions and actual practices of collective bargaining institutions in the United States and Britain with respect to the shareholders sovereignty-cum-collective bargaining model; to the statutory framework of German co-determination and the Bullock proposal with respect to the participative management model; and, finally, to the American, British, and

Japanese corporate statutes and practices as regards the corporative managerial or managerial discretionary model.

Our main concern in the remaining three chapters will be to enquire whether or not the three stylized models of the decision-making structure of the firm are institutionally efficient. An institutionally efficient structure can achieve the organizational equilibrium (co-operative solution), provided that a choice is made from the set of internally efficient outcomes in such a way as to balance the powers of the body of shareholders and the body of employees. Conversely, if the firm is homeostatic in the sense of tending to approximate the state of organizational equilibrium, the decision-making structure internalized therein is institutionally efficient and its outcome is always internally efficient. By assuming that the balancing of the powers is not very problematic, I will henceforth concentrate on the efficiency aspects of organizational equilibrium, and employ the terms 'organizational equilibrium' and 'internal efficiency' interchangeably in a somewhat loose manner.

Chapter 9

The Shareholders' Sovereignty-cum-Collective Bargaining Model

Zero-sum game?

We noted at the end of the last chapter that the shareholders' sovereignty-cum-collective bargaining model consists of two elements, one related to the role of the managers and the other to the scope of collective bargaining (joint decision-making). As regards the former, it is assumed that management acts as a surrogate of the shareholders' body. Many economists are fond of referring to the shareholder–management relationship as an agency–principal relationship. Judicially speaking, however, the agency–principal relationship requires two things: that the authority of an agent can normally be terminated by his principal at any time; and that an agent must normally follow his principal's instructions (see the quotation from Eisenberg (1976) on p. 37). As we shall see in Chapter 11, corporate statutory provisions in general do not guarantee both, or even one, of these conditions in the shareholder–management relation; moreover, doubt is cast on the shareholders' ability to control management in reality, even if the statutes provide for it. We shall not pursue this issue of controllability at present, but are concerned only with the theoretical implications of shareholders' control, if any, over the management imposed in the form of the value-maximizing discipline.

As regards the second element of the model, we recognize a line between the scope of bargaining or joint decision-making on the one hand, and the scope of unilateral decision-making by the management, i.e. the scope of what is often referred to as the 'management prerogative', on the other. As the expression 'shareholders sovereignty-cum-collective bargaining model' is somewhat awkward, and since the following discussion focuses upon the impacts of a collective bargaining framework on internal efficiency, I shall hereafter refer to this model simply as the 'collective bargaining model', although it neither captures the specific character of the management motive nor refers to a limited scope of bargaining, thus lacking an explicit reference to the scope of the unilateral decision-making power of the management on behalf of the shareholders. As we shall see, the manner in which this unilateral power is exercised is a crucial factor affecting the internal efficiency of the model.

The traditional economists' view of a labour union is that of a labour cartel. Collective bargaining is seen as an instance of bilateral monopoly and a struggle between employees and employers for larger pieces of the pie in a zero-sum game. From this viewpoint, the adjective 'adversary' (Eisenberg, 1976, p. 23) may be suggested to qualify the model of the decision-making structure of the firm under consideration. But this is a biased viewpoint; as we have seen, and shall argue once more below, it overlooks the possibility of Pareto-improving (mutually beneficial) trade-offs between the current wage level and the security of sustained employment, as well as the chance for employees to improve their positions through an expansionary managerial policy of the firm. Using Raiffa's expression, the bargaining within the firm may be not of a 'competitive' type, but of an 'integrative' nature. 'It is no longer true that if one party gets more, the other necessarily has to get less: they both can get more. They can cooperate in order to enlarge the pie that they eventually will have to divide' (Raiffa, 1982, p. 131).

Also, although trade unionists in the United States and elsewhere may traditionally have been hesitant to expand the scope of collective bargaining, or the subjects of collective agreements, into managerial policies, they have been quite aggressive and successful in participating in the making of various procedural rules regulating managerial prerogatives regarding allocation and the monitoring of employees. This penetration into the rule-making process, or 'joint regulation' (Flanders, 1968, p. 10), was not necessarily forced upon the management against its will; the view of collective bargaining as an adversary relationship overlooks the possibility of employers' having an interest in joint rule-making. Some system of rules – what Dunlop (1958) and Kerr (1964) have called a 'web of rules' – is essential for the operation of a modern bureaucratic firm. It is essential in order to control the actions of subordinate members of management in dealing with workers in a way consistent with overall organizational orientation; it is also essential in eliciting the employees' willingness to co-operate by preventing favouritism, nepotism, victimization, and arbitrary discrimination of any sort by managers.

Although these systems of rules exist in non-unionized firms as well, in the form of unilateral administrative rules or customs, joint rule-making through collective bargaining serves as a mechanism by which the employees' explicit consent to those rules can be obtained. Implicit in agreements about rules is the acceptance of the management's authority to impose those rules. In other words, the joint rule-making process is an exchange process between the acceptance of the authoritarian nature of an employment relationship and a democratic participation in drawing up the rules through which such authority is exercised. The ethical principle underlying this process is, as Neil Chamberlain and James Kuhn put it, the 'principle of mutuality' (1965, p. 134). It seems thus narrow and misleading to view the collective bargaining relationship only as an adversary one. True, the agreed rules are not subject to changes until the time of re-negotiation, and this rigidity tends to hinder flexible and efficient adaptation to technological progress – an often made criticism of unionized rules. However, rapid technological progress itself will not make the necessity for rules obsolete, and whether management and the unions can adapt themselves to new technological imperatives by devising a new system of more flexible rules is yet to be seen.

The collective bargaining model finds popular support as the more desirable decision-making model among academics, jurists, and trade unionists alike in American society. Economists presuppose that the simple rule of long-term profit maximization subject to bargained wages can lead to an internally efficient use of resources. Jurists find merit in the simple and coherent role of the union in the collective bargaining model, in which the union represents the interests of employees squarely, as opposed to the participative model, in which the union is seen to play dual and possibly conflicting roles by participating with management and having a seat on both sides of the bargaining table. For instance, Detlev Vagts of Harvard Law School observes: 'Most American commentators find a system in which management and labor bargains as representatives of conflicting interests less likely to produce pressure and conflicts within individual roles, and see a major reconstruction of the labor relation structure on the German model as undesirable' (Vagts, 1966, p. 76). The trade unionists are afraid that the participative management will encroach, or even usurp, the autonomy of the union. Thomas Donahue, Secretary-Treasurer of AFL–CIO, expressed this view: 'We do not seek to be a partner in management, to be, most likely, the junior partner in success and the senior partner in failure. We do not want to blur in any way the distinctions between the respective roles of management and labor in the plant' (1978, p. 9).

On the other hand, managements tend to view collective bargaining as being restricted to wage determination, and joint rule-making as the maximum allowable intrusion by the union into the management's freedom and discretion in ordering the affairs of an enterprise. I shall not be concerned directly with these issues of 'conflict of interest', 'union autonomy', and 'management prerogatives', but will touch on them indirectly, while discussing the performance characteristics of the collective bargaining model from the viewpoint of institutional efficiency in three respects.

First, as was emphasized in the preceding analysis, the institutional efficiency of the collective bargaining model is not self-evident. If the employees' interests lie in current earnings only, the residual maximization after wage bargaining — that is, the share-value maximization subject to some level of agreed wages — will provide the management with a clear-cut guideline for serving the shareholders' best interests (see pp. 67–8 above). However, even in this case, if the endowment patterns of firm-specific resources are not identical among firms, and if there are differences in the produced amounts of organizational rent, the balancing of power (a co-operative solution) ought to differ for each firm. If the wage is determined at supra-enterprise level, say between the employers' association and the trade union, an agreement cannot satisfy the organizational equilibrium conditions of all the firms involved all at once. In fact, in most industrialized nations, decentralization of bargaining to the enterprise level seems to be a general tendency, as will be discussed presently. Even in places where more centralized bargaining at national or regional levels has been traditional, supra-enterprise agreements tend to be subject to adjustments and supplements by plant-level negotiations, and/or by enterprise-level negotiations. Institutional factors accelerating or impeding enterprise-level bargaining are thus chosen as the first subject to be discussed in this chapter.

Second, as the employment structures of the firm become more deeply internalized, the employees' welfare may be affected directly and indirectly by managerial policies such as on the lay-off rate and the investment rate. Should the determination of these managerial policy variables become the subject of collective bargaining? There has been, in every country, a more or less well-defined line between the scope of collective bargaining and the scope of management prerogative. However, this line is becoming somewhat more fluid, and there seems to be a tendency, particularly in Europe, towards a shrinkage of management prerogatives. How can we evaluate this tendency? Does broadening the scope of collective bargaining lead to more institutionally efficient decision-making? Or does it deter the efficient operation of the firm? This is the second topic to be discussed below.

Third, even if we admit that the subjective intention and/or imposed obligation of the management team is to serve the shareholders' interests, it is one thing for the management to co-ordinate wage-setting and policy-making so as to realize as high a share value as possible *vis-à-vis* the union's demand for higher employees' welfare, and another for it to choose managerial policy so as to maximize the share value *posterior* to collective bargaining exclusively concerned with the wage rate. As I have repeatedly argued, the former may be conducive to the achievement of institutional efficiency, but the latter is not. Thus, the timing of decision-making may constitute another factor affecting the performance characteristics of the collective bargaining model. Specifically, we shall discuss an efficiency implication of prolonging the duration of collective agreement in the final section of this chapter.

The level of bargaining

This section begins our discussion about the performance characteristics of the collective bargaining model by making an enquiry into the level – industrial, enterprise, or shop – at which the most relevant bargaining is likely to occur. The argument will be illustrated by referring mainly to practices prevalent in two representative collective bargaining institutions: the American institution, which is relatively young, and the British institution, which is, in its origin, among the oldest. The framework of the former has been shaped considerably by unique statutory provisions, while that of the latter, to a great extent, has been conditioned by a more autonomous historical development of industrial relations. In spite of these apparent differences, however, we can discern converging patterns between the workings of the two institutions, which reflect the essential characteristics of the collective bargaining model.

One of the most distinctive features of the American collective bargaining institution is the doctrine of 'statutory bargaining representation'. Section 9 of the Labor Management Relation Act as amended in 1959 (LMRA) stipulates:

Representatives designated or selected for the purposes of collective bargaining by the majority of the employees in a unit appropriate for such purposes, shall be the *exclusive* representatives of all the employees in such unit for the purpose of collective bargaining in respect to rates of pay, wages, hours of employment, or other conditions of employment. (Italics added)

If a majority of the employees in the plant (or in another appropriate unit) want a certain trade union to represent them in collective bargaining and the union can satisfy the employer on this point, the employer may recognize the union and bargain with it. If an employer refuses voluntary recognition of a union and there is a question as to whether the union represents a majority, the matter can be settled by the union's filing a representation petition with the regional office of the National Labor Relation Board (NLRB). Normally the petitioner must establish that at least 30 per cent of the employees in the unit have designated the union as representative. If this and other conditions are satisfied, the question is resolved through an election by secret ballot administered by the NLRB.[1] If the union is chosen by a simple majority of the employees in the unit, it will receive a certificate showing that it is the official bargaining representative of *all* the employees in the unit. Then the union has the exclusive right of representation for the purpose of collective bargaining for a reasonable period of time (as will be discussed later). As a countervailing obligation to such strong rights, the union owes a legal duty to represent fairly all the employees' interests in the group in question.

Section 8(c) of the LMRA, commonly called the 'free speech' provision, allows the employer to engage in a campaign during the election process to influence its outcome, within limits set down by the law and NLRB rulings. However, once the union has won the election and been certified, the employer has no choice but to bargain with the recognized union 'in good faith': it is an unfair practice to refuse to do so. The obligation does not require an employer to concede to the union's demands, but it does require acceptance of the act of bargaining with good intention of reaching an agreement. If agreement is reached with the recognized union, it applies to *all* employees in the bargaining unit, whether or not they are union members. The employer can make no deal with any of non-union members that is different from the terms of the union agreement.[2]

In general, this 'ballot box organizing' makes work organizational units such as plants, establishments, or enterprises logically appropriate units for union recognition in many industries, although examples of craft units can also be observed. A union organization representing an appropriate unit usually constitutes a local union affiliated with an industrial union. The most prevalent bargaining relationships are between one employer and one local, or between one employer and multi-locals of a single international (e.g. motor cars, communications), although bargaining between one employer and locals of multi-internationals (co-ordinated bargaining), between multi-employers and one international (e.g. coal mining, construction), or between multi-employers and multi-internationals (e.g., longshoremen on the West Coast of the United States) are also found. If a large multi-plant firm bargains with separate locals of a single international, often a conference board will be formed by the international to which each local sends representatives. The conference board bargains with the firm centrally for a master agreement to be supplemented by local agreements with plant managers on local issues. According to the 1976 Bureau of Labor Statistics (BLS) survey of collective agreements covering 1000 or more workers, 2.8 million workers in manufacturing are covered by agreements with single employers, while only 0.6 million workers are covered by agreements with multi-employers. Even in all those industries, including construction, coal mining, trucking, and retail trades, in which multi-employer agreements are prevalent, the ratio is 3.7 million workers to 3 million. This predominance of single-employer agreements (what Lloyd Ulman, 1974, calls 'connective bargaining') over multi-employer agreements (what he calls 'competitive bargaining') is a characteristic of the American collective bargaining institution, although the recent trend in Europe is also towards enterprise-level bargaining, as we will see shortly.

In countries such as France and Italy, where the labour movement formed in clusters around the ideologies of communism, socialism, and catholicism, representation elections and the application of majority rule would have been very difficult to operate effectively. In contrast, American workers are less committed ideologically and tend to assess the utility of unionization on more pragmatic grounds. Uniform setting of wages and other employment conditions at an industry-wide level are practical and effective only in those industries where technological characteristics are fairly uniform throughout, so that job classifications can be standardized and the sizes of enterprises therein are not so diverse. Otherwise, industrial-level bargaining can determine at most the minimum of wage rates and other working conditions, and industrial agreements must be adjusted and supplemented by enterprise- and/or plant-level negotiations which will take local conditions into consideration. Thus, for practically oriented American employees, the natural focus of the union–management relationship is the individual plants or enterprises, in which the trade union can have a more tangible impact on the lives of employees by helping to determine their actual earnings and other working conditions as well as solving grievances, unless a centralization of negotiations at the industrial level can strengthen the union's bargaining power.

From a historical angle, this tendency can be explained as follows. The characteristics of the stage of industrial development at which the industrial labour movement began on a large scale were to have an enduring effect on the later development of the collective bargaining institution. In the United States, powerful trade unions did not arise in major industries until production was highly concentrated in a few large corporations. Derek Bok observes:

These firms were generally strong financially, and they could protect themselves against organizing efforts and bargaining demands in particular plants, since their operations were often dispersed among a number of installations, only some of which were organized. Such giant employers were under much less pressure to band together than they might have been if a strong union had emerged before the process of concentration took place. (Bok, 1971, p. 1406)

The managements of those strong corporations could afford to share some portion of the monopolistic gains with their own employees in order to elicit their willingness to co-operate. Also, as work organizations of those large firms were specific to a certain degree because of their monopolistic positions, their management could benefit from running their own industrial relations. In fact, an embryonic form of present-day plant-based union organizations can be traced as far back as the management-sponsored 'employee representation plans' (ERPs) during the 1920s, when activities of large corporations thrived. These plans allowed employees to select their representatives to meet with management concerning grievances, as well as matters of wages and employment conditions. The ERPs were far from autonomous and independent, but they had a feature common to present-day local unions in that representation was on a plant-by-plant basis and along neither occupational nor craft lines. One of the strongest industrial unions at present, the United Steel Workers, initiated itself by capturing these ERPs and converting the management-sponsored representation electorates into a membership basis in the turmoil of the 1930s.[3]

In Japan, where the large-scale independent union movement did not flourish until the end of the Second World War, this decentralization tendency of bargaining is more clearly discernable. An aspiration to organize industrial unions along European lines, largely inspired by academic advisors, had been subdued by the time of rapid growth in the 1960s, and the dominant bargaining pattern now is between management of individual enterprises and enterprise-based unions. These enterprise-based unions are not local branches of industrial unions; in fact, the industrial unions in Japan are nothing but federations of enterprise-based unions, associated for the purpose of co-ordinating bargaining tactics and political activities, exchanging information, and so on. The enterprise-based unions differ from the so-called 'company union' under the ERPs in that they satisfy statutorily provided conditions of independence from the management.[4] They do not, however, enjoy the exclusive representation right of the American type, and although more than half of them have agreements pertaining to 'union-shop' clauses, court judgements state that these agreements are not enforceable once non-members have been organized into different unions. In fact, in the labour turmoils before the relative stability of the 1960s, splits of employees in one enterprise into rival unions were not rare. Thus, the present-day enterprise-based unions in Japan are not the product of legislations or the remnant of exotic and paternalistic industrial relations; rather, they represent an institution that has spontaneously emerged through adapting to the modern form of business organization.

In Britain, on the other hand, where collective bargaining got its earliest start, the adaptation of bargaining institutions to contemporary situations has not been smooth. Industrial-level bargaining machinery first appeared in the 1880s, when industries were still composed of many small firms whose mutual interests *vis-à-vis* emerging trade unions were represented only by employers' associations; small employers banded together to deal with relatively strong unions outside factory gates. The First World War gave a great impetus to industrial bargaining machinery in Britain because the war brought into being the centralized state control of industries for the fulfilment of war efforts. In the period after the First World War, industry-wide bargaining and national unionism became firmly established.

When British industry was competitive, with many small firms concentrated in particular regions and workers mobile among them, multi-employer (regional- or industrial-level) agreements were highly relevant to the determination of individual employment contracts. However, as the size of firms became larger, internalizing more specific employment structure and more diverse activities, firms could benefit from breaking away from multi-employer bargaining, settling for higher wages, and running their own industrial relations. By the 1960s the multi-employer agreements came to be regarded as fixing only minima, on top of which employees expected improvements based on 'domestic bargaining'. Also, managements of some large companies did not necessarily want to delegate the authority of settling intra-factory matters, such as disciplinary rules and appeals, work practices, the use of job evaluation, etc. to the employers' association.

On the other hand, there was an increase in the bargaining strength of unions and work groups, and shop-level bargaining machinery was developed autonomously throughout the Second World War and thereafter. At the shop level, shop-stewards, who were elected by their fellow workers to represent them *vis-à-vis* management (foreman) and were accredited by the union as its representative, conducted negotiations for changes in working conditions and personal practices as problems arose. This grass-roots access of negotiation was used as well to supplement – often to supersede – the standard wage rates determined by multi-employer agreements. According to a 1964-6 survey by the National Board for Prices and Incomes, such supplementary payments in the form of piece-rates, bonuses, and incentive pay amounted to one-third of the total earnings of workers. The *ad hoc* nature of fragmented negotiations gave rise to anomalies, however, in the treatment of different groups of workers within a plant, and those anomalies became sources of grievances for workers. Any change of pay somewhere triggered further demands elsewhere. The loss of control over the determination of actual earnings of workers by the formal bargaining apparatus was called the 'wage drift'.

Also, workshop-level bargaining conducted by shop-stewards was often associated with a large number of wildcat strikes, slow-downs, and other short-lived industrial actions by work groups as they pressed their claims. These industrial actions were called 'unconstitutional' in the sense that 'they occur before the various stages of the appropriate procedure for dealing with disputes have been able to deal with the matter, often indeed before any of the stages have been used' (Donovan Commission, 1968, p. 19, para. 70). The wage drift and wildcat strikes are Siamese twins.

The Donovan Commission (Royal Commission on Trade Unions and Employers' Associations), appointed by the Labour government in 1965 to investigate British industrial relations and to propose recommendations for their reforms, identified the shifting of collective bargaining power from the national centre to the periphery as the principal evil at the time of its *Report* in 1968. The problem was that this fragmentation of bargaining left a sort of vacuum at the enterprise level. But it is at this level that crucial managerial decisions affecting employees directly or indirectly, such as on employment, innovation, pensions, location, and investment, are made. Some traditional bargaining matters may be also more appropriate for enterprise-wide arrangements, such as redundancies arising from the relocation of plants and even wages. In fact, W. E. J. McCarthy, who did research for the Donovan Commission, noted that 'the [shop] steward has an interest in short-circuiting the lower levels of the procedure because he finds that the things he wants can so often only be decided, and decided quickly, at the top' (McCarthy, 1966, p. 31). What was desired was a more systematic approach to enterprise-level bargaining.

But the Donovan Commission was cautious as regards the idea that a stroke of the pen by legislators could solve the problem; it recommended the enactment of the Industrial Relations Act as a first step, which would oblige the 'boards of directors' of corporate enterprises of a certain size to register collective agreements with the Department of Employment and Productivity as their 'public duty'. Initially, companies would be able to register the industry-wide agreements to which they were parties if enterprise-level agreements were lacking. But industry-wide agreements would be unlikely to contain certain matters recommended by the Commission to be registered, such as agreements regulating the positions of shop-stewards, the handling of redundancy and disciplinary matters, and so on. Consequently, it was expected that managements would have to negotiate and register their own agreements on these matters, thereby gradually altering the bargaining structure.

But the Conservative government elected in 1970 did not follow the cautious advice of the Donovan Commission and enacted the Industrial Relations Act of its own version, which put the burden of rehabilitating ailing industrial relations primarily on the shoulders of the trade unions. The Act, enacted in 1971, restricted the legal freedom of employees to engage in unofficial and unconstitutional strikes, put severe restrictions on the closed shop, linked the procedure of union recognition by employers with the settlement of inter-union conflicts, and made the enforcement of union recognition conditional on union registration with the Registrar. Since the Act contained provisions to allow the Registrar to scrutinize union rule-books, it caused a determined effort by the Trades Union Council (TUC) to have member-unions boycott the registration.

'Moreover, [employers] shared the union leaders' dislike of legalism' (Phelps Brown, 1983, p. 191). The Act became ineffectual, and was finally repealed in 1974. The whole episode was a good instance of a point made by the Donovan Commission that legislation cannot create desirable patterns of industrial relations; rather, the patterns of behaviour and customs in industrial relations should have fundamental impacts on the emerging legal structures.

Enterprise- or plant-level bargaining has not been unknown, however, in Britain. So-called 'productivity agreements', initiated at Esso's refinery in the 1960s, were agreements at enterprise or plant level which purported to revise work practices and provide for more efficient uses of manpower and plant in return for concessions on pay. In that decade several companies left their associations in order to sign productivity agreements with the unions. Also, dominating companies in certain industries, such as the National Coal Board or Imperial Chemical Industries Ltd, negotiated with unions to the exclusion of employers' associations, and some large British subsidiaries of American corporations such as Ford disapproved of the employers' associations.

A further important development was the Employment Protection Act (EPA) 1975, which replaced the Industrial Relation Act 1971, and defined the 'recognition' of a union as an act of a single employer (or 'associated' employers) and not of an employers' association. This of course indicates a preference for the method of bargaining by individual enterprises.[5] Also it should be added that, when bargaining by white-collar workers developed in the 1970s, it was usually based on company-level agreements rather than on bargaining at either plant or industry level, because white-collar workers were more mobile between plants within the company (Davies and Freedland, 1979, p. 24). Since information-handling is becoming a relatively increasing part of any enterprise's activities, the extention of bargaining to white-collar workers, as well as the white-collarization of blue-collar workers, may become an important contributing factor to the development of enterprise-level bargaining.

Although there still seems to be some confusion and controversy over the significance of industry-wide agreements, it appears to be in eclipse. In a valuable paper, Brown and Terry (1978) point out that in many cases the minima fixed by national agreements are not even 'floors', but 'safety nets':

When a floor is raised it raises everybody standing on it, even if they are standing on something that raises them off it; when a safety net is raised, on the other hand, the result is merely that those above (unless they are very close to it) have less far to fall. (Brown and Terry, 1978, p. 122)

Using a carefully prepared statistical analysis, they argue convincingly that nationally determined wage schedules are thus becoming pretty irrelevant to workers of large enterprises; it is only small enterprises that are zealous of following multi-employer agreements.

Brown and Terry also pointed out that 'formal' bargaining has been replacing the fragmented bargaining that the Donovan Commission saw as the principal evil of industrial relations in the 1960s. One of the outstanding features of the rise of formal enterprise and work-place bargaining has been the spread of job evaluation. Under this scheme, through a more or less sytematic analysis of job content, the relative pay for different jobs within an enterprise or work-place can be established in a way acceptable to the individual workers affected. So Brown and Terry go on to argue that 'the expression "wage drift" should be buried altogether' (1978, p. 132).

As a twin to the emerging formalization of pay structures, shop-steward's roles are also becoming more formalized. An increase in the number of shop-stewards engaged full time on trade union activities has been observed. Also, Brown, Ebsworth, and Terry (1978) report the development of shop-steward organizations such as joint steward committees, in which shop-stewards from different unions sit together, and these tend to become better at coping with inter-union differences. Thus, even in Britain, where such prewar inheritances as industry-wide bargaining and national unionism are still visible, the comprehensive determination of wages and other working conditions has moved away from national or regional industry-wide levels and gravitated towards enterprise level, or plant level in the case of multi-plant enterprises.

That the tendency towards a gradual eclipse of multi-employer agreements by single-employer agreements is becoming universal (with a few exceptions such as in Belgium and Sweden) is documented in many recent works, including a study conducted by Norman Dufty (1975) for the OECD. Even in France, where the aforementioned ideological cleavage among unions, and possibly the relative weakness of grass-roots organizations *vis-à-vis* managements, has made supra-enterprise-level negotiations and state regulations traditionally more relevant to the determination of wages and other working conditions, collective bargaining and workers' organizations at enterprise level have become visibly stronger and more important, particularly since May 1968. The philosophy of the union movement has shifted as well. A commitment to worker self-management as a goal first by the socialist CFDT and then, more reluctantly, by the communist CGT has led to more interest in enterprise affairs by trade unionists.

As I have argued, this trend is an inevitable consequence of many factors developing within large corporate firms: the generation of the organizational rent (monopolistic gains) to which employees may have legitimate partial claims; the need for more comprehensive and formal pay structures accompanying internal employment structures and serving as sure foundations for managerial policy-making; the emergence of white-collar employees as bargaining partners who have a stake in their employing enterprises, as well as the white-collarization of blue-collar workers; the increasing impact of managerial policy on the welfare of employees; and so on. In order to cope with these factors, enterprise-level bargaining surely serves better than industry-wide bargaining or fragmented workshop-level bargaining.[6]

Of course, to say that there is a general tendency towards enterprise-level bargaining is neither to deny that there are countervailing forces working towards a recentralization of bargaining or a further decentralization of it, nor to suggest that the outcomes of enterprise-level bargaining are completely independent of the conditions of the economy and the industry in which the enterprises are embedded. For instance, in Britain, the enterprise-level agreements of large companies are now often negotiated on the labour side by a team of full-time national union officials and senior shop-stewards from various plants (Edmonds, 1977, p. 140). This increasing concentration of decision-making authority in the hands of national officials was also observed in the United States after the Second World War (see MacDonald, 1967, pp. 561–3). 'Recentralization' in this sense is an inevitable reaction of the union trying to exert a countervailing power against mighty corporations by using the bargaining expertise of trade union officials more effectively. However, whether this recentralization on the union side will necessarily accompany the recentralization of bargaining authority to employers' associations is doubtful. When we talk about the general tendency towards enterprise-level bargaining, we are concerned with the fact that agreements tend to be more with a single employer than with multi-employers, and not with whether bargaining agents on the labour side are employees of the enterprise concerned.

Some may also argue that the widely observed, so-called 'pattern bargaining' is a variant of industry-wide bargaining. This procedure allows the (national) union first to negotiate a favourable settlement with any one of a few key corporations; this settlement then becomes the 'pattern' of major competitors and the target for smaller firms in the industry of firms in related industries. As negotiations move onward from the pattern-generating firms to smaller firms, deviation from the pattern can normally be expected. However, how is the pattern generated at the outset at the key firm? How are the inter-enterprise margins determined? It is one thing to say that the determination of wages and employment conditions is affected by external conditions (which my analytical model does not deny), and it is another to say that the wages can be treated as exogenous data to enterprises (which it does).

The employees' influence in the decision-making of the firm may also be exercised through administrative and legislative regulations. In France, for example, many work-rules that in the United States would be the subject of collective bargaining are specified in law and administrative regulation, and enforced by the state. Also, provisions such as those on minimum wages negotiated by a portion of an industry can be extended by administrative regulations to the rest of the industry and made enforceable.

Some attribute the origin of this centralized control over the labour market and industrial relations to the relative weakness of grass-roots organizations within shops and enterprises at the time of the historical formation of collective bargaining institutions.[7] Kahn-Freund (1977) submits a thesis ('with great caution') that '[i] t is sometimes (but not always) the case that, as the union gets industrially stronger, the significance of collective bargaining grows and that of legislation diminishes' (p. 39). We can now risk the converse of this proposition:

a weakening of union organization may lead unions to seek to use their political power to influence the conduct of enterprises through the enactment of laws or the promotion of government regulations. Employees' aspirations of exercising influence over issues not recognized as bargainable may imply the same tendency.

The increased political activities of trade unions in the United States in the 1970s, seeking government regulation of occupational safety, control over exports of capital and technology by US companies (e.g. the Burke–Hartke proposal), and so on, might have been due partly to the weakening of union power at enterprise and plant level, and/or the relative limitation of mandatory bargainable subjects.

But legislated rules tend to be rather rigid and sweeping because of their inevitable general formulation. Further, in the United States, where the decentralization of administrative power is the tradition, government regulation tends to be dispersed among a large number of agencies. The increase and dispersal of regulations and regulatory agencies have given rise to management complaints of multiple inspection, overlapping jurisdiction, conflicting policy goals, and so on. A strong case can be made in such a country for a flexible decentralized system in preference to the assertion of central control by executive authorities.

Finally, within multi-plant enterprises the bargaining focus may be moving towards a further decentralization to plant level if technological innovations of enterprise activities are very rapid, diverse, and uneven.[8] In such cases, enterprise-level bargaining may not be able to cope with the need for a comprehensive determination of wages and other working conditions. Also, enterprise-level rule-making may impede the efficient operation of relatively newer plants. In such cases, the management may choose plant-level negotiations instead of uniform enterprise-level negotiations. However, plant-level negotiations have more in common with enterprise-level negotiations than with fragmented workshop-level negotiations, in that they are more formalized and that a bargaining partner is often the top management, who is responsible for the co-ordination of decision-making within the firm.

This final point suggests one difficulty associated with enterprise-level bargaining: that is, how can a single union fairly aggregate the preferences and opinions of possibly disparate constitutents? Age differences aside, the craft union represents a relatively homogeneous group; whereas large enterprise-based bargaining units are likely to comprise diverse employees in terms of jobs, ages, employment status, and other characteristics. In a democratic framework of the union based on the majority vote principle, union leaders are likely to be more sensitive to demands of the average employee (the median voter). As Freeman and Medoff (1979) argue, this mode of representation is more conducive to internal efficiency if public goods problems, such as safety provisions on the shop-floor, are at issue; for the efficient allocation of public goods requires the aggregate of marginal benefits over all employees to be set equal to the marginal cost of producing public goods. The union's voting mechanism clearly serves the purpose of approximating the average preference better than the competitive mechanism, which values the preference of the marginal employee. But this merit may turn to demerit in other respects. For instance, the interests of younger employees in job security may be given less weight in relation to wage and pension benefit demands of relatively senior employees. Also, managerial concessions to relatively senior employees may have a spill-over effect on wages of relatively younger employees within the same firm. Then the problem of the 'classical' unemployment may be aggravated — the type of unemployment caused by too high wages. (I have discussed this already at the end of Chapter 7.)

The diverse preferences arising from different types of jobs may be represented by separate unions based on different constituent units even within the framework of single-employer bargaining. But if one enterprise–one union is a conventional rule, as in Japan,[9] the problem of fair representation may become difficult to cope with as the firm size increases. In Japan, there is a clear tendency for enterprises to spin-off divergent activities in the form of subsidiary firms and subcontracting rather than to integrate diverse activities under the umbrella of a single corporation. As a result, the average size of Japanese firms tends to remain small relative to, say, the typical American firm in terms of employees.[10] There are many efficiency and cultural reasons to account for this quasi-disintegration tendency of the Japanese firm, but clearly the desire of management to deal with a relatively homogeneous group of employees is one of most importance.[11] This decentralization of bargaining is tacitly consented to by the union leader and employees of major Japanese firms who have vested interests in their exclusive participation in the organizational rent produced therein.

Thus, the tendency towards enterprise-level bargaining, albeit more conducive to *internal* efficiency, may spin-off some of the difficult problems to the macro-level, with the consequences of classical unemployment, unequal wages and other working conditions between larger and smaller firms, etc. A more detailed treatment of these issues in the macro-dimension is regrettably beyond the scope of this study.

The scope of collective agreements

As the bargaining level gravitates to the enterprise level, institutional efficiency may become potentially more accessible, but of course this is not guaranteed. The institutional efficiency of the collective bargaining model crucially hinges upon what subjects are talked about at the bargaining table (and written into agreements).

Statutorily, the range of joint decision-making in collective bargaining is somewhat tersely defined in the United States. As quoted already, the management and the employees' representatives are obliged to 'bargain in good faith with respect to wages, hours, and other terms and conditions of employment'. The phrase 'other terms and conditions of employment' is capable of various interpretations. According to NLRB rulings and court decisions, the union can compel the management to bargain before deciding on such measures as replacing part of the work-force by a subcontractor and introducing labour-saving machinery likely to lead to redundancies. However, decisions about closures and relocation of the plant do not seem to constitute mandatory subjects for bargaining unless they are devices to avoid a collective agreement, although there may well be obligations to bargain about their effects on employees, such as severance pay. Basic managerial decisions as to what to produce, what to invest, and how much to charge for outputs has clearly fallen outside the range of mandatory collective bargaining.

As for matters other than mandatory subjects, here each party is free to bargain or not to bargain. In many cases the range of bargaining is defined by both parties, by assigning decision-making on certain matters explicitly to 'management rights'. Some management rights clauses enumerate those items belonging to managerial prerogatives in concerete details; other clauses only state a general principle, such as 'the management of business in all its phases and details shall remain vested in the employer.' Managements favouring the short form feel that the enumeration of rights is dangerous lest it is not exhaustive and some unforeseen decision is omitted. According to the 1976 BLS survey, 918 agreements out of 1570 agreements covering 1000 workers or more included management rights provisions in one form or other.

This practice of management rights provisions and the statutory definition of mandatory subjects of collective bargaining have tended to limit the range of employees' influence through collective bargaining in the United States. Of course, in spite of these formal limitations, implicit or explicit dealing may take place concerning managerial decisions of significance to employees. Since, as indicated above, American collective bargaining is usually conducted at the enterprise or plant level, it is hard to believe that the management would make a major policy decision without reflecting on the union's possible reactions to it. In fact, the management must bargain with the union if the decision in question will have a significant adverse impact on employment conditions in a narrow sense (hours, job security, etc.). Yet, in general, the influence of unions on managerial policy-making has been rather limited and indirect; furthermore, unions themselves have failed to show an interest in extending the scope of collective bargaining into policy matters until recently. Thus, the frequently made assertion that the American collective bargaining institution is equivalent to European co-determination in scope and coverage tends to be doubtful.[12]

There has however recently emerged a very interesting sign of change in this regard. In the 1982 negotiations with the General Motors Corporation and Ford Company, the United Automobile Workers proposed a reduction in sales prices of products and an increase in job securities in exchange for restraint on wage rates. This development should be recognized as a noteworthy and positive phenomenon, in that the trade unionists abandoned their traditional negative attitude towards the tradability of wage rates for managerial policy changes, and management agreed that such managerial decisions as pricing could be an official subject of negotiation. Such broadening of the scope of collective bargaining would be likely to contribute to an improvement of its institutional efficiency, as suggested by proposition 2 on p. 119.

The statutorily provided scope of collective bargaining in Britain is not much broader than in the United States.[13] Section 126 (1) of the EPA 1975 defines collective bargaining between a recognized union and an employer (or two or more associated employers) as 'negotiations related to or connected with one or more matters specified in Section 29 (1) of the 1974 Act'; and that section of the Trade Union and Labor Relation Act 1974 [TULRA] specifies, in addition to matters related to procedual rules, such matters as: '(a) terms and conditions of employment, or physical conditions in which any workers are required to work ... [and] ... (b) engagement or nonengagement, or termination or suspension of employment or the duties of employment of one or more workers'. The trade union and its members are immune to actions in tort in respect of any industrial action connected with these 'trade disputes'.

Thus, it may appear that issues over employment fall in the range of 'joint regulation' by the management and the union recognized by it. However, the substantive obligation imposed on management seems to be only to consult. The employer must give to the union, in advance of dismissal, the information specified in section 99 (5) of the EPA 1975, notably, 'information about the reasons for the proposed dismissals, the numbers and types of workers involved, and the proposed procedures for selecting the employees and carrying on dismissal'. In some cases the process of consultation may develop into bargaining, but the law does not require the management to seek agreement with the union on this matter: the decision formally belongs to management.

One noteworthy feature of the statutory arrangement of British collective bargaining is an extensive disclosure requirement imposed on management. Under section 1721 of the EPA 1975, an employer is obliged to disclose to a union recognized by it information that is necessary for carrying on collective bargaining. The Advisory, Conciliation, and Arbitration Service (ACAS), which is an administrative agency providing facilities for non-coercive settlement of collective disputes, sets forth a sort of guideline on items that have obvious relevance to traditional wage bargaining. They include such managerial matters as 'planned changes in work methods; available manpower plans; investment plans', and performance-related matters such as 'productivity and efficiency data; savings from increased productivity and output; return on capital invested; sales and state of order book' (ACAS Code of Practice 2, Disclosure of Information to Trade Unions for Collective Bargaining Purposes, para. 11).

However, the implication of these informational disclosures is yet to be seen. Some expect that a frank disclosure of information regarding the affairs of a company will enable unions to clarify the objective bargaining situation to employees, prevent rumours, create a greater sense of employees' involvement with the company, and increase the incentive for effort. Others argue that the union may wish to utilize the disclosed information only to derive better terms in wages, provide ideological and agitational reinforcement for claims, etc. In any case, the statutory requirement of information disclosure may, by compelling management to justify its managerial decisions, involve the union potentially in management decisions.

A further and more formal union involvement in managerial policy-making is advocated by some. When the Industrial Relations Act 1971 was repealed in 1974, the Labour government announced its intention to expand 'industrial democracy' — that is, to extend workers' influence over managerial policy-making. One conceivable mechanism serving this purpose is the appointment of employees' representatives on the board of directors, such as was subsequently proposed in the ill-fated Bullock Report (1977) of the Committee of Inquiry on Industrial Democracy (to be discussed in the next chapter). The other idea is to extend the scope of collective bargaining to the area of managerial policy-making beyond the traditional realm of wages and other conditions of employment.

In Europe this type of extension of the scope of collective bargaining is not unknown. In Italy, for example, some experiments occurred in making collective agreements which purported to regulate managerial prerogatives in regard to investment. This process began with the Fiat agreement of 1973 and was followed by Montedison, Olivetti, and others. While those agreements are voluntary, one of the most influential unions in Britain, the General and Municipal Workers Union (GMWU), sought, albeit unsuccessfully, the enactment of 'a general requirement on all employers to establish a procedure whereby strategic planning decisions can be jointly determined with representatives of organized trade unions.'

If 'joint regulation' over managerial policy-making is sought bilaterally and voluntarily by both bargaining partners, it will undoubtedly constitute a factor contributing to institutional efficiency. However, it would not seem wise to legislate for the general obligation to bargain on managerial policy. The reason is, above all, the difficulty of devising an efficient and effective sanction against the management that fails to bargain (in good faith).[14] In traditional bargaining it is ultimately the union's ability to make a credible threat of industrial action, in case of failure to reach an agreement, that moves the management towards a compromise. However, when the employees' concern is with more job security and fewer lay-offs, is it a good tactic for the union to appeal to industrial action, particularly in places where employees engaged in such action will not be protected legally from their employers' possible retaliation?

The application of arbitration procedures to managerial policy issues in dispute will not be wise, either. As exemplified by the fact that courts have been reluctant to make any judgement on managerial policy issues in any circumstance (the so-called 'business judgement rule'), the third party generally finds it difficult to adjudicate on such questions. The application of arbitration procedure on this matter will only entail costly and inefficient bureaucracy. Thus, unless developed voluntarily and bilaterally, the statutorily imposed extension of collective bargaining into the realm of managerial policy decisions is not likely to be effective.

An alternative measure to collective bargaining for extending the union's influence on managerial policy-making is the establishment of a joint committee or consultative machinery. The joint (management and union) committee defines problems, finds facts, and, if possible, seeks solutions in a co-operative manner, which may sometimes be impossible in the confrontational atmosphere of formal collective bargaining. Through consultative machinery the management explains to, consults with, and possibly seeks the consent of employees on managerial policy matters that are the prerogative of management. This type of consultation has been operating quite effectively in unionized enterprises in Japan. In Germany, formal consultative machinery is provided statutorily, as we shall see in the next chapter, although the role of unions in it is informal.

However, the famous Human Relations Committee (HRC) set up in the American steel industry in 1959 illustrates the pitfalls of joint committee machinery in the United States (see McDonald, 1967). The HRC initiated many innovations in industrial relations. Among them was an agreement providing that any recommendation made by the HRC during the term of the agreement would take effect immediately. Thus the HRC substituted a more flexible and continuous form of bargaining for the rigidities of traditional negotiation procedures. However, such empowerment with the HRC generated resentment among the rank-and-file as being undemocratic, and in the 1965 election the union leadership associated with the HRC lost to a rival slate of officers pledged to return to the traditional collective bargaining framework. Ever since, trade union leadership has been rather cautious about joint committees.

There also appears to be a statutory constraint against broadening the scope of joint committees in the United States. Managerial interference with the formation and administration of a labour organization is unlawful, as is insistence on bargaining about a matter that is not within the scope of legal obligation; and this must be born in mind by any management that seeks to develop procedures for involving employees in the decision-making process of the firm. There is a danger that such machinery will be held to be an employer-dominated or -assisted labour organization.

Thus in the United States there have been at least some inhibitions to broadening the scope of joint-committee responsibilities. Nevertheless, it seems doubtful that a reversion to the exclusive use of traditional collective bargaining machinery could successfully meet two recent major challenges. In the early 1970s there first arose a public concern with the level of workers' dissatisfaction in the work process; and since the late 1970s even more serious concern has been voiced over productivity slow-downs in traditional industries. These two problems are regarded by many as being capable of solution only through greater labour–management co-operation. Labour–management committees may serve to provide opportunities for co-operative and rational discussion of problems and their possible solutions. They may also enable workers to understand the affairs of the corporation and to improve morale and cost consciousness, as well as creating a greater sense of involvement and identification with the corporation, without spoiling the autonomy of the union. In fact, the rhythm of development in that direction appears to be felt.

Is this just crisis management? Or is it more likely that the joint-committee approach is developing or is likely to develop as a US-style approach to employee participation in the firm? An answer to these questions seems premature; however, it would appear that a prima facie case can be made to the effect that greater management–union co-operation is emerging even in the land of functionalism.

The duration of collective agreements

According to the 1976 BLS survey, to which we have had occasion to refer, 1094 agreements out of 1574 had been in effect for thirty-six months or more. One agreement had been in effect for as long as eight years. In contrast to this, no fixed duration has prevailed traditionally in Britain. However, some movement has been observed recently towards British fixed-term agreements, normally for one-year periods, in part arising from the increasing prevalence of more formal enterprise-level bargaining and in part arising from the impetus of the recent incomes policy with the so-called 'twelve-month rule' restricting renegotiation to an annual basis. In Germany and Japan annual revision of agreements is normal. In Japan any agreement in effect for more than two years is not enforcible. Thus, one may say that the duration of collective agreements is relatively longer in the United States. What, besides the obvious administrative cost of renegotiation, accounts for the prolongation of American agreements? What kind of efficiency implication does it have?

As noted, once a union is selected by an appropriate unit and certified by the NLRB, it has the right of exclusive representation. But for how long? In the normal principal–agency relationship, the authority of an agent can normally be terminated by the principal at any time. Under the principle of majority rule, however, dissident members of the unit lose the power to act for themselves, unlike an ordinary principal, as long as the union retains its representation right. How often are members given the opportunity to repudiate an unsatisfactory representative and either revert to individual bargaining or substitute another agent? As Archibald Cox stipulates, 'The issue is to turn on striking a balance between the interest in stability and the values of freedom of choice' (1958, p. 8). The law provides that no election can be conducted in any bargaining unit in which a valid election has been held during the preceeding twelve months. This provision guarantees a stability in the relationship between employees and employers at least for this period of time. But not only that. The NLRB has now established what is called the 'contract bar' doctrine. This states that a valid collective agreement will ordinarily prevent the holding of an election among employees covered by the agreement. The bar is, in general, for three years.

In other words, the petition for a new election is untimely if it is filed during the term of an existing contract, with a three-year maximum in the case of contracts that run for more than three years. Thus, the union is motivated to enter into agreements with the management that extend at least for three years so that its representation right will not be challenged for the maximum period of time.

On the other hand, management is usually protected from industrial action by no-strike, no-lockout clauses during the period in which the agreement is effective. According to the 1976 BLS survey, more than 90 per cent of contracts surveyed contained some kind of provision for strike and lockout bans. Since lockouts are a less significant feature of industrial relations, the peace obligation is more important as a remedy to assist the management. Any dispute arising during the peacetime regarding the interpretations of the agreement or matters not covered by agreements can be relegated to arbitration procedures. The arbitrator, like a judge, relies on statutory law (the legally enforceable collective agreements) or formulates 'just and reasonable' laws from the practice of the parties and the mores of current employment relations. Hence the peace obligation provision will predictably affect industrial relations for years to come, giving a more stable environment for managerial decision-making.

There are, then, bilateral and mutual interests for both management and union to extend the duration of agreements within a reasonable bound, say three to five years in the United States. During that period, the union's authority as an exclusive representative of the employee is guaranteed; and management is assured of its discretionary decision-making power within the bound limited by the agreement and is given a sure foundation for cost calculation necessary for managerial policy-making. The prolongation of the agreement period should be seen as a natural consequence of the unique framework of the collective bargaining institution in the United States.

Long-term agreements fix the wage rates over the contract period, only subjecting them to automatic adjustments at scheduled dates in the future through a cost-of-living escalator. However, because the cost-of-living adjustment (COLA) is limited in its coverage and extent, the real wage rates are susceptible to influences of outside variables. Some economists, such as Fischer (1977), and Bruno and Sachs (1979), argue that in the United States, where overlapping, long-term wage agreements are prevalent, a monetary expansion can reduce the real wage and ease the profit squeeze because of the limited effect of wage indexation.

Thus, there may be a strong linkage between monetary policy and output in the United States; in other words, there is a potential role for the pursuance of an activist monetary policy. On the other hand, in countries like Japan and Germany, where wage negotiations take place annually, the real wage rates tend to be adjusted more by the bargaining partners themselves, leaving limited room for activist monetary policy. I do not intend to go into this macroeconomic issue here, but my concern below will be the impact of long-term agreements on the internal efficiency of the unionized firm. I would like to argue that *de facto* exogenization of wage rates during the contract period tends to spoil internal efficiency in the world of uncertainty.

As the analysis in Part II indicated, internal efficiency requires that the determination of real wage rates and managerial policy-making relevant to the welfare of employees, as regards employment and investment, must be coordinated in a particular way. Speaking more technically, the efficiency locus, or the Edgeworth contract curve, from which an efficient bargaining solution must be chosen lies in the space spanned by an axis representing the wage rate and an axis representing relevant policy variables (see Fig. 6.1). In the world of uncertainty, the contract curve will shift as events evolve during the agreed period of contract. Notwithstanding this possibility, if the bargaining partners have such forecasting power as to enumerate all potentially possible states of the world and to predict how the contract curve will shift depending on states of the world, they will settle for an agreement specifying a point (i.e., a schedule of both wage rates and managerial policies) on the shifting contract curve for each state of the world, the actual adoption of which is contingent upon the occurrence of the relevant state.

If such an ideal contingent agreement were possible, then we would not have to worry about possible inefficiency, i.e. the possibility of a dislocation off the contract curve during the contract period. However, such ideal contingent agreements may be too cumbersome, complicated, and beyond bounded rationality. Collective bargaining agreements are rarely contingent on outside events. The only important exception is the partial indexing of wages to the cost of living, already referred to.

In spite of the absence of explicit contingent agreement, however, there is a case in which *ex post* adjustments of managerial policy for a fixed real wage rate remain a bargaining game equilibrium. That is the case in which the equilibrium (efficient and fair) wage rate remains unchanged in spite of changes in external variables and only the managerial policy variables (other than wages) ought to be adapted to business cycle fluctuations (see p. 98-9; also proposition 3 in the introduction to Chapter 8). In this case, a long-term wage agreement with ideal indexing may remain efficient and power-equilibrating in spite of the pre-fixing of money wages, provided there is an implicit agreement between the parties regarding the way in which the managerial policy variables are to be adjusted by the management as events evolve during the contract period. The internally efficient adjustment must always be a point on the moving contract curve that requires management to employ more workers and to make a greater investment than the *ex post* maximization of share value subject to the predetermined wage rate would require. To adjust the managerial policy as events evolve so as to maximize the share value for a fixed wage rate is a 'bad' strategy from the organizational point of view in the following sense. It will lead to an inefficient outcome, that is to a point off (to the left of) the contract curve (in terms of Fig. 6.1), although it may increase the shareholders' benefits at the sacrifice of employees' interests.

Thus, the institutional efficiency of long-term wage agreements seems to hinge upon whether the management is bound by an implicit agreement as described above regarding the adjustment of managerial policy. If its motivation is in the pursuit of a unilateral *ex post* share-value maximization, the outcome is likely to be inefficient and unfair from the organizational point of view.

Is the management of the American unionized firm subject to strong pressure for *ex post* value maximization? Or is it bound by an efficient implicit agreement with the union to stay on the contract curve during the prolonged period of the agreement? This is an empirical question which I am not ready to answer.[15] Yet the impression gained is that there seem to exist many factors operating in the American economy motivating the management in the ceaseless pursuit of value maximization. For example, the extent and speed of information-handling by security analysts has been accelerated by the development of information technology, and the management of large corporations is closely monitored to ensure that they follow the value-maximizing objective continuously; this information is of course fed into the board room as well as to the potential take-over bidders. Furthermore, the managers' personal interests are linked to the current price of shares through stock option plans. In addition, the diversification and multinationalization of corporate activities is making management control by means other than financial control more difficult.

The increasing dominance of financial specialists (the financial committee) in the management teams of large corporations may be interpreted as an indicator of the strengthening of value-maximizing discipline imposed on management. Paradoxically, however, apparent efficiency in making a continuous value-maximizing policy, if combined with the rigidity of wages set by a long-term collective agreement, may result in a more fundamental inefficiency from the organizational point of view. The often talked about 'short-sightedness' of financial managers may be taken as referring to this possibility.

As another side of the same coin, if the union is excluded from voicing itself in the sphere of managerial policy-making, and employees are barred from making gains in job security and long-run chances of promotion, the union is naturally compelled to mobilize its bargaining power only for securing higher current wages. In fact, the conservatism of union leaders frequently leads them to bargain away even their bargaining rights on certain bargainable subjects for more visible wage gains. In some cases, the union resorts to the imposition of work rules, limiting the scope of jobs that individual workers can be assigned to and restricting flexible transfers of workers between jobs for the purpose of job security. Such inadequate substitution for direct bargaining over employment is bound to lead to technologically redundant employment and is apt to foster a misplaced resentment of the management against trade unionism itself.

Thus the higher wages, higher lay-offs (and less investment), and adversarial industrial relations that seem to have stagnated some of the American unionized industries in the 1970s may be attributable partly to the inefficient, noncooperative framework of their collective bargaining institution. The preceding theoretical model suggests that revitalizing those industries requires broadening the scope of the collective bargaining institution and, possibly, more flexible bilateral wage adjustments therein.

Summary

This chapter has identified three factors that affect the performance character-istics of the shareholders' sovereignty-cum-collective bargaining model: (1) the level of collective bargaining, (2) the demarcation between collective bargaining and managerial prerogatives, and (3) the duration of the collective agreement. It has been maintained that the achievement of organizational equilibrium (co-operative solution) requires major agreements regarding at least wages and other employment conditions to be concluded at the enterprise level or plant level. The brief survey of major collective bargaining institutions in the United States, Britain, and elsewhere indicates that the general tendency is in fact towards an increasing importance of enterprise-level bargaining and the gradual eclipse of national and fragmented bargaining. However, it has been also suggested that some important issues at the macro-level remain unresolved, or are even aggra-vated, under this development. Among those issues, the possibility of classical unemployment caused by high wages of incumbent employees and the issue of fair distribution at the societal level were mentioned.

As for the demarcation between collective bargaining and managerial pre-rogatives, it was indicated that the scope of collective bargaining tends to be somewhat broadened and/or that managerial consultations with the employees' body regarding managerial policies are developing in many places. Such official or unofficial broadening of the scope of joint decision-making would contribute to an approximation of organizational equilibrium, provided that the develop-ment is voluntary and bilaterally consented to by both the union and manage-ment.

The prolongation of the duration of collective agreements in the United States has been analysed as a natural consequence of the unique statutory frame-work for the collective bargaining institution therein. I have argued, by referring to the model analysis in Chapters 6 and 7, that the fixation of wages over a prolonged period, coupled with the discipline of short-run value maximization on management, is likely to lead to instituional inefficiency in the world of uncertainty.

Chapter 10

The Participative Management Model

Politics and ideologies of participation

In the last chapter we found that, when collective bargaining was conducted at the supra-enterprise (territorial, national, or regional) level, a vacuum was created for joint regulation at the enterprise level, which is the very level at which crucial decisions affecting the economic welfare of employees are taken. We also found that, even if collective bargaining was in fact conducted at the enterprise level, its scope could well fall short of the breadth necessary to cover managerial policy issues relevant to employees. For these reasons, the institutional efficiency of collective bargaining may deteriorate. One way out of this difficulty is of course to develop efficient bargaining at the enterprise level; but another alternative is to involve employees in the managerial policy-making process of the enterprise through the organ of corporate governance.

We refer to this scheme as 'participative management', and question whether the quality of a firm's decision-making from the viewpoint of efficiency is improved once it is instituted. The answer depends mainly upon (among other things) the institutional framework of the corporate organ and the industrial relational tradition in which such a model is embedded. Let us take up two prototypes of the model, which are contrasted in these two respects: the one defined by the West Germany Co-determination Act 1976 (Gesetz uber die Mitbestimmung der Arbeitnehmer), and the other proposed by the majority of members of the Bullock Committee in Britain in 1977.

The German experience of workers' participation in corporate governance, known as co-determination, can be traced back to the period of Allied control after the Second World War, during which the more important enterprises of the coal and steel industries (called the 'Montan' industry), most of them located in the British occupied zone, practised co-determination. According to this scheme, the supervisory board or *Aufsichtsrat*, a unique corporate organ which had functions similar to those of the board of directors of a corporation or company under Anglo-American law, consisted of five shareholder representatives, five employee representatives, and a 'neutral' chairman. According to the German trade unions, this parity representation had 'broken down the authoritarian attitudes which were particularly prevalent' in the coal and steel industries.[1] On 16 May 1950 the Allied High Commission transformed those industries to new ones established under German law. This could have meant the end of co-determination, because German corporate law did not provide for it; however, threatened with a strike by the unions, the German Parliament introduced a scheme of co-determination applicable to the Montan industry, modelled after the Allied practice. In other industries a minor form of co-determination was introduced in 1952 by the Works Constitution Act (Betriebsverfassungsgesetz). This Act gave employees only a minority of votes on the supervisory board and preserved the traditional shareholder control over management. After intense parliamentary debate, however, a new law of co-determination for non-Montan industries was introduced in 1976 which allocated employees half of the seats of the supervisory board of all German corporations having more than 2000 employees.[2] Notwithstanding the adoption of this Act, for reasons given later, the Montan industry continues to be governed by the special Co-determination Act 1950 for the industry.

If German co-determination was originally intended as a means of democratizing the authoritarian structure of the Montan industry, the setting up of the Bullock Committee in Britain in 1977 was to a great extent a matter of political expediency. In 1972 an important document was released by the European Community Commission (ECC) regarding employees' participation, namely the *Draft Fifth Directive on Harmonization of the Company Laws of the Member States*. The EEC Treaty Article 54 empowers the European Council to issue directives in order to harmonize the national laws of member-states. Such directives are binding upon the member-states only as regards the result to be achieved: consequently, some implementing action on the members' part is required.[3] This means that, once proposed directives by the Commission are unanimously adopted by the European Council, the member-states' laws have to comply with them. The original version of the Draft Fifth Directive provided that companies with more than 500 employees should have a minority representation of employees on a supervisory board of the German type, or that the supervisory board should co-opt its members, to which the representative body of employees may have veto power.[4] A leading authority on British industrial relations, H. Clegg, had this to say as regards the impact of the Draft Directive on the British scene:[5]

at that time Mr Heath was very much an advocate of going onto Europe, ... Because he felt that, having tried the Industrial Relations Act, and having tried a statutory incomes policy, there must be *some* way of improving British industrial relations, and conceivably this [the introduction of a participative management model] could be it. When it became known by the General Council [of the TUC] that Mr Heath was going to propose supervisory boards with one-third representation for workers, Jack Jones [the TUC General Secretary] said to his colleagues, 'Look, the one thing you cannot do is to say "No" . . . . That's not the way to negotiate, as you know . . . .' Anyway, he said fifty per cent, and everybody . . . assured that worker representation would never be implemented, said, 'Yes, let's go for fifty per cent', as a proper reply to this kind of offer from the Conservative government. (Clegg, 1977, p. 5.21)

But in 1974 the Heath government fell, and there followed a Labour government, a 'social contract', the repeal of the Industrial Relations Act, and commitments to trade unions and industrial democracy. '[A]ccepting the need for a radical extension of industrial democracy in the control of companies by means of representation on boards of directors, and accepting the essential role of trade union organizations in this processes, to consider how such an extension can be best achieved', the Committee of Inquiry on Industrial Democracy, headed by Lord Bullock, a historian from Oxford, was appointed by the government in 1975. The Report (Bullock Committee, 1977) was completed within a year and a half, and was published in January 1977 subject to the dissent of its three industrialist and banker members.

Before the Bullock Report had been made public, however, portions of it had found their way into the national press accompanied by harsh comments from the Confederation of British Industry (CBI). The unions were not as unanimous about the desirability of employee participation in corporate management as they had appeared. Some powerful unions, such as the GMWU, accepted the idea of extending the unions' involvement in managerial decision-making, but proposed to achieve this objective by an extension of traditional collective bargaining. The government did not seem to be serious about the Bullock proposal, either. It reacted to the Bullock Report and subsequent debates with a compromised White Paper, *Industrial Democracy* (UK Government, 1978). According to this, the statutory right to board representation for employees was to be introduced only after a transitory period during which the management was only obliged to discuss the corporate planning with a committee representing the employees. However, no action was taken even on this diluted proposal before the Labour government fell in 1979.

Meanwhile, faced with criticism on the original draft of the Fifth Directive from Britain, Italy, and France, the ECC published a so-called 'Green Paper' on 'Employee Participation and Company Structure' (ECC, 1975b), in which it recognized the need for flexibility in implementing the objective of employee participation in corporate organs. Subsequently, in 1978 a working document was prepared by the Commission for the European Parliament, in accordance with the 'Green Paper', to modify the Draft Fifth Directive. According to this, the national legislatures of member-states would have a certain degree of freedom in designing corporate structures allowing employee participation during the transitional period of five years. They could even choose a system of one-tier boards of the Anglo-Saxon type, without employee participation 'but combined with an institution representative of the employees'. This was interpreted as allowing the option of extending collective bargaining to the sphere of managerial policy-making.

The Legal Affairs Committee of the European Parliament considered all those documents prepared by the Commission and, in November 1981, finally adopted the motion for a resolution in Parliament to approve a Fifth Directive. The parliamentary discussion on the motion began in 1982. If Parliament passes the motion, the matter will be forwarded to the Council of the European Communities for a final decision. It may still take some time, however, for the Council to act on the Directive. This lack of urgency may be reflected in the legislative inaction on a participative scheme in Britain; and it now seems that the introduction of a participative scheme to UK companies in the near future will be more on a voluntary and experimental basis.[6]

Although the Bullock proposal is politically dead, the discussion surrounding the Report provides useful material for a theoretical comparison of the collective bargaining model and the participative management model. It illustrates just how difficult it is to introduce statutorily a participative scheme in an economy where a strong trade union tradition exists, and to draw a clear line of demarcation as to what matters are to be discussed through participation and what matters are relevant for discussion through collective bargaining.

The admission of employees' representatives to the corporate organ surely implies a divergence from the traditional Anglo-American common law philosophy that the company (the corporation) is the property of, and is to be managed in the sole interest of, the shareholders, towards a philosophy that sees the interest of the company as being formed by a balancing of the interests of the shareholders and the employees. Article 3 of the ECC Draft Fifth Directive states that 'all the members of the management and supervisory organ shall carry out their functions in the interest of the company, having regard to the interests of the shareholders and the employees.' There seems to exist more than one way of interpreting this dry expression according to various national traditions and ideological beliefs.

For instance, in Germany, prior to the introduction of the participative scheme, Article 70 of the Companies Act (Aktiengesellschaftgesetz) 1937 had already provided that: 'the management board is to manage the corporation as the welfare of the enterprise [*Betrib*] and its workers and the common benefits of folk and Reich demand.' It did not refer to the shareholders explicitly, but they may be implied in the word 'enterprise'. The 1965 Act dropped this provision. It is generally believed that the legislator wanted to avoid the provision because of its fascist connotation. According to an account by a German authority of company law, however, the provision was dropped because there was controversy regarding the order in which those diverse interests were to be listed in the relevant sentence; but there was no disagreement whatsoever as to the principle itself.[7] Some point out that this philosophy of regarding the company as a *Gemeinschaft* of different constituents is in accord with traditional Christian teaching. This doctrine is expressed, for instance, as follows:[8]

where capital owners and workers depend on each other both sides have rights of co-determination. Workers have no less a share in an economic enterprise than the owners of capital. . . . Many managers of such companies know that the duty owed by them on human grounds to their fellow workers is as great as the duty owed to the shareholders. They would be better able to discharge this dual responsibility if their legitimation did not depend on the shareholders alone. Dependence on one side alone can mean that the problems of managing men, of co-operation and living in harmony, may be pushed into the background. (quoted from Biedenkopf Commission, 1979, p. 78)

In Britain, where company law evolved from the unincorporated partnership technique, the new concept of the company's interests is also derived from an extension of the partnership principle. The Bullock Report states: 'if our proposals are adopted, the new concept of a partnership between capital and labour in the control of companies will supersede the idea that a company and its shareholders are one and the same thing' (Bullock Committee, 1977, p. 80). The participative management may be legitimized from a more unorthodox view of corporatism as well. For instance, Hadden (1972) argues that more progress might be made in dismantling the current ideological base of the capitalist system by developing the conception that management is employed by both employees and investors.

Finally, the 'Green Paper' by the ECC starts from the premiss that employee participation is a necessity from the 'democratic imperative that those who will be substantially affected by decisions made by social and political institutions must be involved in the making of those decisions'. Such a democratic and human rights concept seems to have formed the accepted foundation for the introduction of participative schemes in the Scandinavian countries.

Whatever the ideological ground for participative management, the model is now in operation in one of the most developed areas of the capitalist economy, while its introduction in others is under discussion. It thus seems high time to understand the economic implications of the participative management model.

Monitoring management: The German model

The design of the participative management model begins with constituting the corporate organ(s) in which various decision-making powers are vested and specifying the degree of employees' participation in it (them). In so doing, two important questions arise:

1   Should the role of employees in the organ be limited to monitoring management and gathering information? Or should employees involve themselves in actual managerial policy-making? If so, how should a line of demarcation be drawn between subjects of participative management and subjects of collective bargaining?
2   Should the employees' representatives remain as a minority in the participative organ *vis-à-vis* shareholder representatives, or should they share decision-making power equally with shareholder representatives in terms of seats in the participative organ?

These issues may be clarified by contrasting the German model and the Bullock model. Since 1870 German corporate law has required the corporation (*Aktiengesellschaft*) to have two corporate organs in addition to the shareholders' meeting: a supervisory council (*Aufsichtsrat*) and a management board (*Vorstand*). This two-tier system was originally introduced for reasons that had nothing to do with industrial democracy, but with the aim of giving shareholders more effective control over management than they could exercise through a general meeting. According to this model, the management board is responsible for the direction of corporate activities, and it alone has the power to represent the corporation *vis-à-vis* third parties. Members of the management board are appointed by the supervisory council for a maximum of five years, and can be dismissed for good reason by the supervisory council or by a resolution at a shareholders' meeting (Section 84). All actions of management are subject to the broad supervisory powers of the council. Particularly important is the council's obligation to examine the financial record of the corporation. Also, the council must receive regular reports from the management board regarding managerial policy-making, profitability, important transactions, and so on. In principle, the role of the supervisory council is to oversee and monitor the way in which the corporation is run, but not to get involved in running it. But the management board may be required to seek the council's approval to certain kinds of action specified by the council or by the corporation's charter. A refusal by the board to give approval can be overruled, however, by three-fourths of the votes at a shareholders' meeting (Section 111 (4)). Members of the management board cannot be members of the supervisory council and vice versa.

According to the 'received' legal model of the Anglo-American corporation (company), the board of directors manages the corporation's business and makes policy decisions; the officer (the managing director) acts as an agent of the board and executes its decisions. The authority of the officer can be terminated by the board. In contrast, the managing board of the German system is not an agent of the supervisory council, but an independent institution. The supervisory council has no legal powers to give binding instructions to the managing board on policy matters. As noted above, even when the council has reserved to itself the power of approving or vetoing certain transactions, it can be overruled if the management board can obtain the agreement of 75 per cent or more of shareholders voting at a shareholders' meeting.

Thus, German law establishes two levels of control in the corporation. Its aim is to separate the responsibility of monitoring management from the actual managing of the corporation. This system is sometimes referred to as the two-tier system, whereas the Anglo-American model is referred to as the one-tier system, although, as we see presently, some argue that the Anglo-American corporation also operates a *de facto* two-tier system and that the difference between the two systems is not great.

German corporate law limits the employees' participation in the corporate structure to a supervisory role. The 1976 Co-determination Act stipulates that the supervisory councils of all corporations employing more than 2000 workers are to be formed of equal numbers of shareholder representatives and employee representatives, the precise numbers of council members specified by the law depending upon the size of corporations in terms of employees.[9] Prior to the 1976 Act, employees elected one-half of council members in Montan industry but only one-third elsewhere. The employee seats on the council are allocated to blue-collar workers (*Arbeiter*) and white-collar employees (*Angestellte*) in proportion to their shares in the whole work-force. One of the white-collar employee seats is reserved for a high-level management employee (*leitender Angestellte*) because this group is generally not numerous enough to elect a candidate of its own. Also, employee representatives must include two or three (depending upon the size of the corporation) representatives from the trade union. The employee representatives other than union representatives are chosen by secret ballot, directly by constituent employees or indirectly by an electoral college representing each constituency, through a complicated and elaborate procedure. Union representatives are elected by employees from a list of nominees prepared by the trade union. Any council member can be dismissed by a three-quarters vote in each constituency.

If the council contains equal numbers of employee representatives and shareholder representatives, how can deadlocks be overcome? The shareholder representatives on the supervisory council have the right to elect the chairman of the council. Generally, all resolutions require a majority of votes cast. In case of a deadlock, however, a second ballot must take place in which the chairman has an additional vote. As the chairman is elected by the shareholder members, this provision results in a majority for the shareholder members provided that they are unanimous among themselves. The selection and dismissal of members of the management board must initially require a majority of two-thirds of all council members. If this majority cannot be obtained, the matter is referred to a special committee consisting of two shareholder members and two employee members, which within one month must make a proposal regarding the selection or dismissal of the board members. Then the council convenes and decides on the matter by a simple majority vote, allowing a second vote for the chairman in case of a deadlock.

Since the shareholder representatives may find it imprudent to force a candidate into office by means of this cumbersome procedure, the procedure in effect is likely to result in a veto power of employee representatives. Apart from this, the employees' power in the corporate organ is limited as regards the actual formulation of managerial policy. But they do derive a direct utility from participation in the supervisory council in an enhanced ability to gather information useful for negotiations conducted elsewhere. Particularly relevant are negotiations conducted at the plant level through the machinery of works councils (*Betriebsrat*).

In Germany, standard wage rates (*Ecklohn*) are determined by collective agreements between trade unions and employers' associations normally acceded at regional or national level. Since two or three employee representatives in the supervisory council should be elected from a list of union nominees, it may be thought that an important communication channel is set up through which accurate and revealing information regarding business performances of the enterprise and managerial plans flows to union negotiators. But the extent to which trade union representatives can disseminate information gained from their directoral role is actually limited, for they may not breach rules and norms of confidentiality. Certainly, the Biedenkopf Commission (1970, Part III, para. 61), charged by the government of the German Federal Republic in 1968 with a study of co-determination, could find no cases of serious breaches of confidentiality or of any greater risk of such breaches on the part of worker representatives as compared with other members of the council. Moreover, court rulings have stressed that the employee representatives' primary responsibility is to the company. Thus, the extent to which information is fed into extra-enterprise wage negotiations by trade union representatives may be limited to information concerning the enterprises' ability to pay, more general managerial plans, and the like. Still the Biedenkopf Commission reported that

[it] was explained to the Commission that workers' co-determination at the supervisory council level has led to the trade union as a bargaining party being given more information as to the economic position of the company and its productive capacity. According to the statements of those questioned, this has had the effect not only of unions raising their demands but also of unions, in stringent economic conditions, being prepared to take into account the actual economic position of the company. (Biedenkopf Commission, 1970, p. 53)

On the other hand, although the standard wage rates are determined through the union negotiation system and collective agreements are binding on the parties that accede to them, additional payments in the form of bonuses, piece rates, and so on are negotiable at plant level. The law (Betriebsverfassungsgesetz 1952 and 1972) requires that employee representation in the form of works councils be instituted in all establishments (*Betriebe*) that normally have five or more permanent employees. Members of the works councils are directly elected by the employees in a particular organizational unit, normally a shop or factory. Enterprises with more than one establishment must also set up a central work council to which other work councils send delegates and which deals with matters concerning the enterprise as a whole.

The law stipulates that 'the works council has right of co-determination of job and bonus rates and comparable performance-related remunerations including piece rates' (Section 87 (11)), but it cannot deal with remuneration and other working conditions of employment that have been fixed or will normally be fixed by collective bargaining (Section 77 (3)). Also, management cannot settle the wide range of intra-establishment issues without the consent of the works council. These include working hours, wage payment procedures, holiday arrangements, safety, criteria for job evaluation, recruitment and selection standards, transfers, redeployment, dismissal, redundancies, closing down, and production procedures. The management and the works council must discuss matters at issue 'with the earnest desire to reach agreement', and 'acts of industrial warfare . . . shall be unlawful' (Section 74). Whenever the need arises, a conciliation committee must be set up for the purpose of settling differences of opinion between the parties.

In addition to the co-determination function on these issues, works councils also deal as consultative bodies with investment plans and manpower plans. Thus the German works councils have far-reaching rights of co-determination and consultation at plant level. However, as suggested by the discussion regarding British industrial relations in the 1960s (see pp. 136–7), such decentralized 'co-determination' on wages, employment, and so on will be internally efficient from the viewpoint of the enterprise only if the settlements of individual issues are properly co-ordinated. Employee participation in the supervisory council may help, through its information-gathering and -spreading functions, to prevent the works councils from indulging in plant-ego and shop-ego strategies and to clarify local bargaining situations from a broader perspective. Thus, employee participation in the supervisory councils may contribute to the internal efficiency of the enterprise if it is combined effectively with the machinery of works councils.

There is a clear line of demarcation between the union negotiation system and the statutorily provided machinery of the works councils, although the latter have some resemblance to American union locals in that they are organized on the principle of 'one establishment–one representative institution'. Historically, this demarcation was the result of a determined opposition by German trade unions to any form of 'syndicalism' and their fear, at the very inception of the development of the works councils in the 1920s, that such an institution might encroach upon their collective bargaining function. But it is said that the unions are becoming less hostile to works councils, and that trade unionists are tending to be more active within the councils to enhance their influences at shop and plant level. Further, as noted already, works councils are not allowed to take industrial action by law, although wildcat strikes, go-slows, and other forms of unofficial industrial actions are not entirely unknown.[10] Thus it may be that differences between the works councils and the union organizations should not be over-emphasized in terms of their functions.

The impact of employee participation in the supervisory council on the selection of management can be varied. If the council is passive and reactive, then the nomination of new members of the management board by incumbent board members may prevail, and the management board may perpetuate itself. But this possibility is not unique to the participative management model. There is always the risk that management will become an autonomous organ, free of surveillance by its corporate constituents.

On the other hand, in more active cases the employee representatives can have a *de facto* veto power regarding the choice of the management board, as remarked already, and the employees' body may be able to exert considerable influence on the general orientation of managerial policy-making. Particularly if senior managers on the board are recruited from within the promotional hierarchy of high-ranking managerial employees, as in most non-financial corporations, the management may have internalized the preferences of employees and may give increased weight to the employees' interests in managerial policy-making. For instance, the Biedenkopf Report observed as follows:

"the commission gained the impression that a special role is played by the fact that companies are to an increasing extent recruiting directors from the ranks of their own trainee managers". "In the hearings, supervisory board chairmen and directors often expressed the fear that parity constitution of the supervisory board has had an unavoidable negative influence on trainee managers. The latter could be at pains to cultivate close contact with the officials of co-determination in order to obtain the particular support of the workers' representatives on the supervisory board thus enhancing their own chances of promotion. (Biedenkopf Commission, 1970, Part II, para. 59)

The greater weighting of the interests of incumbent employees may result in a slowing down of growth and sticky adjustments in employment levels (consult proposition 1 on p. 119). This seems to be an inevitable 'dilemma of industrial democracy'. The Biedenkopf Report presented the view that 'the company-oriented attitude of the supervisory council members elected by the work-force can lead to a certain works egoism .... the extra works aspects are not sufficiently considered. ... It can happen that short-term measures are given priority over long-term considerations and planning' (Biedenkopf Commission, 1970, p. 35; see also p. 104). This observation is in accord with our analytical conclusion.

As a remedy, the Biedenkopf Report suggested a role for trade union representatives, whose presence was expected to have the effect of correcting company-oriented attitudes of representatives from within the corporation. In particular, the trade union would represent the interests of a pool of workers both in and out of particular companies, with one of its objectives being to increase employment from the pool. Union representation was seen as being particularly effective in reducing unemployment resulting from the exploitation of monopolistic advantages by employed workers in collusion with shareholders. The 1976 Act now includes the aforementioned provision that the supervisory council must have two or three extra-enterprise nominees from the trade unions.

However, one may fear that the participation of trade union nominees on the supervisory council as a safeguard against 'works-ego' or 'enterprise-ego' may have an adverse effect on allocative efficiency. For instance, when Mr Douglas Fraser, then President of the United Automobile Workers (UAW), was elected to a board seat at the Chrysler Corporation in the spring of 1980, most of the controversy surrounding it focused on the potential conflicts of interests inherent in the position of a union official-cum-director, but some other questions were also raised. If Mr Fraser succeeds in gaining a directorship at Chrysler, could the UAW be expected to stop at that point, or would the next demand be that he or other union officials be placed on the boards of the General Motors and Ford Motor Corporations? Further, would not similar demands surface in other industries? (see Steuer, 1979). Although Section 8 of the Clayton Act prevents individuals from participating on the boards of competing corporations, it has not been held to apply to similar activities by corporations or organizations such as unions and foundations, and industry-wide union representation on boards could create an unreasonable risk of restraining fair competition in the industry.

In Germany, also, a fear of unions' exercise of monopolisitc power has been expressed, albeit in a somewhat different form. The Biedenkopf Report stated: 'Almost all the arguments brought forward against qualified co-determination express the fear that co-determination will strengthen the influence and power of the union to an unprecedented degree. The most serious objection of opponents is a development of the "union state"' (Biedenkopf Committee, 1970, p. 25). It is particularly feared by some that an involvement of unions in the selection of management personnel may result in their exercising control or influence on personnel selection on ideological grounds or the like. Such does not seem to have been a real problem so far, however, for the trade unions have been self-restrained in the process of managerial selection. It should also be pointed out that, as the stock voting power is concentrated in the hands of three giant banks in Germany, trade union representation may act as an effective countervailing power within the enterprise.

Thus, trade union representation on the German supervisory council has many different facets: the intermediation of managerial information to supra-enterprise wage negotiators; the restraint of enterprise-centred interests of the employees; a potential impediment to fair competition in industry; a counter-balance to the centralized power of financial institutions on the shareholders' side of the enterprise; and possibly others. The trade union appears to be a rather complicated institution of interest mediation in the context of co-determination, and a satisfactory treatment of it is far beyond the scope of this study. However, in very general terms, one may conjecture that the German co-determination model may reduce allocative efficiency (slower growth than the neoclassical value maximization would predict, and upward as well as downward rigidity in the adjustments of employment levels and sales price), since the interests of incumbent employees are more effectively voiced and weighed within the firm, particularly through their influence on the management selection process. On the other hand, the model may improve internal efficiency if it is combined with an effective substructure of works councils, as this would facilitate efficient, internal co-ordination of managerial decisions. Internal efficiency can promote the growth of the firm to a greater extent than value maximization subject to predetermined wages would prescribe; the balance of the counteracting effects of allocative inefficiency and internal efficiency on growth of the firm must of course be empirically ascertained.[11]

Extending collective bargaining? The Bullock model

An elaborate debate was conducted around the Bullock Report as to whether the introduction of employee representation on the corporate organ should be accompanied by the introduction of a new 'two-tier' board of the German type or retain the 'unitary' board found in current British law and practice. The majority of the Bullock Committee rejected the introduction of a two-tier board and opted for including employees' representatives on the unitary board of directors.

Some argue, however, that the difference between the one-tier and the two-tier board systems is over-emphasized (see, e.g., Vagts, 1966; Batstone and Davies, 1976; and Davies, 1978). The reason is that the board of directors in Britain (and the United States) tends to delegate more of its authority to the senior manager or to various committees (executive committee, financial committee, etc.), which the managing director, who is both a senior manager and an influential member of the board, dominates; and the board itself tends to recede to perform the function of monitoring the senior manager. (I shall discuss this tendency more fully in the following chapter.) Yet, from the viewpoint of the employees' relationship to managerial policy-making, there seems to be an appreciable difference between the two systems in that the two-tier system enables the employees to be involved only in the *supervision* of the company's affairs, leaving the management board free to make managerial policy; whereas the unitary system, at least potentially, enables them to exert direct influence over important managerial policy-making. From this perspective, 'the crucial question is [as Paul Davies, 1978 put it] perhaps not one-tier versus two-tiers, but the functions of the board upon which the employees will be represented' (p. 257).

Present British company law requires certain fundamental decisions (such as those listed under function 1 on p. 125) to be taken by the shareholders alone; whereas the management functions, conferred upon the board through the company's constitution, may be delegated to senior management. The division of power between the board and senior management is a matter for the board itself to decide. However, if the introduction of employee representatives on to the existing unitary board is to be effective, the distribution of power will need to be altered. The Bullock Report therefore recommended that the board have certain 'attributed functions'. Specifically, it proposed that company law should specify certain areas where the right to take a final decision would rest with the board, which could not then delegate authority to senior management. These areas were the appointment, removal, control, and remuneration of senior management; the allocation or disposition of resources; and changes in capital structures, such as the issues of securities on a take-over or merger. On the other hand, as regards the relationship between the board and the shareholders, the Report recommended that in some fundamental decisions the power of initiative should lie with the board, while the shareholders would retain a veto power. Decisions in these areas included the winding up of the company; the alteration of its memorandum and articles; certain changes in its capital structure, such as a reduction or an increase in the authorized share capital; and the disposition of a substantial part of its undertakings. The decision on payment of dividends was arranged in a likewise manner.

Except for the attributed functions, the Bullock Report designated no detailed and precise allocation of decision-making functions between the board and senior management, leaving that as a matter for the board itself to determine. It is possible, then, that the board could decide that important policy matters, such as on major investments, should be at least discussed and approved at board level. Can shareholder-directors and employee-directors agree on such issues? There may exist a mutuality of interests between shareholders and employees under certain circumstances. For instance, I have pointed out the possibility that both shareholders and employees may be better off when the target growth rate of the firm is increased to more than the level at which the share price is maximized subject to a predetermined wage rate, which would have the effect of making employment more secure and improving share price, provided that the wage rate was adjusted downward at the same time. However, even in this case, as soon as the parties reach a Pareto-efficient solution (a point on the contract curve), the concert of interests will disappear. One can gain only at the expense of the other.

Even if decisions on wages are set aside for negotiation outside the board room, the mutuality of interests between the parties is not perfect. The matter cannot be settled in a simple two-step procedure, either — making the board maximize some kind of 'joint' surplus, and then allowing the distribution of its outcome. Conceptually, there cannot be such a thing as 'joint' surplus except in the extraordinary case of the stationary state (see pp. 67–9). In general, equilibrium policy-making within the firm always involves the weighting of interests between the shareholders and the employees, which was the main theme of our study in Part II. How, then, is this weighting to be specified in the board room according to the Bullock proposal?

The Bullock Report stipulated that there must be a joint approach to policy-making at the board based on an equal representation of employees and shareholders. However, in order to avoid possible deadlocks, the board should include odd numbers of additional members co-opted by the shareholder-directors and employee-directors. This formula for board composition has come to be called the '$2X + Y$ system', where X is the number of shareholder-directors and employee-directors and Y is the number of co-opted directors. Although the Bullock Report required that Y be greater than one, the German Montan model corresponds to a special $2X + Y$ system for which $Y = 1$, and this co-opted member holds the chairmanship of the supervisory council. Obviously, under a $2X + Y$ system the employees have relatively stronger voting power *vis-à-vis* shareholder representatives in comparison with the 1976 German model. The co-opted members are required to be chosen by the support of majorities of both shareholder-members and employee-members. If both bodies cannot agree on a choice, the proposed quasi-public organ, the Industrial Democracy Committee, initially conciliates; if the conciliation fails, a choice of the Committee prevails.

Another controversial point of the Bullock Report centred on the issue of selection of employee-directors. The employee representatives of the German supervisory council are chosen from different constituencies, and each permanent employee participates in the selection of his/her own representative, directly or indirectly. In contrast, the Bullock Committee proposed that a union-based organization function as a 'single channel' in selecting the employee-directors. More specifically, it laid out that a Joint Representation Committee (JRC) be formed in each company where the introduction of the Bullock model was accepted and that this new body comprise all the independent unions recognized by the company for the purpose of collective bargaining. The Committee recommended that members of the JRC be not full-time union officials but rather shop-stewards. The JRC would determine the method of selecting employee-directors: at one extreme it could decide to hold a general election by all the employees, and at the other extreme it could decide to choose the directors itself. It is most likely that the JRC would act as an electoral college.

From this, however, one should not jump to the conclusion that non-unionists will not play any role at all in the institution of the Bullock model. The introduction of the Bullock model was not supposed to be mandatory, as is the German model, but was to be introduced only by a majority vote in a ballot in which all the employees, irrespective of union membership, could participate. This preparatory voting process was called the 'triggering mechanism'.

Three issues arise regarding this elective process of employee-directors. First, although non-unionists and minority members of the company's work-force could participate in the triggering mechanism, they would most likely be excluded from selecting their own representative to the board. The triggering mechanism resembles the process of union recognition in the United States in that it is based on the principle of majority voting. However, once a US union is approved by the employees in an appropriate unit by majority votes, that union owes the obligation of fair representation to all the employees in the unit, and this obligation is enforceable. The Bullock Report was careful enough to point out that all the directors should be required to take account of the interests of employees and shareholders, but its terms of reference seemed to be oriented more towards regarding the employees-as-a-whole versus the shareholders, rather than towards a fair representation of different components of the firm's work-force.

The Bullock Report also stipulated that an employee-director would be in breach of his duty if he voted in a particular way solely on union instruction; but at the same time a somewhat contradictory provision is found to the effect that a union-appointed director can be removed from his office if all the unions represented on the JRC so demand. Thus, the risk remains that a minority view or a non-unionist view will not be well reflected on board discussion and that the specific interests of such minorities will be subsumed under the general interests of union members. In particular, as white-collar employees and management employees are not well organized into unions or, even if unionized, remain a minority, the reflection of their preferences may become problematical. In the 1976 German model, as noted above, employees' seats on the supervisory council are allocated to blue-collar workers and white-collar employees in proportion to their representation in the whole work-force, but one white-collar employee seat is always reserved for a high-level management employee (*leitender Angestellte*). The inclusion of this *leitender Angestellte* was insisted on by the minority partner of the Social Democrat–Free Democrat coalition government whose constituency is that part of work-force. As a result, *leitender Angestellte*, which have an estimated 5 per cent share of total employment in West German companies, have the right to 16 per cent of employee representation on the supervisory councils.

High-ranking management and white-collar employees are likely to benefit more from the growth of a company, because of their higher promotability, than are blue-collar workers, who are more likely to be concerned with current pay levels. Since shareholders normally prefer higher growth than employees (see p. 112), the representation of high management and white-collar employees on the councils may function as intermediation between the interests of shareholders and of workers. On the other hand, the exclusion of this portion of the work-force from the determination of managerial policy may result in keener conflict between the two X groups, while senior and particularly middle managers, who are the backbone of the internal organization of the firm, are devoid of a means of effectively expressing their interests in managerial policy-making. The board room will bear down on them from one side, and the shop-stewards and unions from the other. Under this situation they will not fail to be demotivated, and this will have a serious consequence on the efficient operation of the internal organization of the firm.

The second issue involving the use of union-based machinery (JRC) in the selection of employee-directors is that of possible union rivalry. Since manual and white-collar workers are normally organized on occupational, professional, craft, and general bases, there may be a large number of recognized unions, sometimes as many as ten or more, in one company, each representing different groups of the work-force. Then, in both the initial triggering mechanism and subsequent discussions in the JRC, a degree of union conflict may emerge. For instance, Kahn-Freund wonders if the proposed procedure will not possibly embitter rather than abate inter-union conflicts. Suppose, for instance, that at the triggering stage there was in a given firm one big union committed, and another opposed, to board representation, the former encouraging its members to vote in favour and the other to vote against: what effect is this going to have on future relations on the shop-floor? (See Kahn-Freund, 1977b).

Inasmuch as all the recognized unions are in favour of the introduction of a participative scheme, however, there is a reason to be a little more optimistic. In proposing that the JRC be organized by shop-stewards, the Bullock Committee seemed to want to give official sanction to the combined shop-steward committee. A recent study of shop-stewards' reports on the possible effect of the development of such inter-union organizations on inter-union differences maintained:

as steward organizations develop, they tend to become better at coping with inter-union differences. Put more tersely, multi-unionism stimulates the development of steward organizations, and steward organizations, as they develop, become more able (and probably find greater necessity) to cope with multi-unionism. (Brown, Ebsworth, and Terry, 1978, pp. 150-1)

Such gradual evolution in accommodating inter-union differences may also be bred through the development of the proposed JRC.

The third and last issue is also related to the Bullock proposal that the JRC be organized not by trade union officials, but by shop-stewards. By this, the Committee seemed to wish to root its system of board-level representation in the existing structure of collective bargaining machinery at plant or shop level. However, as noted in the previous chapter, there is an obvious and fairly well developed trend towards enterprise-level bargaining, particularly in large companies; and when enterprise-level bargaining is established, the people who lead the trade union side are usually full-time union officials (see p. 140). Under this development, the Bullock proposal may have the effect of separating union officials from the participative management as well as separating the employee-directors from wage negotiation.

Thus, in spite of the Bullock Committee's expressed aim of setting up a single channel for employee representation, two channels may be created instead, particularly in large companies, where plant- and shop-level bargaining is increasingly subsumed under enterprise-level bargaining (see pp. 136-9). This separation of bargaining and participative management may also have a serious consequence on the efficiency of decision-making within the enterprise, as we shall see presently.

Having overviewed the main features of the Bullock model, we now turn to properties of decision-making patterns that are likely to emerge from it. In the Biedenkopf Report's summary of the German experience of participative management (1970, Part IIB, para. 19), it was stated that the councils' decisions were often unanimous. We have seen however that in Germany the council's power is limited in the area of managerial policy-making — the problem of redundancy, for instance, does not always come to the council. Also, the German model is designed in such a way that the autonomy of collective bargaining and the institution of co-determination are not to be mixed. The true value of co-determination is to be found in its being an instrument through which important and accurate information relevant to collective bargaining, consultation, and co-determination at the work councils can be disseminated. In contrast, the Bullock model does not clearly separate the respective jurisdictions of participative management and collective bargaining.

Furthermore, the Bullock scheme was intended to be introduced into a company only if the unions recognized by that company took the initiative, and the selection of employee-directors was also controlled by the unions. Thus the unions would have to carry out a double-edged mission, encompassing both bargaining and participative management, and a clear line of demarcation was not drawn between the two. The union's entry in participative management would then bring an aspect of collective bargaining into the board room.

For instance, an important investment decision would presuppose some future wage structure as a basis for budgetary calculation and would imply a certain manning plan. Thus, the board discussion on the investment decision would inevitably have a collective bargaining connotation; the two X members, i.e. the shareholder-directors and the employee-directors, may well find themselves unable to reach an agreement, particularly if it involves redundancies, redeployment of workers, and so on. How is a conflict of this sort to be resolved? The Y component of the Bullock board could be expected to provide an automatic arbitration body. But this may not necessarily be a good solution, because it may remove the incentive for the two X groups to try to reconcile their differences. It is difficult to see how the firm could be run efficiently if automatic arbitration were to become the normal method of resolving conflict.

Anticipating such objections, the Bullock Report pointed to a 'positive' role that the Y group could play. They not only saw the function of the co-opted members as one of tie-breaking in the case of a deadlock, but also expected them to provide 'an important means by which special experiences and expertises can be brought into the board room from inside and outside the company' (Bullock Committee, 1977, p. 96). Thus, the co-opted members were expected to play the role of enlightened co-ordinators who would intermediate in the interests of shareholders and employees. However, in order for this idealistic prescription of the Bullock proposal to be realized, it seems that a new generation of mediator-cum-managers, with different orientations, training, and legitimation from the traditional proprietor-cum-managers, will need to be bred.

Suppose, next, that an important managerial decision has somehow been reached at the board through compromise, arbitration, or otherwise. The agreement may be interpreted as a joint commitment to accept the consequences of the plan. Specifically, the employee-directors might have agreed tacitly to a certain wage rise and manning plan reasonable in the coming year. But when the time comes to bargain about wages applicable to the level of manning, the union negotiatiors, most likely different persons from the employee-directors, may wish to reserve the right to negotiate without any commitment to the managerial decision. Particularly, in a large company a number of unions may be found representing different groups of workers, and some of them may not have been represented on the board. Those unions will certainly want to negotiate as entirely free agents. As a result, bargained wages and manning may diverge from the prior commitment of the employee-directors, and decisions of the firm as a whole may lose their consistency from the internal efficiency point of view.

It may also happen, as Mr John Edmonds of the Research Department of the GMWU pointed out, that union negotiators under pressure to accept lower wage increases than the rank-and-file wish may hint that one of the reasons why the unsatisfactory settlement occurred was because of a budget decision in which the worker-directors had participated. A situation may even become bitter, when a board decision involves a plant closure or similar. Faced with such an unpopular decision, shareholder-directors may hint that the unions had been involved in that decision through the worker-directors. Thus, as Mr Edmonds put it, 'the worker-directors are going to be the natural scapegoats for the things that go wrong in the industry.'[12]

The possible inefficiency of decisions within the firm as a whole, and the difficult position of employee-directors, arise from the fact that the union must play a dual role and that no clear line of demarcation can be drawn between participative management and collective bargaining. Ironically, this difficulty may be resolved in practice by the board's receding from its position as a managerial decision-making body.

For instance, in 1978–80 there was an important experiment of worker participation in the board with a parity representation at the Post Office in Britain. This experiment was carefully studied by Batstone, Ferner, and Terry (1983). Although the Post Office was a public corporation constrained by public accountability through ministerial control, this study reveals many interesting points which may arise in the application of the Bullock-type model. Particularly noteworthy is the size and complexity of the Post Office organization, which significantly limited the board's ability to play a strategic role; the top management was able to govern the internal organization and to set up their own initiative outside the board. According to Batstone *et al.*, '[t]he existence of the union nominees led management deliberately to keep certain issues away from the Board and to "censor" their presentation of information to the Board' (Batstone et al., 1983, p. 72) On the other hand, confronted by the uncertainty over the demarcation between participative management and collective bargaining, employees' representatives were careful to be involved in neither managerial decision-making nor board room bargaining, and maintained close links with represented unions. These were not shop-stewards, as the Bullock Report prescribed, but trade unionists of long standing from unions mostly recruiting members only in the Post Office. Thus the link between unions and employee-directors was close and extensive.

If the board cannot play the active role in managerial decision-making, as the Bullock Report optimistically anticipated, the difference between the one-tier structure and the two-tier structure may be blurred. The board may recede to a position as, at best, a supervisory machinery and, at worst, a mere source of legitimation. This is my reading of the study by Batstone and his colleagues.

Of course, the experiment of the Post Office might have been greatly affected by its very nature as a public corporation. In particular, the board chairman, whose selection was a key form of ministerial control over the Post Office, had a very powerful statutory position and acted as chief executive. He was able to control the term of debate at the board, thus limiting the board's power to challenge managerial actions. The strict application of the Bullock model assigning the 'attributed functions' to the board may however mitigate the reduction of managerial reliance on the board in the private company, but the degree to which this occurred would depend upon the specific contexts in which board representation was located.

Since external pressures from other EEC countries for incorporating the requirement of employee participation in law has not ceased, and since unions have not abandoned their aspiration for involvement in the decision-making process of the firm, the introduction of some form of participative scheme or 'joint regulation' in the near future seems inevitable in Britain, in spite of the burial of the Bullock proposals and the demise of the Post Office experiment. However, employee participation has been, is being, and will be in near future, introduced in a voluntary and decentralized manner. The issues such as one-tier versus two-tier, parity versus minority, collective bargaining versus board representation, single-channel versus proportional representation, and others will be settled through such decentralized and diversified experiments, and an appropriate statutory framework of employee participation will emerge only out of those. That seems to be more in accord with the traditional British way.

In spite of its enormous contribution to the clarification of issues involved in the participative management, the Bullock Report might have committed the same sin as the Industrial Relations Act 1971, in the sense that it tried to create a theoretically desirable pattern of industrial relations by a single act of legislation.

Summary

This chapter identified two stylized models of participative management: the 1976 German model, characterized by a two-tier governance structure with minority representation of employees, and the Bullock model, characterized by a one-tier governance structure with parity representation of employees. I have argued that the two tier-system combined with a substructure of works councils may be effective in the dissemination of managerial information to the employees, clarifying the objective bargaining situation to them: an undoubted prerequisite for the approximation of organizational equilibrium (co-operative solution) within the firm. Employees' direct influence over the managerial policy-making process may be limited, but the employees may be able to exert indirect influence by participating in the process of management selection. If the internal bargaining power of the employees' body is substantially strengthened through this route, the analysis of Part II indicates that the equilibrium growth rate of the firm may be slowed down and the adjustment of employment, as well as sales prices, may become downwardly rigid, although a safeguard against this dilemma of industrial democracy is instituted in the German system in the form of the inclusion of outside trade union representatives on the supervisory council.

The introduction of the one-tier system with parity representation would change the balance of internal bargaining power in favour of the employees' body, and the dilemma of industrial democracy might manifest itself in even a sharper way, provided the board retained substantial decision-making power. One of the main difficulties specifically associated with the one-tier system is that the line of demarcation between collective bargaining and participative management is hard to draw. Particularly when employee-directors and the bargaining representatives are two separate agents, this difficulty might lead to a undesirable consequence for the approximation of organizational equilibrium.

It might be advised, therefore, that this model is to be experimented with on a voluntary basis before any legal attempt is made to enforce it. In practice, top management might appropriate actual decision-making power, by relying less on the board. Then the board representation of workers may not have direct advantages to workers and unions except for possible access to managerial information released to the board. Whether this access of information could lead to greater opposition to management or to greater co-operation would depend upon the specific context in which the model is instituted.

Chapter 11

The Corporative Managerialism Model

This chapter deals with the corporative managerialism model of the firm. It conceptualizes the firm as a system composed of two basic constituent units, the shareholders' body and the employees' body, with an integrative and interest-mediating machinery, identified as the *management*, which welds the units into an interdependent whole. As we saw in Chapter 3, the original idea of viewing the firm in this way can be traced back to the managerialism first expounded by Dodd (1932). But, particularly among economists, managerialism has come to be identified more with the view of management taking over the corporation and running it to its own benefit. Therefore I add the adjective 'corporative', to stress the nature of management as an integrating and mediating machinery. But this characterization of management should be amplified and qualified in at least two respects.

First, although management is conceptualized as an interest-mediating machinery, it should not be taken to imply that management is passive in defining the set of bargain possibilities between the two basic units. Rather, management actively tries to expand the bargain possibility set by formulating more efficient combinations of resources and specifying Pareto-improving internal distributions appropriate to those combinations. How is management motivated to perform this task? The manager, as the personification of the integrative and interest-mediating machinery, is presumed to derive his primary satisfaction from his enhanced status and legitimacy, which is vested in him for doing his job skilfully, efficiently, and professionally. This is not to deny that the manager as an actual person has his own pecuniary and other personal motives. But, generally speaking, the manager's income tends to be positively related to the shareholders' gains and/or employees' earnings. In other words, explicit consideration of the managerial pecuniary motive does not seem to add a particularly new dimension as regards the behaviour of the firm. Rather, I consider it more fruitful to understand the essential nature of management as a unique and indispensable machinery of the firm, and then to proceed to consider how deviant managerial behaviour can be recognized and dealt with. This leads me to the second point.

Management in the corporative managerialism model is neither a mere agent of a basic unit (the shareholders' body) of the firm, as in the shareholders' sovereignty-cum-collective bargaining model, nor a direct composite of basic units, as in the participative management model. However, this does not imply that management in this model is free from control by the basic constituent units. On the contrary, while management has certain discretionary and authoritative power over the internal allocation and monitoring of firm-specific resources, it is at the same time subject to a variety of reciprocal controls exercised by the basic constituent units. Control reciprocity is necessary in order for management to perform its integrative and interest-mediating roles efficiently, and to prevent it from indulging in the pursuit of self-interest at the sacrifice of the basic units. It is necessary also in order that management can win consent and legitimation from its constituents for the exercise of its prerogatives.

The traditional theories of the firm, as reviewed in Part I, recognize the form of discipline imposed on management in terms of either an imposed 'maximand' or a 'constraint'. For instance, the neoclassical theory posits that the shareholders control the management effectively so as to let it maximize the share values on their behalf, while the employees control management only so as to let it observe their reservation wages or bargained wages. The managerialist theory posits that the shareholders control management only indirectly, through the stock market in the form of the minimum share value to be maintained. In contrast, the form of discipline imposed on management in the model of corporative managerialism is neither a fixed constraint nor an unmodifiable objective. The internal demands of the basic constituent units are variable, and striking a balance between them is the essential function of management. This view of management was already formulated in the model of Part II, and its theoretical implications to corporate behaviour were examined. In this chapter therefore I shall discuss only some important institutional issues related to the model.

First, I shall sketch the evolution of statutory recognition of management as an institution independent of the shareholders' body, as well as of the emerging *de jure* and/or *de facto* recognitions of the employees' body as a basic constituent of the firm. These recognitions are considered to be a reflection of a gradual 'corporatization', in the sense of an evolutionary tendency towards the actualization of the corporative managerialism model as theoretically defined, and its examination will put the purely game-theoretic model of the firm of Part II into a more concrete institutional perspective.

Next, I shall overview some of the important mechanisms operating inside and outside the firm for controlling and legitimizing the authoritative power of management. From one point of view, collective bargaining with management, as well as supervision of management by the participative organ, may be viewed as constituting varieties of such controlling mechanisms. However, the corporative managerialism model is theoretically distinguishable from the collective bargaining model as defined in a previous chapter by the managerial motive. In the collective bargaining model, the management is recognized as nothing more than the shareholders' agent; whereas in the present model the equilibrium balancing of employees' power (exercised through collective bargaining) with shareholders' power (exercised through the stock market, general meetings, and so on) is the primary concern of management. Evolutionary changes in the attitudes and positions of management, from the ones described by the collective bargaining model to the ones described by the corporative managerialism model, may be viewed as one way of corporatizing the firm. By the same token, the management of some of the participative management models, such as the management board of the German co-determination model or the *Y*-members of the Bullock model, may function as an interest-mediating machinery; and therefore the introduction of such schemes may be regarded as another way of corporatization. Because of their distinctive statutory characteristics, however, the participative models merited separate treatment in the last chapter.

Statutory tendency towards corporatism

In Britain, until the turn of the century, it was generally assumed that the general meeting was the company, and that directors were merely agents of the company subject to the control of the company in the general meeting. This classical assumption was projected on to the frame of economists' thinking, and seems to have survived until now. However, as the company grew larger and its management grew more complicated, it became increasingly difficult for the shareholders' meeting to give managerial instruction to the board of directors. As a result, the power of decision-making started to shift gradually to the board. At the beginning of this century it became recognized that the division of power between the board and the company in the general meeting was a matter to be decided by the articles of association, and that, where power had been vested in the board, the general meeting could not interfere with the exercise of that power (see Gower *et al.*, 1979, pp. 143-7).

One way in which shareholders can exercise control over the board, in spite of their surrender of important decision-making authority to the board, is by dismissing its directors. Until 1948 this 'dismissal right' depended upon whether the articles of association attributed such power to the general meeting; since then it has become statutorily possible to remove a director by an ordinary resolution of a general meeting at any time. Subject to this shareholders' control, the board of directors is now theoretically responsible for the management of the company except for fundamental matters specifically reserved for the general meeting (such as listed under function 1 on p. 125).

This wide delegation of the company's power is to the directors as a body, not to individual directors. But, here again, it is obviously not practical to hold a formal board meeting whenever the need for a managerial decision occurs. Therefore, under the normal articles of association, the board of directors is empowered to appoint one or more of its members to the office of managing director for such period and such terms as they think fit. In practice, many of the company's powers that have been primarily delegated to the board of directors are sub-delegated to the managing director. The function of the board is receding to that of formulating managerial policy in general terms and monitoring the managing directors.

In the United States, the relative autonomy of the board has been clearly visible since the inception of corporate statutes. While English company law evolved from the concept of mutual agreements among the providers of capital (the company), the American corporation was recognized at the outset as a grantee of state power (see Gower, 1956). During the nineteenth century, when American corporate law was moulded, legal writers did not distinguish business corporations from municipal corporations, and this tendency seems to account for the rule unique to the United States that the shareholders of a corporation may *not* dismiss directors at will. Arthur Traverse explains this as follows:

> it could be readily concluded that the aldermen of a municipality should be insulated from the electorate between elections. Since it was their job to regulate the behavior of that very electorate, fulfilling that function would inevitably cause irritation among citizenry. Some degree of independence had to be afforded them if their regulatory tasks were to be performed. (Traverse, 1967, p. 362)

Thus the aldermen were made unremovable for a term of office. This rule was rather mechanically applied to business corporations serving different functions. State statutes provided that shareholders should elect a corporation's directors for a term of office set forth in statutes or in the corporation's bylaws. Between elections, the business and affairs of a corporation were to be managed by the board. The shareholders' right was only to review the performance of each director when he stood for re-election and to refuse re-election of those who performed badly, in the shareholders' judgement (except for making some fundamental decisions involving a change in corporate character).

Although economists tend to view the shareholder–director relationship as one case of the principal–agency relationship, the board of directors was thus not instituted from the outset as an agent of the shareholders in the general meeting (see Ballantine, 1946, p. 119); for in the normal agency relationship the authority of an agent can be terminated by his principal at any time and an agent must normally follow his principal's instructions.

Lately there has been some tendency towards a statutory provision permitting a majority of shareholders to remove directors with or without cause, but in most cases such provision is left optional.[1] Further, the powers of decision-making, even on fundamental issues, are increasingly being removed from the sphere of shareholders' authority. Under Delaware's General Corporation Law, for instance, shareholders have lost nearly all powers to initiate corporate changes, and only the board of directors may propose charter amendments, a merger, or the sale of a substantial portion of corporate assets.

On the other hand, original American state statutes did not provide clear-cut provisions, as did British law, under which the board can delegate whatever power it thinks appropriate to the managing director. Common law also hesitated to allow the delegation of the management function of the board, 'involving the exercise of discretion'.[2] However, this principle is rather vague, and leads to contradictory and confusing cases. Therefore recent common law and corporate statutes have increasingly adopted the view that the board can delegate a wide range of decision-making power to third parties. For instance, when the Model Business Corporation Act Annoted was initially drafted by the American Bar Association in 1950, its section 35 declared only that 'the business and affairs of a corporation shall be managed by a board of directors'; but that section of the revised Act 1974 now reads: 'All corporate powers shall be exercised by or *under authority of*, and the business and affairs shall be managed *under the direction of*, a board of directors' (italics added). A substantial change in connotation is clear, and the board is not obliged any longer to manage the corporation by itself. In fact, it has become common practice in most large corporations for the board of directors to delegate most of its managerial policy-making to various sub-committees. From the viewpoint of managerial policy-making, the most important of these are the executive and finance committees, and they are dominated by executive officers-cum-directors (see McMullen, 1974). Section 35(2) of the Model Act 1974 further defines that, in order to perform his duty, a director shall be entitled to rely on information and reports supplied by a duly elected committee. If a director pays sufficient attention to the reliability of a committee, he is not liable to any damage to the corporation caused by misjudgement or wrong opinion of the committee. This 'right of reliance' is adopted, for instance, in section 309 of the California Corporate Law 1976.

Thus, the function of the board of directors has been receding to that of moderate supervision. Myles Mace (1971) concluded his authoritative research on American boards by saying: 'In most companies boards of directors serve as a source of advice and counsel, serve as some sort of discipline, and act in crisis situations if the president dies suddenly or is asked to resign because of unsatisfactory management performance' (pp. 178-9). Mace found that in most medium- and large-sized corporations managerial policies are established not by the board of directors, but by management.

Managerial dominance appears to take an even more acute form in Japan. The Commercial Code provides three corporate organs in addition to the shareholders' general meeting: the board of directors (*torishimari yaku*), whose function is to make corporate decisions except for those reserved to the general meeting (such as on fundamental changes in corporate character and dividends payment); the office of representative director (*daihyo torishimari yaku*), which represents the corporation *vis-à-vis* third parties and is responsible for the execution of corporate decisions; and the office of auditor (*kansa yaku*), whose function is to audit the activities of directors. The general meeting can remove a director with or without cause by a more than two-thirds vote. The representative director(s) is (are) elected by the entire board. The Code does not prevent corporations from setting up a sub-structure of the board by articles of association to which the function of the board is delegatable, except for matters specified by the Code as belonging to the entire board (e.g., the election of representative director(s) and decisions on new share issues within the limit of authorized capital). Such sub-structure, normally called the board of full-time directors (*senmu torishimari yaku*), is composed of representative directors and a few other senior directors. Since most of the 'plain' directors (*hira torishimari yaku*) are junior members of the management, and normally only a few outsiders sit in the board room, and only decoratively,[3] the relation between the two boards is reversed in practice from the statutory arrangement, and the board of directors becomes *de facto* the sub-structure of the management system subordinate to the board of full-time directors.

Thus, everywhere the management team (as headed by managing directors in Britain, executive officers in the United States, the management boards in Germany, and full-time directors in Japan) seems to be vested with important decision-making powers. Even decisions on fundamental matters traditionally within the sphere of the shareholders' authority can be (in many cases, as in Delaware) put on the agenda of the general meeting only by a management initiative.

What is implied by this apparent concentration of decision-making power in the hands of management? A popular notion is that management has acquired discretionary decision-making power for carrying its own objectives, and that it tends to abuse this power at the sacrifice of other constituents of the firm and public welfare. Such a view is, as is well known, presented forcibly by Ralph Nader and his associates in the United States. Some academic managerialists display similar apprehensions, although more prudently, and propose possible remedies to make management more accountable and responsible.

However, it is one thing to recognize that the constituents of the firm, as well as the public, assign major decision-making powers to management, and it is another to conclude from this that an abusive use of decision-making power by management is inevitable and the rule. It is rather unlikely that an arbitrary and anti-social exercise of decision-making power by management can be sustained and viable in the long run at the sacrifice of allocative as well as internal efficiency. Rather, by being made subject to various control and accountability mechanisms, management does, or at least can be made to do, approximate the corporative objective of striking a balance between the interests of the various constituents of the firm (and the public welfare) fairly and efficiently. A more fruitful approach, then, would be to seek good workable mechanisms for inducing the management to be accountable for the corporative objectives.

From this theoretical perspective, the traditional notion that the corporation is the property of shareholders and that the board of directors shall manage the corporation as a trustee of the shareholders does not seem very helpful. The anachronistic nature of the notion is dramatically illustrated by the case of *Parke v. Daily News Ltd* (1962) in Britain, which was extensively discussed by Gower *et al.* (1979) in their *Principles of Modern Company Law*. This case arose out of the sale of the ailing *News Chronicle* and *Star*:

The Cadbury family, who controlled the selling company, wished to distribute the whole of the purchase price among the employees who would become redundant. At the suit of one shareholder they were restrained from doing so. To the argument that 'prime duty must be to the shareholders; but boards of directors must take into consideration their duties to employees in these days', Plowman J. answered tersely: 'But no authority to support that proposition as a proposition of law was cited to me; I know of none, and in my judgement such is not the law. (Gower, *et al.* 1979, p. 579)

In Britain the need to overcome this anachronistic view has been recognized by all parties since then, and finally the following corporatist view crystallized on to the statutory book. Section 46 of the Companies Act 1980 now reads: 'The matters to which the directors of a company are to have regard in the performance of their function shall include the interests of the company's employees in general as well as the interests of its members.' Although how this duty is to be enforced is·by no means clear from a reading of that section, section 74 additionally provides that the company can make payments to employees out of profits available for dividends or out of assets available to shareholders on winding up, even if doing so is 'not in the best interests of the company'.

Thus, *Parke v. Daily News Ltd* has now been reversed, statutorily at least, in reasoning. But the practical importance of it has yet to be seen. One of the contestable issues regarding this provision is that such gratuitous payments can be made by a resolution of the directors only if a provision in the articles or memorandum of the company authorizes them to do so. Otherwise, the action must be sanctioned by a resolution of the general meeting. Thus, the recognition of the employees' position in the company is still conditional on shareholders' voluntary action (see Prentice, 1980, pp. 342–53).

The antedated nature of the traditional view of shareholders' sovereignty was recognized even by a leading spokesman for the American business community in the following statement. Responding to an inquiry by the Securities Exchange Commission (in 1977) on the problem of 'how the corporation can best be made more responsive to their shareholders and the public at large', Mr Ralph Lazarus of the Business Round Table commented:[4]

the board's responsibility is to direct the enterprise in the interest of the owners, subject to the constraint imposed by law. However, the interest of shareowners cannot be conceived solely in terms of short-range profit maximization. The owners have an interest in balancing short-range and long-term profitability and in the political and social viability of the enterprise. Moreover, shareowners and directors alike have an interest in behaving ethically and as good citizens. The board's duty, then, to consider the interests and views of non-shareholder groups arises not out of some ill-defined and extra-legal obligation to these groups, but out of responsibility to act in the interest of shareowners.

This statement, albeit eclectic and somewhat confusing, may be interpreted as an expression of the corporative managerialism ideology. Such revisionist ideas have found their way even into some corporations' articles of association. For instance, the 1978 annual meeting of the shareholders of the Data Control Corporation narrowly adopted a new provision stating that, in evaluating an offer by another party of tender offer, merger, and purchase of all or a substantial portion of corporate assets,

> the board of directors . . . shall, in connection with the exercise of its judgement in determining what is in the best interests of the corporation and its shareholders, give due consideration to all relevant factors, including without limitation the social and economic effects on the employees, customers, suppliers, and other constituents of the corporation and its subsidiaries and on the communities in which the corporation and its subsidiaries operate or are located.

The main opposition to the addition of this provision is said to have come from institutional shareholders (see *Wall Street Journal*, 4 May 1978, p. 38). Some may regard this addition as an effort by management to create a base for legitimizing its opposition to unwanted tender offers and perpetuating itself. But if management can successfully legitimize its action by appealing to the interests of constituents other than the shareholders, that may be said to reflect a real change in the power balance within the firm.

Of course, whether a particular firm is in fact managed so as to strike a balance between the various claims of its different constituents fairly and efficiently, and whether potentially abusive exercise of managerial power therein is properly controlled, are matters to be scrutinized case by case. However, it would seem unwise to deny the evolutionary trend of corporatization and not to seek the best use of the politico-legal situation by clinging to the anachronistic doctrine of shareholders' sovereignty.

In Japan, the corporative managerialist philosophy has been formalized neither into the Commercial Code nor into the articles of association of corporations; but the view that management ought to pay due regard to the welfare of its employees is now taken for granted. One noteworthy statutory provision relating to the present subject is found, however, in the Corporation Reorganization Act. When a business corporation falls into financial difficulty, yet there is a prospect of its revival, the corporation can apply, upon resolution of the board of directors (or by request of shareholders having more than 10 per cent of its shares or of creditors lending more than 10 per cent of its corporate assets), to the court for initiation of a reorganization procedure. If the court finds it reasonable to initiate such a procedure, it will appoint a reorganization custodian and hold a general meeting of interested parties comprising shareholders and creditors. The custodian will then manage the business of the corporation during the reorganization process and will formulate a reorganization plan, while the general meeting will decide on a final plan to be submitted to the court for approval. (A reorganization plan may include, in addition to a plan of payment of liabilities, such fundamental changes as merger, dissolution, partial liquidation, changes in the articles of association, the setting up of a new corporation, etc.) The employees of the corporation are not members of the general meeting or interested parties, since contractual obligations arising from employment are payable prior to any other liabilities, including tax obligations. In spite of this preferential treatment of employees, the Act provides that the court must hear the opinion of the labour union representing the majority of employees regarding the submitted reorganization plan before making a final decision upon it (section 195). The court is not bound by the expressed opinion of the labour union, but can reject a plan if it judges that disregard of the union's opinion will make the plan not 'fair and equitable' (section 233.1(2)).

In the examples quoted above, the position of employees in the corporation is recognized statutorily only in such unusual cases as dissolution, tender offer, and reorganization. However, by the same token as studies of anomalous political situations, e.g. wars and revolutions, illuminate the essence of the state, the legal treatment of employees' positions in these crisis situations may reveal what is latent in the normal course of affairs; that is, notwithstanding the survival of the antedated philosophy-cum-theory of shareholders' sovereignty, the alternative model of corporative managerialism may be permeating itself.

Mechanisms for controlling management

We have seen that, statutorily, the decision-making powers originally vested with the shareholders and thence with the board of directors are slowly being assumed by management, in parallel with the gradual infusion of a corporative managerialism view in the society at large. However, can management be made responsible for the integrative and interest-mediating role?

In this section I would like to enlist some of the important mechanisms for inducing management to be more accountable for its stewardship and for 'fair' and efficient interest mediation. As the present study excludes customers and the general public from being explicitly recognized members of the firm, important mechanisms exercised on management by these sectors, such as customer relations, administrative regulations, and public opinion, are not considered here. The main focus will be on internal control mechanisms exercised by the shareholders' body and the employees' body.

The issue of controllability, thus limited in scope, involves two interfaces: that between management and the shareholders' body, and that between the management and the employees' body. The issue in the former is often discussed under the theme of 'shareholder democracy'[5] and that of the latter under the theme of 'industrial democracy'. Should they, however, be treated separately, at the neglect of each other? As was discussed in the last chapter, the expansion of industrial democracy to the board room will require an overall adjustment of the corporate structure. It will not only change the composition and selective process of the board of directors, but will also necessitate some adjustment in the role of the shareholders' general meeting in fundamental decision-making (for this see p. 163). If corporatization is to develop through the alternative route of expanding the scope of collective bargaining, the traditional attitude of shareholders exhibiting interest in short-run value maximization must be modified, as was discussed at the end of Chapter 9. On the other hand, although the expansion of industrial democracy may have an aspect of remedying the historically antedated imbalance of powers within the firm, the neglect of democracy on the side of the management–shareholder interface may yield management–employee (union) collusion, not only at the expense of share-holders' interests but also at greater cost in the form of allocative inefficiency, resulting in stagnant growth, a restriction of new employment, higher sales prices and so on (see proposition 1 at the beginning of Part III).

Thus, the expansion of industrial democracy and of shareholders' democracy cannot be made in isolation. Restructuring the firm in the process of managerial corporatization may then require some simultaneous adjustments in the share-holder–management and the employee–management interfaces. As Clive Schmitthof put it, if effective management control mechanisms are developed, 'there may well be a coalescence of the law of company management and owner-ship with some aspects of industrial relations' (1978, p. 27). With this general comment, we now turn to a critical examination of some of the important mechanisms of controlling management and recuperating from the organizational disequilibrium.

Exit

One mechanism available to the constituents of the corporate firm for disciplining management is, in the terminology of Albert Hirschman, to 'exit' from the firm when they are dissatisfied with the management. For shareholders, this means selling shares in a corporation whose managerial policies they do not agree with. If this occurs on a large scale, it will affect the share price and have a significant impact upon the manager's personal finances, will make corporate finances more difficult and expensive, and will lead to pressure on the board to take corrective action. At the point where dissatisfaction is clearly demonstrated, changes in management occur either through board action or take-overs. For employees, 'exit' means, needless to say, quitting jobs at the firm and seeking other jobs in the external market. The exodus of firm-specific human resources is costly to management in terms of recruiting and retraining, and will weaken the firm's competitive position.

The exit mechanism is the only controlling mechanism that has been ex-plicitly treated in traditional economics. It is of course a potentially powerful instrument, but exclusive reliance on it may be neither as efficient nor as effective as the traditional doctrine holds. On the shareholders' side, it is gener-ally believed that the exit mechanism will induce management to maximize share prices in order to secure its position. But we have already seen in Chapter 3 that value maximization is not a policy supportable unanimously by the share-holder in the world of uncertainty, if the firm is large and unique relative to the economy. In other words, the value-maximizing objective is not a desirable way of aggregating the individual preferences of shareholders. Furthermore, there is a circumstance in which the imposition of 'short-run' value maximization discipline leads to an internally inefficient outcome. This is the case we have frequently referred to, namely the case in which contracted wages are kept fixed for a prolonged contract period (for this see particularly pp. 149–50).

The effectiveness of the exit mechanism is also limited because the constituents of the large firm, shareholders and employees alike, are partly 'locked into' it. For the employees, such phenomena are evident. As discussed in Chapter 2, the internal organization of employees replaces the working of the market mechanism when it can save on the various costs of using the spot labour market. In particular, in order to save risk cost as well as to gain from the collective accumulation of firm-specific human resources, continual association of a substantial portion of employees with the firm is essential. In order to 'attach' employees to the firm and to distribute a share of the saved cost thereby, devices are developed in which the employees receive various benefits related to their tenures with the firm, in the form of seniority rights, pension benefits, and the like. If an employee quits his job in the middle of his career, he will lose these attained seniority rights; his pension benefits may not be portable further, his skills and professional knowledge may be firm-specific to some extent, and their economic value may be partly lost if he changes jobs. Thus, unless the skill of an employee is universally valuable, significant costs may be imposed on exiting employees, and these costs may retard the actual exodus of those who are dissatisfied.

On the shareholders' side, 'locked-in' phenomena have manifested themselves through the growing importance of institutional shareholders. The growth of institutional shareholdings and the accompanying concentration of voting power in financial institutions in the United States has already been referred to in Chapter 3. In Japan the dominance of institutional shareholdings is even more clearly visible: 41 per cent of the total stock listed at the Tokyo Exchange at the end of March 1981 were held by financial institutions and 21 per cent by non-financial corporations, while only 31 per cent were held by individual investors. Under the present Japanese personal and corporate tax system, the banking sector seems to be able to achieve higher gains if its portfolio corporations finance their investments by debt-financing beyond the level warranted by the share price maximization.[6] In this respect, there is a conflict of interests between financial shareholders and individual shareholders; whereas the latter are likely to be concerned more with share prices, shareholdings of financial institutions seem to be used as an instrument to maintain and expand credit relationships with portfolio corporations. As a consequence, share trades by banks are extremely limited.

In Japan, several corporate groups emerge out of webs of financial as well as non-financial intercorporate shareholdings. Some of these corporate groups are reminiscent of the old 'Zaibatsu' conglomerate. After the Second World War, the mighty holding companies at the cores of the Zaibatsu were dissolved, and the organization of a pure holding company has been outlawed ever since. But grouping of major corporations along the line of the old Zaibatsu have been dextrously manufactured through mutual shareholdings of member corporations with commercial banks as their nuclei. In addition, new corporate groups have emerged with giant manufacturing corporations (such as Toyota and Shin Nippon Steel) as apexes and with many subsidiaries and quasi-subsidiary subcontractors as subordinates. The typical large Japanese firm today has ten or twenty important institutional shareholders, in which it in turn holds shares. Unlike Western institutional shareholders, which invest largely for dividends and capital gains, Japanese institutional shareholders tend to be business partners and associates.[7] As Rodney Clark put it, 'shareholding is the mere expression of their relationship, not the relation itself' (1979, p. 86).

The extent as well as the speed at which the institutional shareholder is formed differs from one economy to another, but the trend seems to be universal. As has already been pointed out, there are many cases in which an institution cannot liquidate its shareholding except at a substantial loss, in terms of either capital value or business relations accompanied with shareholdings, so that it would be better for the institution to try to change managerial policy more directly. The interplay between the management of the corporation and its outside institutional shareholders is becoming more direct and self-sustaining to a large extent.

On the other hand, substantial blocks of stock held by institutional shareholders might have given the management of the corporation a security from take-over. In fact, the take-over seems to be losing its role substantially as a device to cast out bad management; rather, it is becoming a means for large acquisition-minded corporations to take over well-managed small and medium-sized firms (see Scherer, 1983). The traditional view (neoclassical as well as managerial) that the fear of raiders constituted a major discipline on management by shareholders thus seems to need some modification.

If dominating institutional shareholders are 'locked in', exits of small individual shareholders may not have any significant impact on management, unless the institutional shareholders act in concert with them through board actions or otherwise.

The above argument, however, is not to deny the potential importance of the exit mechanism. I only wish to make the point that this mechanism alone would not be sufficient for controlling management as traditionally viewed. As Hirschman argues, the effectiveness of other controlling mechanisms, particularly the voice mechanism discussed below, is strengthened by the possibility of a credible threat to exit (see Hirschman, 1970, p. 37). Further, it is desirable to keep the exit mechanism as effective as possible from the point of view of allocative efficiency, among other things. Tenure-related benefits function as a device for accumulating firm-specific human resources in well managed firms, but they can be turned into a barrier to efficient reallocation of human resources away from badly managed firms. Also, in order to protect individual freedom and dignities from misuses of managerial authoritative powers, the cost of exit to employees should not be excessive.

Voice

An alternative check on management is, again borrowing the terminology of Hirschman (1970), for dissatisfied members of the firm to 'voice' their criticisms, and if possible to make remedial suggestions or proposals through appropriate apparatus built into the firm. On the side of the shareholder-management interface, this apparatus is normally considered to be provided by proxy machinery. But in the large corporate firm, where the number of shareholders is numerous, the proxy machinery is usually controlled by the incumbent management subject only to regulations by security law and the like.

In many countries, it is very expensive and time-consuming for shareholders to gain access to this machinery and to communicate with each other in order to influence managerial decisions. In the United States, Proxy Rule 14a–8 now enables shareholders to gain access to corporate proxy machinery in order to submit certain proposals under certain conditions. But the access so provided is limited to proper subjects for action by shareholders under state statutes, unless a proposal is framed as 'a recommendation or request' (14a–8(c) (1)). Also, the shareholders can make neither a proposal related to an election to office (8(c) (8)), nor one that 'deals with a matter relating to the conduct of the ordinary business operations of the issuer' (8(c) (7)). Thus, even in the United States, where shareholder democracy is considered to be most advanced, the substance of it seems to be limited.

An interesting proposal to vitalize shareholders' participation in fundamental decision-making of the firm has been made by Gower (Gower *et al.*, 1979, pp. 554–5). That is the proposal to hold a postal ballot in order to make an important fundamental decision after shareholders have an opportunity of hearing both sides of the argument at a general meeting. This proposal seems worth serious consideration, as its adoption would restore the substance of the general meeting and shareholders' democratic participation.

For the large institutional shareholders, opportunities for uttering voice within the corporation will not be limited to the use of proxy machinery but will include directorate holdings, informal consultations, advice, and so on. The ability of financial institutions, particularly of commercial banks, to gain influence over portfolio corporations through these methods may be further reinforced by the borrowing of large sums of money by the latter from the former.

However, if the exercise of a bank's influence is made possible through the concentration of trust assets as in the United States, there may arise the problem of a potential conflict of interest between its position as a trustee and that as a lender. For instance, the bank trust department that happens to own a large block of the shares of a corporation that also happens to be a good customer of its commercial department may not sell those shares, even if that is the proper investment decision to make, when this action would jeopardize the bank's business relationship with that corporation. Or the tax structure may be such that the value of the corporation's shares owned by the trust department would increase by more if the corporation financed its investment by the retention of profit, but the commercial department might wish to extend credits to finance such investment.

In the United States, a voluntary restriction called the 'China Wall' is imposed on information exchanges between the commercial department and the trust department in order to prevent this type of conflict-of-interest problem from arising. But many cast doubts on the effectiveness of such voluntary legal regulation (see Allen, 1977, p. 127). In fact, the conveyance of vital information may not require any sophisticated method of communication between the two departments. Even though the exercise of voting rights at general meetings of the portfolio corporation is passed on from the bank to beneficial owners of the trust, the problem may not be resolved if the latter is apathetic.

Turning to the employee–management interface, we can locate channels through which the employees' voice is effectively heard and amplified in the labour union or representative institution, such as the works council in Europe. The role of the union as a voice institution has recently been re-emphasized by a series of works by Freeman and Medoff (1979) and their associates. According to them, the union has 'two faces': one is that of a monopoly institution which may disturb allocative efficiency by raising wages; but the other is of an institution that can contribute to internal efficiency by giving an outlet for better worker–management communication. The union provides workers with a formal grievance system through which they can express discontent instead of walking off the job. Also, the existence of the grievance system may help correct an obvious mistake made by management, with a net gain in internal efficiency. Since employee turnover is costly in terms of recruiting, screening, and training new workers, and since it interferes with the smooth functioning of teamwork on the shop-floor, the reduction of the quit-rate would undoubtedly improve the internal efficiency of the firm.

The co-operative game model of the firm constructed in the last two chapters indicates, however, that the relationship between the 'two faces' of the union may be more subtle than Freeman and Medoff appear to suggest. I have argued that the body of employees deeply internalized within the firm may contribute to the joint production of organizational rent at the firm and thereby have a legitimate claim for the sharing of it. This sharing might assume the form of wage premiums. If the union represents the collective bargaining power of the body of employees and collective bargaining is able to approximate the organizational equilibrium (co-operative solution), as prescribed in Part II, then the two faces of the union, i.e. as a 'monopolistic' institution and as a vehicle of internal efficiency, may not be separable. An inefficient aspect of the union would rather manifest itself, as discussed in Chapter 9, if the bargaining machinery does not transmit the employees' voice in those managerial policies highly relevant to employees' welfare, but only amplifies their current wage demands.

The European works council differs from the trade unions in that it lacks statutory protection from economic torts arising from industrial dispute. Yet its role as a voice institution at plant or shop level never seems to be inferior to that of the union. We have already discussed its impact on efficiency in the previous chapter for the case of Germany.[8]

Watchdog

Still another way of controlling management would be to institute a corporate organ whose function is to act as watchdog, or to supervise, management so that it is accountable for its stewardship and corporatist task. The function of supervision would include hearing reports from management regarding the business and affairs of the firm, evaluating the performances of management, checking the accounts of the corporation, and, finally, reporting any wrongdoing by management to an appropriate organ. The effectiveness of the supervisory task would be strengthened if the supervisory organ were empowered to appoint and, if necessary, remove unfit managers. The supervisory council of the German corporation was set up for this purpose long before the introduction of the co-determination system. Here, I would like to examine the often-held view that the board of directors in Anglo-American corporate statutes also serves as a watchdog organ.

As we have seen, the Anglo-American corporate statutes vest the authority of management in the board of directors, but actually, management is beyond the reach of the board as a body. The board of directors does not direct the corporation in the classical sense. The ambiguity of the role of the board arising out of the gap between the statutory requirement and the technocratic reality of managerial autonomy makes it difficult for the board to perform idiosyncratic roles in the corporate structure, and allows it to remain a passive and reactive body. Some jurists, recognizing the impracticability of the board's full involvement in the management of the corporation, propose that the board's function be made transparent and unique by requiring it to concentrate on independent supervisory functions.

One of the earliest proponents of the introduction of an independent board into the American system was the late Justice William Douglas (1934). He proposed to re-constitute the board with professional directors, who would control the proxy machinery in their own hands as well as 'supervise the management and formulate generally the financial and commercial policies rather than act as operating on managerial heads' (p. 1322). This view was recently vigorously reiterated by the former chairman of the Securities and Exchange Commission, Harold Williams (1979).

Several objections to this proposal have been raised. For instance, how can the board effectively be informed about the operation of the corporation when no managerial members sit in the board room? Will there be enough qualified directors if a full-time outside board is required? On the other hand, if professional directors are allowed to hold multiple directorates, then will they not form an interlocking network of communication among themselves and retard the competitive operation of the market? Separation of those who manage from those who supervise may be possible, however, in a less radical way – at least theoretically – by requiring a clear independent majority of outside directors and vesting in them a control of the proxy machinery and of supervisory committees dealing with such matters as auditing, nominating, and compensation. In this way, it is argued, it may become possible to ensure the structural and psychological independence of outside directors from management and yet to maintain communication between management and outside directors.

In the United States, in law and largely in practice, the selection, tenure, and dismissal of accountants has been in the hands of management. Many commentators are critical of the fact that the responsibility is vested in management also of selecting the accounting principle to be employed, such as between LIFO (last-in-first-out) and FIFO (first-in-first-out) in inventory flow assumptions, which in large measure affects the amount of recorded profits in an inflationary process. Many propose that the selection of accountants and the choice of accounting principle must at the very least be vested in the board as part of its supervisory role.[9] The American corporate system seems to be moving toward this model, if slowly. According to the Corporate Board Survey in 1979 by the New York Stock Exchange, 888 out of 949 respondent companies now have audit committees in the board of directors which are comprised entirely of non-management directors. The function for those committees is to make the nomination of auditors, and sometimes to recommend a choice of accounting principle. According to the same survey, non-management directors comprise the majority of approximately 80 per cent of respondent companies' directors.

One of the crucial issues involved in the formation of an independent board concerns the criteria for the board's judgement of management performances: specifically, whether the board should monitor and discipline the management according to the simple rule of short-run value maximization. If this rule is enforced in a unionized firm that is bound by a longer-period union contract, however, the achievement of internal efficiency may be endangered. If it is employed as an exclusive standard to judge the performance of management in a non-unionized firm, the question arises as to who evaluates the management from the viewpoint of the employees, as well as who ensures that good industrial relations are maintained within the firm. It seems, rather, that the independent board should evaluate management according to how efficiently and fairly it strikes a balance between the different constituents of the firm. The share value could be *a* criterion for judging management performance, but it should not be *the* criterion.

The much publicized model of Ralph Nader and his associates (1976) may be worth a comment in this regard. According to the Nader model, the board should be composed of non-homogeneous outsiders, each of whom is given, 'in addition to a general duty to see that the corporation is profitably administered, a separate oversight responsibility, a separate expertise, and a separate constituency so that each important public concern would be guaranteed by at least one informed representative on the board' (Nader, Green, and Seligman, 1976, pp. 124-5). Each director is charged with one of the following oversight responsibilities: employee welfare, consumer protection, environmental protection and community relations, shareholders' rights, compliance with the law, finances, purchasing and marketing, management efficiency, and planning and research.

An objection that can be raised against such constituency directors is that the board would then be transformed into a political forum and would not be able to function effectively (see Williams, 1979, pp. 11-12; and Business Round Table, 1978, p. 2106). The Nader model is built in such a way that all directors ought to be elected by the body of shareholders through a reformed electoral process, and this may help to bring about the degree of unification necessary for the board to function as an integrative body. However, the essential philosophy of Nader's model-building seems to be that of classical 'pluralism'. Diverse constituents compete for their causes through their representatives, and the basic policy orientation of the firm is to emerge as an equilibrium of open bargaining at the board room.

As regards the efficiency and effectiveness of board room bargaining, some of the discussions regarding the Bullock model would be relevant and suggestive (see particularly pp. 168-9). In contrast, according to the corporatist view of the independent board, directors ideally are supposed to retain relatively autonomous positions, to gain insights into the needs and imperatives of the organization, and to help the management and the constituents of the firm to achieve their needs through enlightened concerts of interest. The efficiency and effectiveness of the corporatist model would depend crucially upon the availabilities of directors who are professionally trained and can internalize the professional ethic of corporatism.

In the firm where the board of directors functions as a *de facto* substructure of the management and does not serve as a source of independent supervision, an independent organ to 'watchdog' director-cum-manager would be necessary. In Japan this task is assigned to the special office of auditor. The Revised Commercial Code 1981 provides that the general meeting of shareholders must elect more than one auditor for the purpose of auditing the management. The auditors individually have a wide range of auditing authority, including that of accounts, but they cannot interfere with the directors' decisions involving discretion. However, in order to prevent the board of directors from making an illegal or seriously unjust decision, auditors have a right to attend board meetings and be heard. When they find a serious wrongdoing by directors, the auditors can initiate a derivative suit for injunction without putting up securities for expenses.

In theory, then, the office of auditor can be a powerful watchdog organ of the Japanese corporation. However, its effectiveness is not ensured unless the auditors are competent and independent of the management. The original draft Revised Code prepared by the Ministry of Justice included a provision that at least one of the auditors must be an 'outsider', who has not been either a director or an employee of the corporation for a certain period of time before assuming the office of auditor. However, this provision was dropped from the final draft enacted, owing to strong opposition from the business community. Without this provision, however, there is the danger that auditorship will become a position junior to directorship, and auditors will face an extremely difficult task in acting as watchdog over senior colleagues. It is yet to be seen whether this 'quasi'-independent organ will be able to perform its supervising function properly.

Judicial recourse

On both the shareholder–management interface and the employee–management interface, judicial and/or quasi-judicial recourses are available to the constituents of the firm with regard to any existing or potential wrongdoing by the management. Actual uses of these judicial mechanisms may be costly in terms of time, resources, co-operative relationships, firm's reputation, and so on. However, even if the actual use of this mechanism is inefficient in resolving disputes and problems, its very existence may serve as an effective device to deter management from misconduct.

Corporate law in general imposes on directors fiduciary duties to the shareholders of loyalty, care, and a modicum of business skills. A breach of these duties can result in a director being sued. But the court has been, and is, reluctant to intervene by substituting its judgement on management for that of the directors. This is often expressed as the 'business judgement rule'. Thus, an effective sanction is lacking against the breach of the director's-cum-manager's duties of care and skill. However, when the corporation is acting *ultra vires*, when personal rights are infringed, or when those who control the corporation are perpetrating a fraud, a litigation may be brought by any shareholder as a plaintiff against the corporation as a defendant. Also, if damage was done to the corporation by the fraud or illegal activities of its directors and the recovery of damages are being sought, the plaintiff-shareholders can act as a representative of the company. This litigation is called the derivative suit in the United States, as the individual member sues on behalf of the company to enforce rights derived from it.

The effectiveness of this mechanism is doubted by some commentators, however. In particular, in many cases shareholders can sue only when what they complain of could not be effectively ratified by an ordinary resolution of a general meeting. Further, the so-called 'securities for expenses' requirement makes litigation very costly. Litigation may be also time-consuming. Finally, the spread of indemnification insurance over the last decade would nullify the effect of the court decision. However, to repeat, the availability of the mechanism itself may serve as a preventative device of apparent fraud and misconduct by the management, for unfavourable publicity from litigation would damage a manager's reputation.

The derivative suit is not unknown in other countries, but in some countries cheaper legal procedures are available. For instance, in Britain, when circumstances suggest the concealment by management of information to shareholders, fraud, or misconduct to shareholders or creditors, the case may be brought to the Department of Trade investigation by anyone who puts up nominal securities for expenses, or by a resolution of a general meeting or by the court. The Department of Trade, if it thinks there is good cause to do so, has the power to appoint an inspector to investigate and report on the affairs of the company. The inspector's report may be published, and if necessary the Department itself can institute civil or criminal proceedings. This is a relatively costless and speedy procedure in comparison to a shareholders' action.[10]

On the employee–management interface, relations are normally regulated by collective agreements, labour relation law, rule-books, customs, 'a well understood, complex, uncodified set of rituals and etiquettes' (Kahn-Freund, 1977a, p. 59), and the like. Whether collective agreements are enforceable or not differs from one country to another. In Japan collective agreements are interpreted as being legally enforceable, since the right of employees to organize and negotiate is derived from Article 28 of the Constitution. In Britain collective agreements traditionally have not been interpreted as legally enforceable contracts, unless the parties so opt and it is clearly stated in writing. It is said that parties seldom opt for this. What the court does enforce is the individual employment contract. However, by entering into a contract of employment the parties normally subscribe to an extensive body of common law and statute law. Also, under certain conditions the substance of a contract is implied by the rules laid down in the collective agreement. For instance, increasingly extensive regulatory laws require that employers specify certain employment conditions and let the employer discharge that obligation by referring to a collective agreement containing relevant terms.[11]

In the United States, the Supreme Court, in its famous ruling on the *United Steel Workers vs Warrior & Gulf Nav. Co.* case, declared that: 'A collective agreement is an effort to erect a system of self-government.' The agreement is 'more than a contract; it is a generalized code . . . [which] . . . covers the whole employment relationship . . . [and calls into being] . . . new common law – the common law of a particular industry or a particular shop' (363, U.S. 574–580 (1960)). Thus, employees' rights under a collective agreement could be enforceable, but, unless there is the breach of a union's obligation to represent employees fairly, the autonomous nature of the dispute settlement is emphasized.

If there is a complaint on the employees' side of the employer's alleged breach of agreement that can not be resolved within an intra-firm grievance procedure, the union can bring the case to an arbitration proceeding in order to settle the difference in interpreting the agreement. There is no Labor Arbitration

Act in the United States, and the arbitration is arranged by voluntary agreement. To initiate the process, the management and the union must create an arbitration tribunal of a single impartial member or a tripatite tribunal composed of additional representatives of disputants. The arbitor is a quasi-judicial institution, and he must possess the judicial qualification of fairness and equity to both parties as well as an extensive knowledge of common law. Once the award is delivered, the matter is settled. Such voluntary administration of arbitration would undoubtedly contribute to the formation of an atmosphere more favourable to the co-operative management of the firm, since arbitration would leave a less severe scar than litigation on industrial relations.

To process and settle employee grievances, the union owes a judicially enforceable obligation to represent employees fairly. When the union breaches this duty, then individual employees can bring the case to law in order to recover damages suffered as a result of alleged breaches of agreement by the employer and the union (see Feller, 1973).

Professional ethics and training

Various management-control mechanisms and the enforcement of legal rules governing the conduct of a powerful management tend to be ineffective unless the content of these controls and rules finds approval in the minds and feelings of the management affected thereby. The code of conduct shared by managers may be called the professional ethics of the management, and internalization of such code constitutes one of the most important aspects of the professional training of managers. These ethics are learned less in school than through the practice of management itself.

Senior managers in large corporations often come up through its internal promotional hierarchy. The process of manager allocation is thus a process of screening candidates for senior positions. As a consequence, modes of internal organization and patterns of managerial conduct tend to be congruent. In the United States, for instance, the internal organization of management is structured more on a functional basis, and managers are required to perform their specialized functions professionally and skilfully; they are promotable on these merits. The greater development of schools of business administration in the United States reinforces this tendency towards professional specialization.

The rise and fall of certain specialist classes within the firm indicates a change in organizational orientation. Until two decades or so ago, marketing specialists dominated the managements of most of American firms, but now it is the financial specialists who so dominate. This change reflects a shift of emphasis from sales growth to value-maximizing strategy. But paradoxically, as the discussion of Chapter 9 indicates, this strategy is internally efficient only if it is counterbalanced by employees' having a voice in the making of policies highly relevant to their welfare. If the firm lacks a union organization, the problem of how management, dominated by financial specialists, can take account of its employees' interests in policy-making becomes an issue worth consideration. Can the issue be met by letting other specialists, e.g. personnel administration specialists or industrial relations specialists, formulate needs arising internally, and by striking a balance between that and financial imperatives through 'quasi-bargaining' between the respective types of specialists within management? Or is there a need for a general change in the business philosophy, so that the corporatist view is more consciously shared by managers, while the high professional standard of specialized skills is maintained?

A very interesting study about the personnel management at large non-union corporations in the United States was carried out by Fred Foulkes (1980, 1981). According to this study, the personnel departments of the corporations studied have access to, and in many cases are part of, top management. The head of personnel often reports directly to the president and in some cases to a member of the board of directors. Many of top managers at these corporations are said to take obvious pride in their egalitarian and less confrontational philosophies and accomplishments. Thus Foulkes concludes his study by saying: 'for a large company to remain nonunion, top management needs to be personally involved in personnel management and to constantly demonstrate . . . its interest and concern for employees' (Foulkes, 1981, p. 96).

In Japan, those managers who are considered the most qualified for senior positions are the ones who, in addition to possessing a modicum of specialized skills, are well versed in the diverse aspects of the firm and excel in the skill of interest mediation. The expression, 'he is just a specialist in such and such (*nani nani ya*)' does not fall too short of being derogatory. In the Japanese firm, career managers are normally rotated over various jobs in the process of training. Since status differentials and social barriers are somewhat blurred between white collars and blue collars, this practice helps managers to become familiar with at least some aspects of the diverse activities in the firm and to realize the organizational need for efficient integration and fair interest mediation. Those who fail in personnel management in any division are apt to be disqualified from further advancement. Such training of managers as generalist-cum-mediators is most effectively carried out in practice, and the business school has never been an important economic and social institution in Japan.

But is this method of training inherent to the unique culture of Japan? Will it continue to work that way? In fact, the explicit acceptance of corporatist philosophy is rather a recent phenomenon there. The typical attitude of Japanese managers towards their employees is often characterized as 'paternalistic' by casual foreign observers. But this characterization really applies only to the labour policies of some of the prewar industrialists. In the process of rapid industrialization in the beginning of this century one of the most serious problems industrialists faced was how to cope with the scarcity of skilled labour and the consequential high rate of labour turnover. In order to reduce the high quit-rate and to cut down on the cost of recruiting and training, some 'enlightened' industrialists adopted a paternalistic policy towards their employees by instituting seniority wages, welfare funds, retirement benefits, and so on after the Russo-Japanese War. Although the philosophy of emphasizing the value of quasi-family relationships is traditional, the policy was undoubtedly purposely designed.[12] This paternalistic policy turned out to be effective in preventing frequent quits and the intrusion of a militant union movement inside the factory gate.

The paternalistic labour policy culminated in the nationwide movement of the Industrial Patriotic Society organized during the Second World War. Although the direct purpose of the Society was to facilitate industrial production serving the war effort by mobilizing employees' efforts, the activities of its branches at enterprise and plant levels had an aspect of forced egalitarianism amidst the scarcity of goods, in assisting families of conscripted employees, in functioning as a machinery to ration limited consumers' goods, and so on.

When the war ended and the Society movement was outlawed, the large-scale experience of this corporative, albeit employer-dominated, organization comprising all employees gave impetus to the rapid formation of independent unions in a short period of time. An equally important change was occurring on the management side. The control by Zaibatsu families, which had already been weakened in the prewar period because of their difficulties in meeting the needs for closely financing the development of capital-intensive industries, was finally annihilated. A large corps of senior managers at those large companies was purged from public office by the Supreme Commander for the Allied Powers. A relatively younger generation, who lacked the sense of rigid loyalty to the Zaibatsu families, took over managerial posts.

But it was only after a painful trial-and-error approach towards industrial relations that Japanese management came to accept the corporatist view. When a militant union movement surged after the Second World War, inexperienced managers were often compelled to yield to pressures from unions and then adopt tough attitudes towards the unions in order to regain their positions afterwards. Industrial relations between management and unions in the late 1940s and early 1950s had an aspect generally characterized more as 'confrontational' than as explicitly co-operative.

However, the era of confrontation was gradually giving way in the process of high economic growth starting in the middle of the 1950s. The landmark of the end of this period was the labour strife at the Mitsui Mining Co. in 1959–60, which ended after 300 days of strike, lock-out, and bloody clashes. Two years after the strife, the mine was struck by a disastrous blast, killing 450 miners. The indirect cause of this disaster was thought to be the severe scar left on the industrial relations by the strife, which had resulted in poor safety provisions and a low work morale.

By this time, managements had begun to accept the philosophy of 'harmony' between management and labour. A parallel shift in the labour side was the take-over of union movements by more economically oriented, enterprise-based unionists, replacing more ideologically oriented trade unionists. And, needless to say, the economic condition that made possible such changes of attitude on both sides was a steady growth of the pie to be shared between them.

Thus, the corporatist task of integrating and mediating between diverse constitutents of the firm became the main function of management in Japan only after a long history of trial and error. On the other hand, the managerial function there has remained relatively undifferentiated. However, recent developments may induce some changes in this respect. For instance, faced with keener international competition, particularly in the financial market, Japanese management is under increasing pressure to develop more sophisticated financial operations. As the gap between Japanese technology and advanced technologies from abroad is narrowed, Japanese firms need to develop new home-made technology to sustain the country's growth. But research and development will require more risky managerial planning. Further, although the management of a firm often recruits some of its membership from *ex*-union leaders who have high abilities in interest mediation, this practice is now becoming less frequent, because of the bureaucratization of union and management organizations.[13] These phenomena and possibly others may induce, or indicate, a gradual change towards greater emphasis on specialized skills in Japanese managers.

Having referred to the American and Japanese managements only cursorily, I shall now risk a broad generalization. Specialization and corporatization (in the sense of integration and interest mediation) are two *complementary* aspects of management under modern conditions of employment structure. Firms that are embedded in specific cultural, historical, social, and economic contexts may have developed either the corporative task or a specialized role as their main function and the other as only an inferior function. The firm that developed the corporative task as its main function may be superior in attaining internal efficiency, whereas the one that developed a market-oriented specialized role as its main function may be superior in attaining competitive efficiency. However, faced with a higher degree of integration of national economies into the world economy and increasing international competition, allocative and internal efficiency may require firms to develop inferior functions more consciously and to combine specialization and corporatization in management in a harmonious way.

Summary

The corporative managerialism model, which considers the role of management of a modern corporation as integrative as well as interest-mediative among corporate constituent bodies, finds its theoretical origin in the legal discourse of managerialism. The adjective 'corporative' is attached here only to distinguish the present model from the discretionary managerialism model as developed by economists.

The development of a legal framework for the corporation, as sketched above, indicates the gradual tendency towards an acceptance of the managerialist idea. In order for management to perform its corporative task internally efficiently and fairly, it must be subject to democratic internal control in both the shareholder–management interface and the employee–management interface. Otherwise this structural model may degenerate into the one in which the manager abuses his discretionary power to his own advantage.

Among various controlling mechanisms, the one that has been most attended by economists is the exit mechanism. But I have cast some doubt on the efficacy of this mechanism in the context of the large modern corporation, in which its constituents are to a significant degree 'locked-in'. Still, the exit mechanism must be kept as operative as possible, because the effectiveness of other mechanisms, particularly the voice mechanism, is strengthened by a credible threat of exit.

The voice mechanism is particularly significant on the employee–management interface, instituted as the labour union, the works council, the joint committee, etc. On the shareholder–management interface, however, there may not be a unanimity of interests between individual investors and institutional investors, and it is quite likely to be the latter who will have the louder voice in the corporate institution.

The watchdog mechanism is currently gaining importance. Reconstituting the board of directors as a supervisory organ rather than assigning it the impractical task of managerial decision-making may make the role of the board more transparent, unique, and thereby effective.

The judicial mechanism is very costly to actually use, but its very existence may be able to deter potential misconduct of management.

Lastly, the various controlling mechanisms would tend to be ineffective unless the content of these controls and rules finds approval and becomes internalized in the minds and feelings of the management as professional ethics. None of the controlling mechanisms discussed above seems to be effective in isolation, but each needs to be utilized in a way supplementing the others.

I would like to conclude this study by mentioning a hitherto-untouched aspect of the management of the modern corporate firm. In the present treatise on the firm, among the many possible roles of the manager, only one particular aspect has been emphasized: his integrative and intermediating role between the shareholders' body and the employees' body. Albeit thus limited in its scope, hopefully we have been able to gain from it a few important insights into the nature of the modern firm which the orthodox approach has disregarded.

However, claiming so is far from implying that the present treatise is satisfactory, even as regards the mediating role of the manager. Particularly noteworthy is the fact that the 'customers' of the firm have been ignored from the nomenclature of the firm's constituents and have appeared in the model only implicitly, in the form of the demand function for the firm's product (in case of current customers) as well as in the growth possibility function (in the case of customers of future products). As repeatedly argued, one consequence of this limited scope is to leave aside the problem of allocative efficiency.

But there is one more important aspect. Throughout this book it has been assumed that the manager is interested in the expansion of the market and the generation of new products only in so far as the benefits therefrom are accruable to the current shareholders in the form of capital gains and to the existing employees in the form of increasing lifetime earnings. However, the firm is considered viable in the long run only when its products are approved by customers over periods. When extraordinary revenues are realized by the expansion of the market or by the introduction of new innovative products, often the firm will not exhaust all the benefits therefrom between the shareholders and the employees. Normally it will retain a significant portion of such revenue and re-invest it in exploring and developing new products to a degree exceeding the immediate interests of current shareholders and existing employees. In a way, this tendency can be regarded as contributing to the potential benefits of unknown future customers. In this view, the manager who has succeeded in satisfying current customers is entrusted to explore potential future benefits for them, so to speak. In so doing the manager may be regarded as playing the *Shumpeterian* entrepreneurial role.

A full analytical treatment of the role of modern management from such a viewpoint is more complicated than the present treatise can afford, but it must certainly be placed among the most important items on the agenda for future study, particularly in this age of rapid technological progress.

Notes

Chapter 1: Introduction

1. See, for instance, Slichter *et al.* (1960), Doeringer and Piore (1971), and Koike (1984).
2. The appraisal right is a right accorded to a shareholder who dissents from certain structural changes of the corporations such as merger: it is the right to require the corporation to buy his shares at their 'fair value' as determined through appraisal proceedings.
3. See a recent study on personnel policy of non-union big corporations by Foulkes (1980, 1981).
4. More comprehensive reviews of the recent literature on 'the theory of the firm', which, however, emphasized somewhat different aspects than the present study, are given by Cyert and Hendrick (1972), Furubotn and Pejovich (1972), Leibenstein (1979), Marris and Mueller (1980), and Williamson (1981).
5. The concept of co-operative game solution used in Part II is a straightforward extension of bargaining equilibrium concept initiated by Zeuthen (1930). Harsanyi (1956) showed that this equilibrium notion is mathematically equivalent to the bargaining solution developed by Nash (1950, 1953). The latter notion is a normative one satisfying the conditions of efficiency, informational economy (the independence of irrelevant alternatives), and fairness (symmetry). Therefore it may be warranted to view our model having a descriptive aspect as well as a normative aspect. This is discussed on pp. 88–9 below.
6. The fourth edition of Gower *et al.'s Principle of Modern Company Law*, published in 1979, contains the same passage as quoted above, but in addition it includes new twenty-eight-page discussion on the topics of industrial democracy and the harmonization of corporate laws within the European Community. A brief historical summary of public discussion surrounding harmonization of company law in EEC nations will be provided in Chapter 10, specifically on pp. 153–5.

Chapter 2: The Neoclassical Theory of the Firm

1. The famous Schumpeterian notion of entrepreneur appears to be unique, but is obviously a brain child of the Walrasian view. The entrepreneur is regarded as an agent who brings in new, more efficient 'black boxes' into the Walrsian equilibrium. I shall refer to this Schumpeterian notion in the concluding section of this book.
2. It seems that the theory of implicit labour contract is based upon such presumption. For instance, see Azariadis (1975, pp. 1198–1200). An exception is D. Gordon (1974): 'With [the existence of quasi-contracts], a *mutual gain* is available to employers and employees if we start from a world of purely auction labor markets' (p. 444; italics are mine). Also see a quotation below (p. 21) from Samuelson (1977).
3. See Marschak (1949) and Hirschleifer (1966) on the liquidity premium as a price for the 'option value'.
4. The optimal risk-sharing condition between two (representative) individuals is given by Borch (1968) and Arrow (1971, pp. 90–120) which requires that the marginal rates of substitution between consumption in any two states be equal for both parties. If $u(.)$ and $v(.)$ summarize the employees' and the employer's risk attitudes, respectively, the Arrow–Borch condition is $u'\{w(i)\}/u'\{w(j)\} = v'\{r(i)\}/v'\{r(j)\}$ for all possible pairs of states of nature, where $w(k)$ and $r(k)$ are wages and profits in state $k(=i,j)$.
5. See Arrow (1971) and Pratt (1964) for the concept of absolute risk aversion. If the measures of absolute risk aversion of the representative employee and the employer are given by constant A and B, respectively, the Arrow–Borch condition is reduced to the

following sharing rule: $\beta^* = nA/(nA + B)$, where n is a fixed number of the employees in the labour pool. See Wilson (1968), Stiglitz (1974). See Aoki (1979) for a rigorous treatment of the following discussion.

6. For the theory of decentralization, see Arrow and Hurwicz (1960), Heal (1973, Part I), and Hurwicz (1973).

7. The idea of the quantity mechanism originates in Kornai and Liptak (1965). See also Marglin (1969).

8. This terminology is originally due to Koopmans (1951), and since then its usage has become standard. See Arrow and Hurwicz (1960).

9. The formulation in Arrow and Hurwicz (1960) is slightly different from the one adopted here in that they distinguish the 'custodians' of resources from the helmsman.

10. Arrow and Hurwicz (1960), in their pioneering work in the theory of decentralized resource allocation, devised a variant of the price mechanism which may be used to co-ordinate activities even in the presence of economies of scale. In this mechanism, each activity unit is required to adjust its activity plan in the direction of positive marginal profitability, using expected prices formed by a simple extrapolation of the past movement of prices. This additional informational requirement is a cost that has to be paid to find an optimal plan, in the presence of economies of scale, which is characterized as a local equilibrium point of the process. When an equilibrium is achieved, however, activity units that would operate under economies of scale would incur negative profit, a well-known difficulty in the presence of increasing returns. But this obvious difficulty in the incentive aspect aside, the Arrow–Hurwicz mechanism may encounter another difficulty in its application: until the equilibrium is exactly located, the demand and supply of each good is not equal, so that tentative activity plans out of equilibrium are not implementable. This defect of the *tatonnement*-like price mechanism was first pointed out by Malinvaud (1967).

11. The following formulation of the quantity mechanism in the presence of economies of scale is due to Aoki (1971a). It is summarized in Heal (1973, pp. 219–20). See also Heal (1969).

12. The formulation of the quantity mechanism in the presence of collective goods in the sense of production externalities is due to Aoki (1971b). This mechanism is also summarized in Heal (1973, pp. 221–8).

13. The relatively higher productivity growth of Japanese industry in the 1970s is regarded as attributable to a great extent to the success of the 'quality control circles', in which voluntary groups of workers participate in plan-making and implementation of the reorganization of work processes. In the same decade, many joint union–management committees on productivity were organized at enterprise and plant level in the United States. According to the US Department of Labor, which analysed 1570 major collective bargaining agreements covering 6.7 million workers in total as of 1 July 1976, 84 agreements covering 1.3 million workers contained provisions for labour–management committees on productivity (US Department of Labor, 1979, p. 21).

14. Such behaviour may be identified as another instance of 'opportunistic strategy' extensively discussed in the transactional cost (or 'new institutionalist') framework of Williamson (1975).

15. How can their concept of the firm be extended from the 'classical' one to the 'corporate' firm? The 'risk-averse' investors spread wealth across many firms and contribute only small portions to a large investment. Therefore, if every one of the shareholders participates in corporate decision-making, 'many would shirk the task of becoming well informed on the issues to be decided, since the losses associated with unexpectedly bad decisions will be born in large part by the many other corporate shareholders' (Alchian and Demsetz, 1972, p. 788). Hence modification in the relationship among corporate inputs is required: instead of policing the shirking of shareholders, decision-making authority is transferred to management. However, the body of shareholders performs the job of the ultimate control by disciplining management with the assistance of the unrestricted saleability of their shares and the accompanying possibility of an outside takeover. Here is the resurgence of the

classical notion of the firm with power resting upon those who have title to the residual. See also Jensen and Meckling (1976).

Chapter 3: The Managerial Theory of the Firm

1. The accepted doctrine at that time maintained that corporate powers were held in trust only for the corporation, but not for individual members of it.
2. Berle's 'ultra-classical' view of the corporation in his earlier writing (1931) was projected in part II of Berle and Means (1932), but part IV of that book already contained the new view as expressed by Dodd. The transition of Berle's view from the classical one to the new one is suspected to have occurred in the process of preparing the book. Berle's own account of the debate is, however, as follows: 'I should not accept his [Chayes's] view of the debate I had in that era with his predecessor, the late Professor E. Merrick Dodd. Dodd believed directors of corporations must (if they had not already) become trustees not merely for shareholders but for the entire community; this admitted them to a far greater power position than I thought they should have. In 1954 [*The 20th Century Capitalist Revolution*] I conceded that Professor Dodd had won the argument.... But when Professor Chayes suggests I conceded that Dodd was right all along, I must protest. It is one thing to agree that this is how social fact and judicial decisions turned out. It is another to admit this was the "right" disposition; I am not convinced it was. Things being as they are, I am unabashed in endeavoring to seek the best use of a social and legal situation whose existence can neither be denied nor changed. (Berle, 1959, p. xii).
3. For the sales maximization hypothesis, see Baumol (1959), Williamson (1964), Galbraith (1973). See also a recent survey article by Marris and Mueller (1980).
4. It was a characteristic of American corporate law until recently that in most states the shareholders had no power to remove directors in the absence of misconduct until the expiration of their term of office. In British law, the whole of the existing board can be dismissed by ordinary resolution of a shareholders' meeting, which can be summoned by an appropriate procedure.
5. This valuation ratio is equivalent to the Tobin's 'q-ratio', if we replace the 'book value' by the 'replacement cost' We refer to this concept in Part II.
6. If vacancies in higher positions of corporate hierarchies are filled by internal promotions, managers' life-term earnings would depend upon their future promotabilities, hence ultimately upon the expected growth rates of their employing corporations. Therefore, it is problematic if it is the salary paid at the bottom level that is determined by the market competition, unless corporations face a uniform growth rate and a uniform pay structure. Otherwise, new entrants would expect different lifetime prospects under a uniform beginning salary, and the question then arises as to why arbitrage would not occur to equalize expected lifetime prospects.
7. This theory is also used to explain the Pareto distribution of personal incomes often empirically observed. See Lydall (1968, pp. 127–33).
8. This also implies that the internal pay structure should be treated as an endogenous variable of the model. The analyses of Chapter 7 below will follow this line of thought.
9. These questions are treated by the so-called 'theory of the possibility of shareholders' unanimity'. See Ekern and Wilson (1974), Radner (1974), Grossman and Stiglitz (1977) and Leland (1974).
10. This is a terminology coined by Radner (1974).
11. See Allen (1977, pp. 584–5, 137–8); and Eisenberg (1976, pp. 56–7).

Chapter 4: The Theory of the Worker-controlled firm

1. On shop stewards, more detailed discussion will be provided in Chapter IX. See also Clegg (1979, Chapter II) and Moore (1980).

2. An only notable exception is Atkinson (1973) which examines implications of the hypothesis of the managerial growth maximization in the worker-controlled firm.
3. The perverse property of the product supply function of the worker-controlled firm may be attributable to special features of the model: the absense of uncertainty and its 'long-term' nature. Miyazaki and Neary (1983) built a notable model in which the worker-controlled firm faces two-stage decision-making under uncertainty: the determination of the size of labor pool in the "long-term" and that of the rate of lay-offs from this labor pool in the "short-term". He showed that the rate of lay-offs does not respond to the price of product negatively in the 'short-term' in his model. However it still looks true that the employment in the 'long-term' tends to be restricted.

Chapter 5: The Organizational Equilibrium

1. To treat the business partners and financial institutions supplying capital to the firm as possible coalitional members of the firm seems to be a very promising approach to the industrial organization theory. I discussed this research orientation in Aoki (1983).
2. See the 'Penrose function' in Uzawa (1969) and the 'sales cost function' in Solow (1971). In the Uzawa's model, perfect competition of the market is assumed so that there is no constraint on the volume of sales at the market-determined price. Therefore, his Penrose function represents only the cost necessary to expand the stocks of equipment and/or to overcome internal constraints on the expansion of the firm as a function of growth. In contrast, Solow's sales cost consists only of pure sales expenditure. This concept can be traced back to as far as Sraffa (1926). Solow's model incorporates the imperfectness of the market competition, but it assumes that the current stocks of capital equipment can be adjusted concurrently to the requirement of a steady-state growth. In the appendix on pp. 82–4 I examine the implications of the relaxation of this assumption, that is, implications of the fixity of durable equipment.
3. I will discuss problems related to the choice of a method of investment financing in a later section of this chapter.
4. This is a simple convention adopted by Keynes (1936, p. 152).
5. On this theorem, see the penultimate section of this chapter.
6. For the case of several possible threats, see Harsanyi (1977, pp. 167–95) and Roth (1979).
7. Still another interpretation of $B_u(W)$ is that it represents the demand price of W in terms of the marginal percentage gain in utility level with the disagreement utility level $\hat{U}$ as the base. See Aoki (1982b).
8. Since the bargain possibility set is not convex outward as depicted in the Fig. 5–1, the weighted sum of employees' earnings and shareholders' wealth is not maximized globally at the equilibrium.
9. The process described above presupposes that the manager as mediator possesses the precise knowledge of boldness of both the employees' body and the shareholders' body. The question may arise then of how the manager can elicit correct information regarding boldness from each player. Put differently, the question may be posed as to whether the players are not motivated to manipulate the information to their own advantages. In the process above, it is certainly to the players' advantages to over-represent their respective boldness if the manager is ignorant of it. However, in (1982b) I constructed a process modifying the present model in which the manipulation of information regarding the boldness would not lead to players' advantages, at least not in the neighbourhood of equilibrium. In other words, the modified process is incentive-compatible in the sense of Hurwicz (1973) in that the equilibrium of the process approximates the co-operative game solution and is at the same time a Nash equilibrium. The gimmick of the modified process is that the manager introduces a random element in the process in such a way that the co-operation of the two players is broken down with a small probability, but the players are allowed to insure against the cost of the breakdown. The overrepresentation of boldness by a player would lead to an insufficient protection of the player against the risk of the breakdown. This

purely theoretical construct suggests that the fear of a breakdown of co-operation may work as a driving force for the truthful revelation of boldness by each player. See Aoki (1982b).

10. That is to say, the so-called Condorcet paradox will not occur. See Arrow (1961, p. 93) for this paradox.
11. For the measurement of an agent's risk aversion see Pratt (1964) and Arrow (1970).
12. In the original formulation by Nash, conditions (2) and (3) are referred to as the conditions of 'independence of irrelevant alternatives' and of 'symmetry', respectively. See Roth (1979) and Luce and Raiffa (1957, Chapter VI) for a detailed discussion of those conditions.

Chapter 6: Equilibrium Bargain and Inefficient Bargain I: The Case of Lay-offs

1. A similar condition is derived in the theory of implicit labour contract: the risk-averse employees accept the wage contract in which the wage rate is equal to the 'expected' marginal revenue product of labour plus the marginal risk premium of lay-offs. See Azariadis (1975, pp. 1183–1202).
2. This view of the nature of unionism is expounded by A. Ross (1948).
3. Symmetrically, another equilibrium condition is given by

$$B_u N \, d\hat{w}/dw + B_v d\{R(L) - wL\}/dw = 0.$$

But this condition and (6.6) yield the relation (6.3).

4. Differentiating both sides of (6.5) with respect to L, we derive

$$u'(\hat{w}) \, d\hat{w}/dL = \{u(w) - u(\bar{w})\}/N.$$

Using (6.2) and (6.5),

$$d\hat{w}/dL = \{u(w) - u(\bar{w})\}/b_u(\hat{w})\{u(\hat{w}) - u(\bar{w})N\} = 1/b_u(\hat{w})L.$$

5. Judicially speaking, the view that the union is an agent of employees is not an accepted doctrine; see Feller (1973).

Chapter 7: Equilibrium Bargain and Inefficient Bargain II: The Case of Employees' Hierarchy

1. Freeman and Medoff (1979) estimate that the approximate amount by which quits are reduced by unionism under which the seniority system is prevalent is between 34 and 48 per cent for manufacturing workers, and that the substantially lower quit rates can explain about one-fifth of an estimated positive union productivity effect of 20–25 per cent.
2. A rigorous proof of this statement is given in M. Aoki, 'The Cooperative Game Theory of the Firm: part II', discussion paper no. 158 (May 1981), Kyoto Institute of Economic Research, Kyoto University, which may be obtained from the author upon request.
3. After the lengthy polemic regarding the distinction between a union's collective utility function and members' private utility functions in the last chapter, I admit that this assumption is not warranted. There is no excuse for it other than for the sake of simplicity.
4. If a corner solution obtains with the constraint (7.8) being binding so that condition (7.12) holds with $\mu \neq 0$, then the marginal rate of promotional gains will have a more complicated formula. See the mathematical appendix.

Chapter 8: Institutional Efficiency

1. Using an estimate by Harberger (1962) of the social cost of monopoly, Leibenstein
    (1966) indicated that the amount of internal inefficiency (X-inefficiency) is possibly
    substantially larger than the allocative inefficiency. Harberger's estimate came to be
    criticized subsequently, particularly for its partial equilibrium approach (see, for
    instance, Bergson, 1973, and Shoven, 1976). However, the point holds that the social
    cost arising internal of the firm is of non-negligible magnitude, although a precise
    estimate of internal inefficiency remains an important research agenda. For a possible
    extension of the intra-firm bargaining model to the general equilibrium framework,
    see Forsythe and Ichiishi (1983).

Chapter 9: The Shareholders' Sovereignty-cum-Collective Bargaining Model

1. For a detailed description concerning the union recognition process in the United
    States, see Beal *et al.* (1976, pp. 171–98).
2. This exclusive bargaining right of the union is often loosely referred to as 'union
    shop'. However, technically speaking, the union shop goes further. A union shop
    agreement requires an employer to make union membership a condition of employ-
    ment for all employees in the bargaining unit. The Taft–Hartley Act 1947 authorized
    a states' 'Right to Work' law, which makes the union shop unlawful. Most southern
    states have passed such law. In those states, collective agreements, if any, usually make
    it a condition of employment that employees pay the union the equivalent of dues as
    a kind of service charge, in return for the union's role as their bargaining agent.
3. For a detailed description of the employee representation plans during the 1920s and
    their transformation into independent industrial unions, see Millis and Montgomery
    (1945, Chapters IV and XI).
4. Section 5 of the Labor Union Act in Japan stipulates that a union can be protected
    by this Act only if it has been recognized as an independent organization by the
    neutral Labour Commission after the scrutiny of its rule-book.
5. I owe this account to Davies and Freedland (1979).
6. Deaton and Beaumont (1980) enlist possible factors that may act as the determinants
    of the bargaining level and estimated those statistical significances for the British
    case. They found that high regional industrial concentration, high union density, and
    multi-unionism are associated with multi-employer bargaining, whereas larger
    establishments, multi-plant firms, foreign owned firms, high concentration, and firms
    with an industrial relations function at senior management level tend to lead to
    enterprise-level bargaining. See also Brown (1982).
7. See Bok (1971, pp. 1427–30). For a somewhat different account, see Piore (1981).
8. Deaton and Beaumont (1980) examine statistically what factors are significant in
    determining the issue of enterprise-versus-plant level. They suggest that 'high labour
    cost' caused by the higher proportion of the work-force that possesses specific skills,
    knowledge, or experience is associated more with plant-level bargaining.
9. In spite of the prevailing view that Japanese unions are characterized by enterprise
    unionism, there is no legal foundation for this convention. It is not rare for multiple
    unions to be organized within an enterprise and to bargain with management, when
    labour–management disputes and/or intra-employees' rivalry become heated.
10. One example illustrates this. While General Motors Corporation turned out 4.62
    million four-wheeled cars in 1981 with 758,000 employees, Toyota Motors Corpor-
    ation produced 3.22 million four-wheeled cars with only 49,000 employees.
11. I discussed this issue in detail in Aoki (1983b, introductory chapter).
12. Such assertion may be found in Vagts (1966), and Eisenberg (1976, pp. 23–4).
13. I owe the following account to Davies and Freedland (1979).
14. This point is emphasized by Davies and Wedderburn of Charlton (1977) in their
    debate with Kahn-Freund (1977).
15. Recently, a pioneering study was made by MaCurdy and Pencavel (1984) testing be-
    tween the efficient bargaining model (which they call the 'contract curve equilibrium

model') and the inefficient value-maximizing model (which they call the 'labor demand curve equilibrium model'). In the case of bargaining involving the International Typographical Union in the North America, their tentative conclusion is that the former model comes closer to providing a satisfactory explanation. Whether this conclusion holds generally in American unionized industries is yet to be seen.

Chapter 10: The Participative Management Model

1. UK Commission on Industrial Relations, Study no. 4, 'Worker Participation and Collective Bargaining in Europe', 1974, p. 22; cited in Clegg (1977, p. 5.10). Also see Batstone and Davies (1976, p. 35).
2. For the 1976 Co-determination Law, English-speaking readers may wish to consult Grunson and Meilicke (1977).
3. Another method of harmonizing legal frameworks within the EEC is by means of a regulation directly applicable to all member-states pursuant to its unanimous adoption of the Council. A proposed *Draft Statute on the European Company* is an attempt to introduce an additional form of incorporation with participative management through a regulation. See ECC (1975a) and Schmitthoff (1973).
4. The latter system was instituted in the Netherlands in 1971.
5. This is a quotation from Professor Clegg's statement at a conference on industrial democracy held at the University of Leicester in 1977 (hereafter referred to as the 'Leicester Conference').
6. One of the most important experiments in recent time is that at the Post Office in 1978–80, which I will discuss later.
7. This is a statement made by a .German authority on corporate law, Professor Würdinger of Hamburg University, at a seminar held at the Japan Institute for Securities and Economy in November 1975. See 'On German Corporate Law', *Shoken Keizai Jiho*, no. 51 (March 1976), pp. 2–4.
8. Council of the Evangelical Church in Germany (ed.), *Socio-ethical Considerations of Co-determination in the Economy of the Federal Republic of Germany*, Hamburg (1968), IV. paras 14 and 18. Quoted from Biedenkopf Commission (1979, p. 78).
9. The number of council members are twelve, eighteen, and twenty for enterprises with less than 10,000, between 10,000 and 20,000, and more than 20,000 employees, respectively.
10. See discussion at the Leicester Conference, in Benedictus *et al.* (1977, pp. 5.15D–5.17D).
11. For empirical studies on the effects of co-determination on the behaviour of the firm, see Svejnar (1981), and Furubotn (1978).
12. From a statement by Mr Edmonds of the Research Department of the General and Municipal Workers Union at the Leicester Conference; Benedictus *et al.* (1977, p. 4.10).

Chapter 11: The Corporative Managerialism Model

1. Section 14(k) of Delaware Corporate Code stipulates: 'Any director or the entire board of directors may be removed, with or without cause, by the holders of a majority of the shares then entitled to vote at an election of directors, except as follows: (i) Unless the certificate of incorporation otherwise provides, . . .'. See also California Corporate Code, section 810.
2. See Cary and Eisenberg (1980, pp. 192–3), and 'Note, Delegation of Duties by Corporate Directors', *Virginia Law Review*, vol. 47 (1961).
3. Well under 10 per cent of total directors on the boards of the 134 Japanese companies surveyed for the Conference Board by Keizai Doyukai are outsiders.
4. Quoted in 'Re-Examination of Rules Relating to Shareholder Communications,

Shareholder Participation in the Corporate Electoral Process and Corporate Governance Generally, Summary and Comments', SEC, undated (1978–80?, p. 105).

5.   Shareholder democracy was an important issue pursued by the Securities Exchange
Commission under the former chairmanship of Harold Williams. The effort of the
Commission culiminated in the revision of Proxy Rule 14(a), enhancing the degree
of shareholders' participation to be discussed below. Also, the *Staff Report on
Corporate Accountability* prepared by the SEC (1980) for the US Senate, is an
important document on this subject.

6.   I analysed this possibility in Aoki (1984b).

7.   For Japanese corporate groups, see Aoki (1984b); Hadley (1970).

8.   For works councils, also see International Labor Office (1981).

9.   See, for instance, Eisenberg (1976, Part III), and American Bar Association, Section
of Corporation Banking and Business Law (1980).

10.   See Gower *et al.* (1979, pp. 1387–9) for comparative advantages of this procedure
over shareholders action.

11.   I rely for this account on Davies and Freedland (1979, pp. 240–9).

12.   See Taira (1970). The traditionalist and culturalist view was emphasized by Abegglen
(1958); but this authority on the Japanese economy has revised his view substantially
since 1970.

13.   According to a survey conducted by the Nikkeiren (the Japan Managers Association)
in 1978, 352 corporations surveyed had 6457 directors in total, among whom 1012
(15.7 per cent) were ex-members of executive committees of enterprise unions.

References

Abegglen, James C. (1958), *The Japanese Factory*. Glencoe, Ill: Free Press.

Akerlof, George (1976), 'The Economics of Caste, and of the Rat Race and Other Woeful Tales', *Quarterly Journal of Economics* 90: 599–617.

Alchian, Armer, and Demsetz, Harold (1972), 'Production, Information Costs, and Economic Organization', *American Economic Review* 62: 777–95.

Allen, Julius (1977), 'The Exercise of Voting Rights by Large Institutional Investors: A Survey', in US Senate (1978): 559–799.

American Bar Association, Committee on Corporate Laws to the Section of Corporation, Banking and Business Law (1950), *Model Business Corporation Act*.

—— (1974), *Model Business Corporation Act* (Revised).

—— (1980), 'The Overview Committees of the Board of Directors', *Business Lawyer* 35: 1335–64.

Aoki, Masahiko (1971a), 'Investment Planning Process for an Economy with Increasing Returns', *Review of Economic Studies* 38: 273–80.

—— (1971b), 'Two Planning Procedures for an Economy with Externalities', *International Economic Review* 12: 403–14.

—— (1979), 'Linear Wage Contracts vs. the Spot Market in their Risk-bearing Function', *Economic Studies Quarterly* 30: 97–106.

—— (1980), 'A Model of the Firm as a Stockholder–Employee Cooperative Game', *American Economic Review* 70: 600–10.

—— (1982a), 'Equilibrium Growth of the Hierarchical Firm: Shareholder–Employee Cooperative Game Approach', *American Economic Review* 72: 1097–110.

—— (1982b), 'An Incentive Compatible Approximation of the Nash-like Solution under Non-convex Technology'. Mimeographed; to appear in the *Hurwicz Festschrift*

—— (1983), 'Managerialism Revisited in the Light of Bargaining-Game Theory', *International Journal of Industrial Organization* 1: 1–21.

—— (ed) (1984a), *The Economic Analysis of the Japanese Firm*. Amsterdam: North-Holland.

—— (1984b), 'Shareholders' Non-unanimity on Investment Financing: Banks vs. Individual Investors', in Aoki (1984a): 193–224.

Arrow, Kenneth (1959), 'Towards a Theory of Price Adjustment', in Moses Abramowitz and others, *The Allocation of Economic Resources*. Stanford: Stanford University Press: 41–51.

—— (1961), *Social Choice and Individual Values* (2nd ed.). New York: John Wiley. First published in 1951.

—— (1971), *Essays in the Theory of Risk-bearing*. Amsterdam: North-Holland.

—— (1974), *The Limits of Organization*. New York: W. W. Norton.

—— and Debreu, Gerard (1954), 'Existence of an Equilibrium for a Competitive Economy,' *Econometrica* 22: 265–90.

—— and Hurwicz, Leonid (1960), 'Decentralization and Computation in Resource Allocation', in R. W. Pfouts (ed.), *Essays in Economics and Econometrics:* 34–104. Chapel Hill: University of North Carolina Press.

—— and Lind, Robert (1970), 'Uncertainty and the Evaluation of Public Investment Decisions', *American Economic Review* 60: 364–78.

Ashenfelter, Orley, and Johnson, George (1969), 'Bargaining Theory, Trade Unions, and Industrial Strike Activity', *American Economic Review* 59: 35–49.

Atkinson, Anthony (1973), 'Worker Management and the Modern Industrial Enterprise', *Quarterly Journal of Economics* 87: 375–92.

Auerbach, Alan, and King, Marvyn (1982), 'Corporate Financial Policy with Personal and Institutional Investors', *Journal of Public Economics* 17: 259–85.

Aumann, Robert, and Kurz, Mordecai (1977), 'Power and Taxes', *Econometrica* 45: 1137–60.

Azariadis, Costas (1975), 'Implicit Contracts and Underemployment Equilibria', *Journal of Political Economy* 83: 1183–202.

Ballantine, Henry (1946), *Ballantine on Corporation,* Chicago: Callaghan & Co.

Batstone, Eric, and Davies, Paul L. (1976), *Industrial Democracy: European Experience*. Two reports prepared for the Industrial Democracy Committee. London: Her Majesty's Stationary Office.

Batstone, Eric, Ferner, Anthony, and Terry, Michael (1983), *Unions on the Board*. Oxford: Basil Blackwell.

Baumol, William (1959), *Business Behaviour, Value and Growth*. New York: Harcourt, Brace & World.

Beal, Edwin, Wickersham, Edward, and Kienast, Philip (1976), *The Practice of Collective Bargaining*. Homewood, Illinois: Richard D. Irwin.

Becker, Gary (1964), *Human Capital*. New York: Columbia University Press.

Benedictus, Roger, Bourn, Colin, and Neal, Alan (eds) (1977), *Industrial Democracy: The Implications of the Bullock Report*. Leicester: University of Leicester.

Bergson, Abram (1973), 'On Monopoly Welfare Losses', *American Economic Review* 63: 853–70.

Berle, Adolf Jr (1931), 'Corporate Powers as Powers in Trust', *Harvard Law Review* 44: 1049.

—— (1959), 'Foreword', in Mason (1959): ix–xv.

—— and Means, Gardiner (1932), *The Modern Corporation and Private Property*. New York: Macmillan; rev. ed. 1962, New York: Harcourt, Brace & World.

Biedenkopf Commission (the commission of experts set up to evaluate the experience to date of co-determination) (1970), *The Biedenkopf Report: Co-Determination in the Company*. Translated from the original German *Mitbestimmung in Unternehmen* (1976), by Duncan O'Neill Belfast: Queens University.

Bok, Derek (1971), 'Reflections on the Distinctive Character of American Labor Laws', *Harvard Law Review* 84: 1394–63.

Borch, Karl (1968), *The Economics of Uncertainty*. Princeton: Princeton University Press.

Brown, Williams (ed.) (1982), *The Changing Contours of British Industrial Relations*. Oxford: Basil Blackwell.

—— and Sisson, Keith (1975), 'The Use of Comparisons in Workplace Wage Determination', *British Journal of Industrial Relations* 13: 23–53.

——, Ebsworth, Robert, and Terry, Michael (1978), 'Factors Shaping Shop Steward Organization in Britain', *British Journal of Industrial Relations* 16: 139–59.

—— and Terry, Michael (1978), 'The Changing Nature of National Wage Agreements', *Scottish Journal of Political Economy* 25: 19–33.

Bruno, Michael, and Sachs, Jeffrey (1979), *Macro-Economic Adjustment with Import Price Shocks: Real and Monetary Aspects.* Jerusalem: Maurice Falk Institute for Economic Research in Israel.

Bullock Committee (Committee of Inquiry on Industrial Democracy) (1977), *Report.* London: Her Majesty's Stationery Office (Cmnd 6706).

Burnham, James (1941), *The Managerial Revolution.* New York: John Day Co.

Business Round Table (1978), 'The Role and Composition of the Board of Directors of the Large Publicly Owned Corporation', *Business Lawyer* 33: 2079–113.

Cary, William, and Eisenberg, Melvin (1980), *Cases and Materials on Corporations* (5th ed.). Mineola, NY: Foundation Press.

Chamberlain, Edward (1962) *The Theory of Monopolistic Competitions* (8th ed.). Cambridge, Mass.: Harvard University Press. First published in 1933.

Chamberlain, Neil and Kuhn, James (1965), *Collective Bargaining* (2nd. ed.), New York: McGraw-Hill. First published 1951.

Chandler, Alfred. Jr (1977), *The Visible Hand: The Managerial Revolution in American Business.* Cambridge, Mass.: Harvard University Press.

Chayes, Abram (1959), 'The Modern Corporation and the Rule of Law', in Mason (1959): 25–45.

Clark, Rodney (1979), *The Japanese Company.* New Haven: Yale University Press.

Clegg, Hugh (1977), 'The Bullock Report and European Experience', in Benedictus *et al.* (1977): 5–13.

—— —— (1979), *The Changing System of Industrial Relations in Great Britain.* Oxford: Basil Blackwell.

Coase, Ronald (1937), 'The Nature of the Firm', *Economica* n.s.4: 386–405; reprinted in G. J. Stigler and K. E. Boulding (eds), *Readings in Price Theory*: 331–51. Homewood Ill.: Richard D. Irwin.

Cox, Archibald (1958), 'The Legal Nature of Collective Bargaining Agreements', *Michigan Law Review* 57: 1–36.

Cyert, Richard, and Hendrick, Charles (1972), 'Theory of the Firm: Past, Present, and Future: An Interpretation', *Journal of Economic Literature* 10: 398–412.

—— and March, James (1963), *A Behavioral Theory of the Firm*, Englewood Cliffs: Prentice-Hall.

Davies, Paul (1978), 'The Bullock Report and Employee Participation in Corporate Planning in the UK', *Journal of Comparative Corporate Law and Securities Regulation* 1: 245–72.

—— and Freedland, Mark (1979), *Labour Law: Text and Materials.* London: Weidenfeld and Nicolson.

—— and Lord Wedderburn of Charlton (1977), 'The Land of Industrial Democracy,' *Journal of Industrial Law* 6: 197–211.

Deaton, D. R. and P. B. Beaumont (1980), 'The Determinants of Bargaining Structure: Some Large-scale Survey Evidence for Britain', *British Journal of Industrial Relations* 18: 202–16.

Debreu, Gerard (1959), *Theory of Value.* New York: John Wiley.

deMenil, George (1971), *Bargaining: Monopoly Power versus Union Power.* Cambridge, Mass.: MIT Press.

Dodd, E. Merrick (1932), 'For Whom are Corporate Managers Trustees?' *Harvard Law Review* 45: 1145–63.

Doeringer, Peter, and Piore, Michael (1971), *Internal Labour Markets and Manpower Analysis*. Boston: D. C. Heath and Co.

Domar, Evsey (1966), 'The Soviet Collective Farm as a Producer Cooperative', *American Economic Review* 56: 734–57.

Donahue, Thomas (1978), 'The Future of Collective Bargaining', quoted in John Dunlop, 'Past and Future Tendencies in American Labor Organizations', *Daedalus* 107: 79–96.

Donovan Commission (Royal Commission on Trade Unions and Employers' Associations) (1968), *Report*, London: Her Majesty's Stationery Office (Cmnd 3623).

Douglas, William (1934), 'Directors Who Do Not Direct', *Harvard Law Review* 68: 1305–34.

Dreze, Jacque (1976), 'Some Theory of Labor Management and Participation', *Econometrica* 44: 1125–40.

Drucker, Peter (1976), *The Unseen Revolution: How Pension Fund Socialism Came to America*. New York: Harper & Row.

Dufty, Norman (1975), *Changes in Labour–Management Relations in the Enterprise*. Paris: Organization for Economic Cooperation & Development.

Dunlop, John (1958), *Industrial Relations Systems,* N.Y.: Holt-Dreyden.

– – (1966), 'Job Vacancy: Measures and Economic Analysis', in *The Measurement and Interpretation of Job Vacancies: A Conference Report*, National Bureau of Economic Research. New York: Columbia University Press.

Edmonds, John (1977), 'The Bullock Committee's Report and Collective Bargaining', in Benedictus *et al.* (1977).

Eisenberg, Melvin (1976), *The Structure of the Corporation*. Boston: Little, Brown.

Ekern, Steiner and Wilson, Robert (1974), 'On the Theory of the Firm in an Economy with Incomplete Markets', *Bell Journal of Economics and Management Science* 5: 171–80.

European Communities Commission (1972), 'Proposal for a Fifth Directive to Coordinate the Laws of Member States as Regards the Structure of "société anonymes"'. *Bulletin of the European Communities Supplement* 10/72.

– – (1975a), 'Statute for European Companies: Amended Proposal for a Regulation', *Bulletin of the European Communities Supplement* 4/75.

– – (1975b), 'Employee Participation and Company Structure', *Bulletin of the European Communities Supplement* 8/75.

– – (1978), Working Document Prepared by the Commissions' Services for Use in the Discussions of the Legal Committee of the European Parliament on the Proposal for a Fifth Directive on 'Company Law'.

European Parliament (1982), 'Second Report drawn up on behalf of the Legal Affairs Committee on the proposal from the Commission of the European Communities to the Council for Fifth Directive', Working Document 1-862/81.

Fama, Eugene (1980), 'Agency Problems and the Theory of the Firm', *Journal of Political Economy* 88: 288–307.

Feller, David (1973), 'A General Theory of the Collective Bargaining Agreement', *California Law Review* 61: 663–856.

Fischer, Stanley (1977), 'Long-term Contracts, Rational Expectations, and the Optimal Money Supply Rule', *Journal of Political Economy* 85: 191–205.

Flanders, Allan (1968), 'Collective Bargaining: A Theoretical Analysis', *British Journal of Industrial Relations* 6: 1–26.

Forsythe, Robert and Ichiishi, Tatsuro (1983), 'A General Equilibrium Bargaining Model of Owner–Labor Jointly Managed Firms: Existence and Optimality'. Mimeographed, University of Iowa.

Foulkes, Fred (1980), *Personal Policies in Large Nonunion Companies*. Englewood Cliffs: Prentice-Hall.

—— (1981), 'How Top Nonunion Companies Manage Employees', *Harvard Business Review*, September–October: 90–6.

Freeman, Robert, and Medoff, James (1979), 'The Two Faces of Unionism', *Public Interest* 57: 69–93.

Furubotn, Erick (1978), 'The Economic Consequences of Co-determination on the Rate and Sources of Private Investment', in S. Pejovich (ed.), *The Co-determination Movement in the West*. Lexington, Mass.: D. C. Heath: 137–67.

—— and Pejovich, Svetozar (1972), 'Property Rights and Economic Theory: A Survey of Recent Literature', *Journal of Economic Literature* 10: 1137–62.

Galbraith, Kenneth (1973), *Economics and Public Purpose*. Boston: Houghton Mifflin.

Gordon, Donald (1974), 'A Neo-classical Theory of Keynesian Unemployment', *Economic Inquiry* 12: 431–59.

Gordon, Robert (1966), *Business Leadership in the Large Corporation* (with a new preface). Berkeley and Los Angeles: University of California Press. First published in 1945.

Gower, L. C. B. (1956), 'Some Contrasts between British and American Corporation Law', *Harvard Law Review* 69: 1309–1402.

—— (1969), *Principles of Modern Company Law* (3rd ed.). London: Stevens & Sons.

——, Cronin, J B., Easson, A. J., and Lord Wedderburn of Charlton (1979), *Principles of Modern Company Law* (4th ed.). London: Stevens & Sons.

Grossman, Sanford and Stiglitz, Joseph (1977), 'On Value Maximization and Alternative Objectives of the Firm', *Journal of Finance* 32: 389–402.

Grunson, Michael and Meilicke, Wienand (1977), 'The New Co-determination Law in Germany', *Business Lawyer* 32: 571–89.

Hadden, Tom (1972), *Company Law and Capitalism*. London: Weidenfeld and Nicolson.

Hadley, Eleanor (1970), *Antitrust in Japan*. Princeton: Princeton University Press.

Hall, Robert, and Lilien, David (1979), 'Efficient Wage Bargains under Uncertain Supply and Demand', *American Economic Review* 69: 868–79.

Harberger, Arnold (1962), 'The Incidence of the Corporation Income Tax', *Journal of Political Economy* 70: 215–240.

Harsanyi, John (1956), 'Approaches to the Bargaining Problem Before and After the Theory of Games: a Critical Discussion of Zeuthen's, Hicks's, and Nash's Theories', *Econometrica* 24: 144–57.

—— (1977), *Rational Behaviour and Bargaining Equilibrium in Games and Social Situations*. Cambridge: Cambridge University Press.

Hart, Oliver (1983), 'The Market Mechanism as an Incentive Mechanism', paper presented to the Bonn-Harvard Conference on Entrepreneurship. Mimeographed.

Hayek, Frederik (1945), 'The Use of Knowledge in Society', *American Economic Review* 35: 519–30.

Heal, Geoffrey (1969), 'Planning without Prices', *Review of Economic Studies* 36: 347–62.

–– (1973), *The Theory of Economic Planning*. Amsterdam: North-Holland.

Hirschleifer, Jack (1966), 'Liquidity, Uncertainty, and the Accumulation of Information', *Uncertainty and Expectations in Economics*: 136–47. Oxford: Basil Blackwell/Mott.

Hirschman, Albert (1970), *Exit, Voice, and Loyalty*. Cambridge Mass.: Harvard University Press.

Hori, Hajime (1975), 'The Structure of Equilibrium Points of Process', *Review of Economic Studies* 36: 47–62.

Hurwicz, Leonid (1973), 'The Design of Mechanisms for Resource Allocation', *American Economic Review* 63: 1–30.

International Labor Office (1981), *Workers' Participation in Decisions Within Undertakings*. Geneva: ILO.

Jensen, Michael and Meckling, William (1976), 'Theory of the Firm: Managerial Behavior, Agency Costs and Ownership Structure', *Journal of Financial Economics* 3: 305–60.

Kahn-Freund, Otto (1977a) *Labour and the Law* (2nd ed.). London: Stevens & Sons. First published in 1972.

–– (1977b), 'Industrial Democracy', *Industrial Law Journal* 6: 65–84.

Kerr, Clark (1954), 'The Balkanization of Labor Markets', in E. W. Bakke (ed.), *Labor Mobility and Economic Opportunity*: 92–110. Cambridge, Mass.: MIT Press.

–– (1964), *Labor and Management in Industrial Society*. Garden City, NY: Anchor Books.

Keynes, John M. (1936), *The General Theory of Employment, Interest, and Money*. London: Macmillan.

King, Mervyn (1977), *Public Policy and the Corporation*. London: Chapman and Hall.

Knight, Frank (1921), *Risk, Uncertainty and Profit*. Boston: Houghton Mifflin.

Koike, Kazuo (1984), 'Skill Formation Systems in the U.S. and Japan: A Comparative Study', in Aoki (1984a): 47–76.

Kornai, Janos, and Liptak, Tamas (1965), 'Two-level Planning', *Econometrica* 33: 141–69.

Koopmans, Tjalling (1951), 'Analysis of Production as an Efficient Combination of Activities', in T. C. Koopmans (ed.), *Activity Analysis of Production and Allocation*: 37–97. New York: John Wiley.

Kouri, Pentti (1979), 'Profitability and Growth in a Small Open Economy', in Assar Lindbeck (ed.), *Inflation and Unemployment in Open Economies*. Amsterdam: North-Holland.

Leibenstein, Harvey (1966), 'Allocative Efficiency vs. "X-Efficiency"', *American Economic Review* 56: 392–415.

–– (1976), *Beyond Economic Man: A New Foundation for Micro-Economics*. Cambridge Mass.: Harvard University Press.

–– (1979), 'A Branch of Economics is Missing: Micro-Micro Theory', *Journal of Economic Literature* 17: 477–502.

—— (1982), 'The Prisoners' Dilemma in the Invisible Hand: An Analysis of Intrafirm Productivity', *American Economic Review* 72: 92–7.

Leland, Haynes (1974), 'Production Theory and the Stock Market', *Bell Journal of Economics and Management Science* 5: 125–44.

Leontief, Wassily (1946), 'The Pure Theory of Guaranteed Annual Wage Contract', *Journal of Political Economy* 54: 392–415.

Lerner, Abba (1933–4), 'The Concept of Monopoly and the Measurement of Monopoly Power', *Review of Economic Studies* 1: 157–75.

Luce, Duncan and Raiffa, Howard (1957). *Games and Decisions.* New York: John Wiley.

Lydall, Harold (1968), *The Structure of Earnings.* London: Oxford University Press.

MacDonald, Robert (1967), 'Collective Bargaining in the Postwar Period', *Industrial and Labor Relations Review* 20: 553–77.

MaCurdy, Thomas and Pencavel, John (1984), 'Testing between Competing Models of Wage and Employment Determination in Unionized Markets'. *Journal of Political Economy*, forthcoming.

Mace, Myles (1971), *Directors: Myth and Reality.* Cambridge Mass.: Graduate School of Business Administration, Harvard University.

Malinvaud, Edmond (1967), 'Decentralized Procedures for Planning', in *Activity Analysis in the Theory of Growth and Planning*: 170–208. London: Macmillan.

—— (1977), *The Theory of Unemployment Reconsidered.* Oxford: Basil Blackwell.

Marglin, Stephen (1969), 'Information in Price and Command Systems of Planning', in Julius Margolis, *Public Economics.* London: Macmillan.

Marris, Robin (1964), *The Economic Theory of 'Managerial' Capitalism.* New York and London: Free Press and Macmillan.

——, and Mueller, Dennis (1980), 'The Corporation, Competition and the Invisible Hand', *Journal of Economic Literature* 18: 32–63.

Marschak, Jacob (1949), 'Role of Liquidity under Complete and Incomplete Information', *American Economic Review* 39: 182–95.

Marshall, Alfred (1920) *Principles of Economics* (8th ed.). London: Macmillan. First published in 1890.

Mason, Edward (1958), 'The Apologetics of "Managerialism"', *Journal of Business* 31: 1–11.

—— (1959), *The Corporation in Modern Society.* Cambridge Mass.: Harvard University Press.

McCarthy, W. E. J. (1966), 'The Role of Shop Stewards in British Industrial Relations: A Survey of Existing Information and Research', Research Papers 1. Royal Commission on Trade Unions and Employers Associations. London: Her Majesty's Stationery Office.

McDonald, Ian, and Solow, Robert (1981), 'Wage Bargaining and Employment', *American Economic Review* 71: 896–908.

McMullen, John (1974), 'Committees of the Board of Directors', *Business Lawyers* 29: 755–804.

Meade, James (1974), 'Labour-managed Firms in Conditions of Imperfect Competition', *Economic Journal* 84: 817–24.

Miller, Merton (1977), 'Debt and Taxes', *Journal of Finance* 32: 212–75.

Millis, Harry and Montgomery, Royal (1945), *Organized Labor.* New York: McGraw-Hill.

Miyazaki, Hajime and Neary, Hugh (1983), The Illyrian Firm Revisited, *Bell Journal of Economics* 14: 259–70.

Modigliani, Franco, and Moller, Merton (1958), 'The Cost of Capital, Corporation Finance and the Theory of Investment', *American Economic Review* 48: 261–97. 'A Correction', *American Economic Review* 53: 433–43.

Moore, R. (1980), 'The Motivation to Become a Shop Steward', *British Journal of Industrial Relations* 18: 91–8.

Muth, John F. (1960), 'Optimal Properties of Exponentially Weighted Forecasts', *Journal of American Statistical Association* 55: 299–306.

Nader, Ralph, Green, Mark, and Seligman, Joel (1976), *Taming the Giant Corporation*. New York: W. W. Norton.

Nash, John (1950), 'The Bargaining Problem', *Econometrica* 18: 155–62.

—— (1953), 'Two-person Cooperative Games', *Econometrica* 21: 128–40.

New York Stock Exchange, Business Research Department (1979), *Corporate Governance: Survey of Corporate Boards, Structure and Corporation*. New York: NY Stock Exchange.

Penrose, Edith (1959), *The Theory of the Growth of the Firm*. Oxford: Basil Blackwell.

Phelps Brown, Henry (1983), *The Origins of Trade Union Power*. Oxford: Oxford University Press.

Piore, Michael (1981), 'Convergence of Industrial Relations? The Case of France and the United States'. Mimeographed, Massachusetts Institute of Technology.

Pratt, John (1964), 'Risk Aversion in the Small and the Large', *Econometrica* 32: 122–36.

Prentice, Daniel (1980), *Companies Act 1980*. London: Butterworth.

Radner, Roy (1974), 'A Note on Unanimity of Stockholders' Preferences among Alternative Production Plans: A Reformulation of the Ekern–Wilson Model', *Bell Journal of Economics and Management Science* 5: 181–4.

Raiffa, Howard (1982), *The Art and Science of Negotiation*. Cambridge, Mass.: Harvard University Press.

Robinson, Joan (1934), *The Economics of Imperfect Competition*. London: Macmillan.

Ross, Arthur (1948), *Trade Union Wage Policy*. Berkeley and Los Angeles: University of California Press.

Ross, Stephen (1973), 'The Economic Theory of Agency: The Principal's Problem', *American Economic Review* 63: 134–9.

Roth, Alvin (1979), *Axiomatic Models of Bargaining*. Berlin: Springer-Verlag.

Rostow, Eugene (1959), 'To Whom and For What Ends Is Corporate Management Responsible?' in Mason (1959): 46–71.

Samuelson, Paul (1977), 'Thoughts on Profit Sharing', *Zeitschrift für die Gesamte Staatswissenschaft*, Special Issue: 9–18.

Scherer, F. M. (1983), 'Growth by Diversification: Entrepreneurial Behavior in Large-Scaled United States Enterprise', paper presented to the Bonn-Harvard Conference on Entrepreneurship. Mimeographed.

Schmitthoff, Clive (ed.) (1973), *The Harmonization of European Company Law*. London: United Kingdom National Committee of Companies Law.

—— (1978), *Commercial Law in a Changing Economic Climate*. London: Sweet & Maxwell.

Schumpeter, Joseph (1934), *The Theory of Economic Development*. Cambridge Mass.: Harvard University Press. English translation of *Theorie der wirtschaftlichen Entwicklung* (1911) by Redvers Opie.

Shoven, John (1976), 'The Incidence and Efficiency Effects of Taxes on Income from Capital', *Journal of Political Economy* 84: 1261–83.

Simon, Herbert (1952-3), 'A Comparison of Organisation Theories', *Review of Economic Studies* 20 :40–8.

—— (1957), 'The Compensation of Executives', *Sociometry* 20: 32–5.

—— (1972), 'Theories of Bounded Rationality', in C. B. McGuire and Roy Radner (eds), *Decision and Organization*. Amsterdam: North-Holland: 161–76.

Slichter, Sumner, Healy, James, and Livernash, E. Robert (1960), *The Impact of Collective Bargaining on Management*. Washington DC: Brookings Institution.

Solow, Robert (1971), 'Some Implications of Alternative Criteria for the Firm', in R. Marris and A. Wood (eds), *The Corporate Economy*. Cambridge Mass.: Harvard University Press: 318–42.

Sraffa, Pierro (1926), 'The Laws of Returns under Competitive Conditions', *Economic Journal* 36: 535–50.

Steuer, Richard (1979), 'Director's Seat for the U.A.W. Stirs Antitrust Issue', *National Law Journal* November 12.

Stiglitz, Joseph (1972), 'On the Optimality of the Stock Market Allocation of Investment', *Quarterly Journal of Economics* 86: 25–60.

—— (1974), 'Incentives and Risk Sharing in Sharecropping', *Review of Economic Studies* 41: 219–55.

Svejnar, Jan (1981), 'Relative Wage Effects of Unions, Dictators and Co-determination', *Review of Economics and Statistics* 63: 188–97.

Taira, Koji (1970), *Economic Development and the Labor Market in Japan*. New York: Columbia University Press.

Tobin, James, and Brainard, William (1977), 'Asset Market and the Cost of Market', in Bella Balassa and Richard Nelson (eds), *Economic Progress, Private Values and Public Policy: Essays in Honor of William Fellner*. Amsterdam: North-Holland: 235–62.

Traverse, Arthur (1967), 'Removal of the Corporate Director during his Term of Office', *Iowa Law Review* 53: 389–419.

Ulman, Lloyd (1974), 'Connective Bargaining and Competitive Bargaining', *Scottish Journal of Political Economy* 21: 97–109.

UK Government (1978), *Industrial Democracy*. London: Her Majesty's Stationery Office (Cmnd 7231).

US Department of Labor, Bureau of Labor Statistics (1979), 'Characteristics of Major Collective Bargaining Agreements, July 1, 1976', *Bulletin* 2013. Washington DC: US Government Printing Office.

US Senate, Subcommittee on Reports, Accounting and Management of the Committee on Government Affairs (1978), *Voting Rights in Major Corporations*. Washington DC: US Government Printing Office.

US Securities and Exchange Commission (1980), *Staff Report on Corporate Accountability: A Re-examination of Rules Relating to Shareholder Communications, Shareholder Participation in the Corporate Electoral Process and Corporate Governance Generally*. Washington DC: US Government Printing Office.

Uzawa, Hirofumi (1969), 'Time Preference and Penrose Effect in a Two Class Model of Economic Growth', *Journal of Political Economy* 77: 628–52.

Vagts, Detlev (1966), 'Reforming the "Modern" Corporation: Persepctives from the German', *Harvard Law Review* 80: 23–89.

—— (1979), *Materials on Basic Corporation Law* (2nd ed.). Mineola, NY: Foundation Press. First published in 1973.

Vanek, Jaroslav (1970), *The General Theory of Labor-managed Market Economies.* Ithaca, NY: Cornell University Press.

Walras, Leon (1954), *Elements of Pure Economics.* Edited and translated by W. Jaffe. London: George Allen and Unwin.

Ward, Benjamin (1958), 'The Firm in Illyria: Market Syndicalism', *American Economic Review* 48: 566–89.

Williams, Harold (1979), 'Corporate Accountability and Corporate Power', the Fairless Lecture Series, Carnegie-Mellon University.

Williamson, Oliver (1964), *The Economics of Discretionary Behavior: Managerial Objectives in a Theory of the Firm.* Englewood Cliffs. NJ: Prentice-Hall.

—— (1975), *Markets and Hierarchies: Antitrust Implications.* New York: Free Press.

—— (1981), 'The Modern Corporation: Origins, Evolution, Attributes', *Journal of Economic Literature* 19: 1537–68.

—— (1982), 'Efficient Labor Organization', mimeographed.

Wilson, Robert (1968), 'The Theory of Syndicates', *Econometrica* 36: 119–32.

Zeuthen, Frederik (1930), *Problems of Monopoly and Economic Warfare.* London: George Routledge & Sons.

Author Index

Subject Index